Literature and Society in Eighteenth-Century England

This book is due for return on or before the last date shown below.

THEMES IN BRITISH SOCIAL HISTORY

edited by John Stevenson

This series covers the most important aspects of British social history
from the Renaissance to the present day. Topics include education,
poverty, health, religion, leisure, crime and popular protest, some of
which are treated in more than one volume. The books are written
for undergraduates, postgraduates and the general reader, and each
volume combines a general approach to the subject with the primary
research of the author.

Currently available

Literature and Society in Eighteenth-Century England 1680–1820

Ideology, Politics and Culture

W. A. SPECK

Longman
London and New York

Addison Wesley Longman Limited
Edinburgh Gate,
Harlow, Essex CM20 2JE,
United Kingdom
and Associated Companies throughout the world

*Published in the United States of America
by Addison Wesley Longman Inc., New York*

First published 1998

ISBN 0 582 265703 PPR
ISBN 0 582 265185 CSD

British Library Cataloguing in Publication Data
A catalogue record for this book is available from the British Library

Library of Congress Cataloging-in-Publication Data
Speck, W. A. (William Arthur), 1938–
Literature and society in eighteenth-century England, 1650–1820 /
W. A. Speck.
p. cm. — (Themes in British social history)
Includes bibliographical references and index.
ISBN 0–582–10316–9 (ppr). — ISBN 0–582–10315–0 (csd)
1. English literature—18th century—History and criticism.
2. Literature and society—England—History—18th century.
3. English literature—Early modern, 1500–1700—History and
criticism. 4. Engish literature—19th century—History and
criticism. 5. England—Social conditions—18th century. 6. Social
problems in literature. I. Title. II. Series.
PR448.S64S65 1998
820.9′355—dc21 97–42979
CIP

Set by 35 in 10/12pt Baskerville
Produced by Longman Singapore Publishers (Pte) Ltd.
Printed in Singapore

Contents

Preface

My interest in the value of literary sources to the historian is of long standing. The first book I wrote under my own name alone, some thirty years ago, was a study of Jonathan Swift. In 1983 Gill and Macmillan published my *Society and Literature in England 1700–1760*. That volume attracted such little notice that I was delighted when John Stevenson approached me, suggesting the present volume and offering a fresh opportunity to investigate the subject over a longer period. I wish to thank John and Andrew MacLennan for their encouragement and support during the writing of this book. I also wish to thank Mary Geiter for reading it in manuscript and offering constructive criticism and reassuring appreciation. If it still contains shortcomings then responsibility for them is entirely mine.

One obvious anomaly is that it devotes more space to the later part of the period than it does to the earlier. This is largely because I did not wish to recycle material from previous investigations, which were mostly confined to the years before 1760. The major exception to this is part of chapter one, which first appeared in *History Review* number 26 for December 1996 and is published here with the editor's permission. In my approach to the theme of History and Literature I have sought to take account of contributions to it in the last fifteen or so years, for the historical and literary contexts of the eighteenth century have been altered almost out of recognition since the early 1980s. I have tried to keep abreast of the historiography of the subject, and trust that my citations of historians are as up to date as possible. But I admit that I have not made a similar effort to keep up with shifts in literary criticism from deconstructionism to post-modernism. I plead in extenuation that I am an empirical historian who believes that the evidence which has survived documents an objective reality, however inadequately. I do not consider all historical documents to be texts admitting of a variety of equally valid readings. And I insist that there is a hierarchy of sources and that the value of literature to historians depends on the nature of the questions they address to it. I even think that the authorship of literary sources is relevant to its significance. If that is incorrigibly old-fashioned, so be it.

I write this Preface in the valley of the Susquehanna river, where Joseph Priestley settled and to which the Pantisocrats planned to travel. They could not have hit upon a more delightful spot to fulfil their aspirations, a fulfilment I seek with her to whom the book is dedicated.

Bloomsburg, Pennsylvania, April 1997

For Ollie

Introduction

'Literature and Society in Eighteenth-Century England' seemed to be a self-explanatory title for this book when I first embarked on it. It soon became apparent, however, that it begs a lot of questions. Indeed, almost every word in it needs to be clarified.

Even what constituted the eighteenth century has caused debate among historians.[1] Few confine it to the period 1701 to 1800. Some start it in 1688 and end it in 1783 or 1789. To these the terminal events are the Glorious Revolution and either the loss of the American colonies or the outbreak of the French Revolution. Yet others claim it began as early as 1660 and ended as late as 1832. To them the Restoration of Charles II and the Great Reform Act of 1832 mark out a distinct epoch.

Those who favour a 'short' century ending in the 1780s argue that the period was marked more by change than by continuity. To them the pace of change became so rapid in the penultimate decade that society was being transformed under the impact of economic and political revolutions. The economy was changing under a variety of stimuli. It was not just urbanisation which was proceeding at a rapid pace in the closing decades of the eighteenth century proper. Communications were improving as the turnpike system was completed and the canal age got under way. Agricultural improvements were revolutionising productivity, enabling the country to feed its rapidly growing population. Indeed, demographic trends are seen by some as the most significant motor of change. The population of England and Wales expanded from roughly five millions in 1700 to about nine and a half millions at the time of the first census in 1801. Most of this increase occurred after 1750, since growth in the first half of the eighteenth century was sluggish and might even have stagnated in the 1720s. Industrial production was also expanding from the mid-century, especially in the coal, iron and textile sectors,

1. See W. A. Speck, 'The eighteenth century in Britain: long or short?', *The Historian* (London, 1996), 38, 16–18.

where the rate of growth justified the notion of an incipient industrial revolution.

At the same time the American and French Revolutions stimulated demands for reform – above all from an urban middle class which challenged the hegemony of the landed elite. The slogan 'no taxation without representation' struck a chord in England as well as in America, since so many subjects were unenfranchised, especially in the emergent industrial towns such as Birmingham, Leeds, Manchester and Sheffield. 'Liberty, Equality, Fraternity' also appealed to those who felt that an hierarchical society was entrenching hereditary privilege unfairly on both sides of the English Channel.

Those who prefer a 'long' eighteenth century argue that the era between the Restoration of Charles II and the eve of the Great Reform Act was characterised more by continuity than by change. The social order remained largely unaffected by economic developments. The so-called 'industrial revolution' did not occur until well into the nineteenth century, if it occurred at all. Meanwhile, the economy remained overwhelmingly agricultural, and this ensured the unchallenged hegemony of the landed classes. For the owners of the means of production were not industrialists but landlords. The owners of great estates dominated the countryside, drawing rents from tenant farmers and controlling the instruments of power such as the county militias and the commissions of the peace. Moreover, the constitution in church and state remained essentially Anglican and monarchical, despite crises such as the Revolution of 1688, the War of American Independence and the challenge of the French Revolution. England was to all intents and purposes an *ancien régime*, characterised by a monarchy, an aristocratic social order and a confessional state. These survived in all essentials until the crisis of the late 1820s, when they capitulated to reform in the form of the repeal of the Test and Corporation Acts in 1828, Catholic Emancipation in 1829 and the Parliamentary Reform Act of 1832.

Superficially, literature offers documentation for both views. The notion of a 'short' century is apparently upheld by the traditional labels which literary historians use to depict the period: 'Augustan' and 'Romantic'. Thus, literature from Dryden to Dr Johnson is dubbed 'Augustan', while from Blake to Shelley it is called 'Romantic'. The two labels are, however, very different in origin. Contemporaries applied the term Augustan to the early eighteenth century, even though some literary scholars find it inappropriate. A Quaker visitor to Britain in the 1770s noted that Hardwick Hall in County Durham had 'a number of fine busts of poets, philosophers and historians of the British Augustan Age'.[2] Clearly, he considered it to be over by then. The notion that the subsequent age was predominantly Romantic was not contemporary but was foisted upon it by the Victorians. Some contemporaries, notably Wordsworth, thought they were making a break with the past. Yet others, such as Byron, were admirers of the so-called 'Augustans'. Even in form Byron's poetry owed more to Pope than to Wordsworth, for as he put it, 'prose poets like blank verse, I'm fond of rhyme'.[3] Byron, in fact, felt much the same contempt for 'the Lakers' as Pope did for the Dunces. It has even been claimed that the world of Jane Austen differed little in essentials from that of Fielding and Richardson – so little that one literary scholar feels that she was an honorary Augustan.[4]

The very terms themselves are now at a discount among literary historians. 'Augustan' seems inappropriate, for Augustus Caesar was associated with the flowering of Latin literature fostered by such writers as Ovid and Virgil, whereas under George Augustus, the king of England, literary genius as displayed by Pope and Swift flourished despite the regime, which significantly failed to patronise major writers. 'Romantic' seems to some to be little more than a general label to apply to almost any poet in the period 1780 to 1830. Attempts to define what, if anything, they had in common tend to break down in a welter of exceptions. Of late, too, the break between 'Augustan' and 'Romantic' has become increasingly blurred as scholars search for the transition in such phenomena as 'sensibility', 'neo-classical' and even 'pre-Romantic'. Although historians have appropriated the term 'Augustan' just as literary scholars were inclined to drop it, they have not done so consistently. It seems to have been adopted as a way of avoiding the awkward expression 'late Stuart and early Georgian', and has been applied to a variety of periods between 1660 and 1760. In view of their lack of precision, therefore, these labels have not been generally employed to categorise the period chosen for the present work, which is from about 1680 to about 1820.

The choice of these years was dictated by the major theme of this study, which is that literature both reflected and formed the

2. *An American Quaker in the British Isles: The Travel Journals of Jabez Maud Fisher 1775–1779*, ed. K. Morgan (London, 1992), p. 179. Fisher was not confusing the house he visited with its namesake in Derbyshire.
3. *Don Juan*, I, 201.
4. Alan Downie, 'I'd rather be reading Jane Austen: The Appeal of the Augustans' (inaugural lecture, Goldsmith's College, London, 1995).

prevalent ideologies of the age.[5] Examining literary works in this light established three ideological contexts during the 'long' eighteenth century to which the literature of the age related.

At the outset, from 1680 to about 1720, there was a contest between the conflicting discourses of tories and whigs. The tory view of divine indefeasible hereditary right was challenged by the whigs who emerged in the Exclusion crisis towards the end of Charles II's reign. To justify their attempt to exclude the king's brother from the succession they advanced the theory that there was an implicit contract between kings and their subjects. If the ruler broke the terms of this agreement then those whom he ruled were no longer bound by it and could replace him with another. As a Roman Catholic, Charles' brother James was automatically in breach of the original contract which in a Protestant country involved the defence of the Church of England of which the monarch was supreme governor. Ultimately, whig ideology was based on the concept of popular sovereignty in opposition to the tory view of divine right. Although unsuccessful in the short run, since James succeeded to the throne in 1685, in the long run whig claims seemed justified by the Revolution of 1688.

However, divine right did not disappear overnight but survived the Revolution settlement and even took on a new lease of life when Queen Anne succeeded in 1702. As long as tories were prepared to overlook the legitimacy of the son born to James II's queen in 1688 – and a surprising number were that way inclined – then Anne could be regarded as the hereditary successor after her father's death in 1701. Anne herself, though she flinched from the idea that she ruled by divine right, nevertheless was more in favour of the tories than the whigs, and under her the tory party enjoyed power for the last time in the eighteenth century. Tory ideology was ascendant in the last four years of Queen Anne's reign, though it was significantly modified by the trial of Dr Sacheverell. He upheld the traditional Anglican doctrines of passive obedience and non-resistance,

---

5. I see no reason to alter this conclusion reached after an earlier study of the use of literary sources to the historian: *Society and Literature in England 1700–1760* (Dublin, 1981). On the contrary, examining the longer period 1680 to 1820 has reinforced it. It could be that I have been guilty of the error exposed by Cowper in his poem 'The Progress of Error':

> When some hypothesis absurd and vain
> Has fill'd with fumes a critic's brain,
> The text that sorts not with his darling whim,
> Though plain to others, is obscure to him.

If I have committed it doubtless other critics will point it out.

even to the point of arguing that there was no resistance to the sovereign in 1688. His defenders put forward the argument that he was right in the sense that the sovereign power was not the king alone but the king in parliament, and since the two houses had not been in existence at the time of the Revolution then they could not have been resisted. This was ingenious, but changed tory doctrine significantly since there can be little doubt that the Doctor had meant by the sovereign the king alone.

The tory ministers were superseded by whigs on the accession of George I. During his reign Britain became almost a one-party state. But whiggism, too, was modified under the strains of the rage of party. Resistance was out of favour, to be used only as a last resort when all else had failed. Many whigs even dropped the idea of the sovereignty of the people. To some extent this was a reaction to the fact that appeals to the people in the form of general elections had by and large returned tory majorities to parliament under William and especially Anne. In its stead whigs were more inclined to advance the sovereignty of the king in parliament. This was not far from the position reached by the tories, albeit by a different route.

Under the first two Georges, therefore, a consensus was arrived at that the constitutional arrangements made in the Revolution settlement were ideal, and the political debate took the form of a dispute over the best means of preserving it. In the seventeenth century whigs had argued that historically the English constitution was one of mixed or limited monarchy. Attempts by monarchs since the Norman Conquest to elevate their powers at the expense of those of the people had therefore been illegal. They had been legitimately resisted in such crises as had produced the signing of Magna Carta by King John or of the Petition of Right by Charles I. The civil war and the Glorious Revolution had both been precipitated by Stuart kings intent on asserting their prerogative over parliament, provoking just resistance. Against this whig view of English history tory historians had asserted that the Normans had been perfectly justified in maintaining that the Crown could rule without restraint, and that the resistance to them and their successors had been unlawful. After the accession of the House of Hanover the debate took a different form. Whig supporters of the Hanoverian government accepted that the ancient constitution was of unlimited monarchy, and that limitations had been imposed upon the Crown at the Glorious Revolution. Their opponents, tories now like Bolingbroke as well as whigs, sustained the thesis that the ancient constitution was of limited monarchy and that the Revolution had restored, not established it.

Despite their disagreement over the origin of mixed monarchy, however, both accepted that this was the basis of the constitution.

This consensus began to break down in the 1760s, but it was not until the impact of the American and, above all, of the French Revolutions that it completely collapsed. Thereafter, the dialogue shifted to one between a conservative defence of the Revolution settlement and a radical critique of it which demanded major reform of the constitution. The conservatives continued to appeal to history to justify the existing institutions in church and state. Radicals leapt out of history to assert universal natural rights. During the French revolutionary and Napoleonic wars the conservative ideology was able to retain its hegemony. This was not solely due to the repressive measures adopted by successive governments, which came increasingly to be described as 'tory', though it was not until the ministry of Lord Liverpool after 1812 that ministers accepted the description. The new toryism was genuinely popular, and the repression of radicalism was widely accepted as justified to save England from the threat of Jacobinism.

From this perspective, therefore, the 'long' eighteenth century was not of a piece throughout. Rather the years 1680 to 1820 are best divided for our purposes not into two eras – 'Augustan' and 'Romantic' – but into three. Hence the book has been arranged into chronological sections encompassing the years 1680 to 1720, 1720 to 1780 and 1780 to 1820. Each section starts with a discussion of the prevailing ideologies before considering how these interacted with literature.

Since the word 'ideology' bears several meanings its use in this context requires explanation. Gerald Newman has provided a useful definition of the term for our purpose: 'a large and interconnected body of doctrines and myths, partly inhabiting the underworld of emotions and pre-conscious suppositions, operating intellectually more as a set of enthymemes than as explicit propositions in argument, broadly uniting some class or group (often against another) and giving directions to collective action'.[6] The classes or groups under discussion need to be identified, for thus broadly defined an ideology could encompass various collective entities. For example, eighteenth-century society was very hierarchical and the notion that 'God made them high and lowly and ordered their estate' was widespread. As Isaac Watts put it, 'the Great God has wisely ordained

6. Gerald Newman, *The Rise of English Nationalism: A Cultural History 1740–1830* (London, 1987), p. 79.

in the Course of his Providence in all Ages, that among Mankind there should be some Rich, and some Poor'.[7] This doctrine was used to justify many forms of subordination, for example male hegemony over females. In this respect, men could be regarded as an ideological group conspiring to keep women subordinate to them, a conspiracy thesis which appealed to some early feminist historians.[8] But the doctrine was also used to defend the subservience of servants to masters, a point driven home by Defoe in the significantly titled tract *The Great Law of Subordination Considered*. Although there were sporadic complaints against subjection of wives and servants to husbands and masters, as we shall see there was no orchestrated ideological campaign against it to match that of the Leveller movement of the mid-seventeenth century until the 1790s.

Before that the major ideologies reflected the philosophies of rival political groups. In the 'first age of party' this took the form of a debate between tories and whigs. They disagreed fundamentally on the nature of the constitution in church and state and on the role of the social hierarchy in maintaining it. Although these persisted into the early Georgian era, they were replaced as the dominant ideologies by a Court whiggism in tension with civic humanism. Both accepted the constitutional settlement in the Revolution of 1688, but disagreed as to whether its ideals were being sustained under the first two Georges. This constitutional consensus was eroded by developments after the accession of George III, but did not disintegrate until the late 1780s under the impact of the American and French Revolutions. Thereafter, a conservative defence of the Revolution settlement was in conflict with a radical critique of it which sought to replace it with a more liberal polity. The defenders of the constitution in church and state successfully resisted challenges to it during the reign of George III. During the 1820s, however, a fresh challenge arose, posed not by the French Revolution and its aftermath but by the consequences of the Union of Ireland with Great Britain in 1800. This altered the political agenda and led directly to the age of reform. The literary agenda also changed around 1820, with the deaths of such leading writers as Jane Austen, Lord Byron, John Keats and Percy Bysshe Shelley. For these reasons, therefore, this study ends in 1820.

Reference to a literary agenda raises the problem of the definition of the term 'literature' itself in an ideological context. Today

---

7. I. Watts, *An Essay Towards the Encouragement of Charity Schools* (London, 1728), p. 14.

8. See, for example, Bridget Hill, *Eighteenth-century Women: an Anthology* (London, 1984).

departments of English literature in colleges and universities distinguish creative from other forms of writing and devote their syllabuses to the former in the form of novels, plays and poems. Were this book to be aimed solely at students following such a curriculum the selection of texts would be relatively easy, and the chapters could all be devoted to genres. Thus, the canonical poets from Dryden to Byron, and novelists from Defoe to Scott, would be dealt with discretely. Certainly, these authors are discussed in the following study. Moreover, since the canon has been challenged of late for its exclusiveness, works by other 'creative' writers are also addressed. For example, apart from the novels of Jane Austen, the canon tended to overlook writing by women.[9] Their contributions to the ideological debates are not ignored.

However, this book is intended to be useful not only to readers of novels and poems but also to students of history. Though it would not be true to say that critics in the eighteenth century made no distinction between creative and other forms of literature, it is valid to assert that from a historian's point of view such a distinction is not particularly helpful.[10] For history students seek to ascertain what light literature throws on the questions informing current historiography. To exempt pamphlets such as Burke's *Reflections on the Revolution in France* or periodicals like *The Spectator* on the grounds that they were not 'creative' is to exclude literary achievements which were as significant contributions to a debate about the nature of eighteenth-century society as *The Dunciad* or *Caleb Williams*. Authors like Defoe did not address one set of questions in tracts such as *The Compleat English Tradesman* or journals like *The Review* and a completely different agenda in *Moll Flanders* and *Robinson Crusoe*.[11] But why stop at pamphlets and periodicals? What about sermons, such as Dr Henry Sacheverell's *The Perils of False Brethren*, which was probably read by more people than any other publication in the early eighteenth century? For religious works still provided the bulk of published material, as the eclectic reading of the bibulous shopkeeper Thomas Turner of East Hoathly reflects.[12] Nor should

9. An attempt is made to redress the imbalance in *The 'Other' Eighteenth Century: English Women of Letters 1660–1800*, edited by Robert W. Uphaus and Gretchen M. Foster (London, 1991).

10. R. Terry, 'The Eighteenth-Century Invention of English Literature: a Truism Revisited', *British Journal for Eighteenth-Century Studies* (London, 1996), xix, 47–62.

11. As James Thompson has demonstrated in *Models of Value: Eighteenth-Century Political Economy and the Novel* (London, 1996), pp. 87–131.

12. *The Diary of Thomas Turner 1754–1765*, ed. David Vaisey (Oxford, 1984), Appendix D., pp. 347–53. Turner read a variety of works including sermons, novels, plays, essays and journals.

prints be omitted, such as Hogarth's hugely successful series like *Marriage à la mode*, *The Harlot's Progress*, *The Rake's Progress* and *Industry and Idleness*. For these undoubtedly influenced novelists like Fielding, who frequently referred to Hogarth's example as a narrator. History painting, too, like Benjamin West's *Death of General Wolfe*, inspired biographers and historians. This was a great age of biography, producing such classics in the genre as Gibbon's *Autobiography* and Boswell's *Life of Johnson*. Gibbon also wrote perhaps the most celebrated history in English, *The Decline and Fall of the Roman Empire*, though at the time Hume's *History of England* vied with it for popularity. Such works cannot be ignored in a study of literature and society in the eighteenth century.

'Society' is another term which poses problems. Even if most historians, unlike some politicians, are prepared to accept its existence, they inevitably disagree about its nature. Among those who write on the eighteenth century there is disagreement about the social structure itself. One group of scholars sees an emergent middle class as so significant that it marks the cutting edge of change, while others dispute the very phenomenon.[13] Since a rising bourgeoisie is alleged to have provided the readership for such productions as newspapers and novels, the debate is crucial to a study of literature and society.

Among those who downplay the emergence of a middle class are the unlikely bedfellows of both revisionist and Marxist historians. Thus Jonathan Clark, writing from a revisionist viewpoint, stresses the survival and even the strengthening of the hegemony of the landed elite.[14] This was an era of aristocratic ascendancy. The owners of large estates virtually monopolised representation in both houses of parliament, and, as militia officers and justices of the peace, ruled the countryside in what was still an overwhelmingly rural England. Apart from London, in his view, there was no significant urban centre or growth to challenge their control of national and local affairs. The late Edward Thompson, writing from a Marxist perspective, saw a struggle between capitalists as the owners of the means of production and those who had to sell their labour in a capitalist market. However, he modified this conventional Marxist model by identifying the capitalist class not with urban entrepreneurs but with the rural elite, who exploited their estates for profit. He even called them an agrarian bourgeoisie.[15] Below them were the

13. For a review of the debate see *The British Journal for Eighteenth-Century Studies* (London, 1992), xv, 131–8.
14. J. C. D. Clark, *English Society 1688–1832* (Cambridge, 1985).
15. E. P. Thompson, 'Patricians and Plebs', *Customs in Common* (London, 1993), p. 84.

landless agricultural labourers. Between these patricians and the plebeians, where the middle class should have been expected, was in fact a vacuum. Towns had not grown sufficiently to generate an urban middle class, and in the countryside they were either clients of the landed elite or made common cause with the plebs.

Urban historians, however, have demonstrated that there was a significant degree of urbanisation during the century.[16] Taking a population of 2,500 as the minimum for a town, they argue that in 1700 one in six of the population lived in towns so defined, while by 1800 the proportion had risen to one in three. London grew from about 500,000 in 1700 to 948,000 by 1800, containing roughly ten per cent of the total population of England and Wales throughout the century. The capital was thus a giant, dwarfing all other towns. None could measure their populations in six figures, while in 1700 only seven reached five figures. By 1800, however, there were fifty such towns, including cities like Birmingham and Manchester with over 50,000 inhabitants. An urban infrastructure thus developed which contained a large and growing middle class. These sustained a bourgeois culture which found expression in public and private buildings. Civic pride was exhibited in town halls, markets, churches and hospitals. Private subscriptions built assembly rooms and theatres, while to cater for their patrons coffee houses and taverns were established. The opening of circulating and subscription libraries demonstrates the existence of a reading public in provincial towns.

The printing presses also catered for this growing public. They were mainly located in urban centres, spreading from London, the two university towns and regional capitals to the emergent industrial cities during the course of the century.[17] The newspaper press saw a similar diffusion. London's first daily paper made its appearance in 1702, and by the end of Anne's reign there were papers in two provincial towns. Over the century the newspaper press expanded until by 1800 London sustained several dailies, evenings, bi-weekly and tri-weekly. The publication of those appearing three times a week was planned to take advantage of post days to the provinces, for the London press was not confined to the capital. In 1770 Leonard Herd's African coffee house in Liverpool subscribed to

16. P. J. Corfield, *The Impact of English Towns 1700–1800* (London, 1981); P. Borsay, *The English Urban Renaissance: Culture and Society in the Provincial Town 1660–1770* (Oxford, 1989); Kathleen Wilson, *The Sense of the People: Politics, Culture and Imperialism in England 1715–1785* (Cambridge, 1995).

17. Wilson, *Sense of the People*, p. 29.

ten London newspapers.[18] This did not prevent the growth of local newspapers, for by the end of the century over fifty provincial towns had their own, some of them two or even three. This essentially bourgeois culture was not confined to urban centres but spread far out into the surrounding countryside, newspapers circulating over wide areas of rural England from the towns in which they were printed.

They also penetrated deep into English society. Literacy, tested by the ability to sign the marriage registers made compulsory by Hardwicke's Act of 1753, extended to sixty per cent of males and forty per cent of females. This was an aggregate figure, concealing great discrepancies between classes and places. Most of the gentry and business and professional men could sign, while most agricultural labourers could not. About eighty-five per cent of urban craftsmen had the ability. But this measured the minimum proportion of those who could read, since reading was taught before writing. The vast majority of urban middle-class men and women in eighteenth-century England could read the works discussed below.

Whether they had access to them depended on several considerations. Price was undoubtedly one. Pope's *Works* cost twenty-seven shillings for the nine-volume set in 1751, and his *Iliad* sold for six guineas. At these prices only 'gentle' readers could afford to read them, many of whom undertook to purchase copies in advance of publication by way of subscription. A breakdown of any subscription list soon reveals how far this end of the publishing trade was still dominated by the social and economic elite rather than by the bourgeoisie. Peers, baronets and knights subscribed to books out of all proportion to their numbers in society. Subscription was thus one step down from the patronage of an individual aristocrat towards the open market for books. Another was the circulating library to which individuals paid to be members, such as the one in Bristol where membership cost a guinea a year. While this brought borrowing within the range of the professional and business classes of towns it scarcely made books generally available. Some libraries, however, charged as little as three pence per book per week, which did make their availability more widespread, especially to women, who made up nearly a third of borrowers. Novels at five or six shillings a copy also penetrated further down the social scale, while chap book versions of *Robinson Crusoe* and *Moll Flanders* circulated at the lowest levels of society. Chap books were not covered in

18. Ibid, pp. 30, 39.

the Reviews which emerged to discriminate for the middle classes between the titles aimed at them which flooded from the presses in the eighteenth century. They did, however, review novels, and there is some evidence that their criticisms had some influence on novelists.[19]

The word 'society' in the title, therefore, is restricted to the readership of the literary works examined in this study. As such it concentrates largely on the urban bourgeoisie and their ideologies. In the early eighteenth century this audience was overwhelmingly London-based. The metropolis alone could sustain a market for literary works aimed at middle-class town-dwellers. But by the late eighteenth century there had been sufficient urban growth to sustain a bourgeois readership even in provincial England.

Finally, the word 'England' itself poses problems in a study of this kind. For while its history has been written with little reference to its Celtic fringe, English literature has never been confined to writers who were born in England. Otherwise Burke and Swift, who were born in Ireland, and Smollett, Thomson, Burns and Scott who were Scots, not to mention Welsh authors such as John ap Rhydderch, would be excluded. Whether they identified themselves as Irish or Scottish or Welsh, or as English or British writers raises the whole question of national identities in eighteenth-century Britain. For as Linda Colley has shown, the period following the Anglo-Scottish Union of 1707 saw a deliberate attempt to develop a British identity.[20] However, as Robert Crawford has observed, by and large English writers did little to promote Britishness.[21] Poets from Pope to Byron, though they might speak of Albion and Britain, used these expressions almost invariably to refer to England.[22] Similarly, novelists from Defoe to Austen, when dealing with episodes set in the British Isles, confined them almost exclusively to England, while their heroes and heroines are quintessentially English. 'The English people are not a little vain of themselves and their country', complained James Thomson, 'Britannia too includes our native country Scotland.'[23] Discussing *Roderick Random*, Crawford notes that 'by choosing a Scot as his hero and making the reader aware of the way in which Scottishness is treated, Smollett is beginning to construct a fiction

19. Frank Donoghue, *The Fame Machine: Book Reviewing and Eighteenth-Century Literary Careers* (London, 1996).

20. Linda Colley, *Britons* (London, 1992).

21. Robert Crawford, *Devolving British Literature* (Oxford, 1992).

22. John Lucas, *England and Englishness: Ideas of Nationhood in English Poetry 1688–1900* (London, 1990), p. 3.

23. Quoted in Crawford, *Devolving English Literature*, p. 49.

that is not English (in the national sense) but both Scottish and truly British.'[24] Burns as 'the Scotch bard' could sign himself 'A BRITON . . . and . . . extol the liberty of the "independent British mind" '.[25] Above all, Sir Walter Scott created in his novels writing which was not just Scottish and English but, perhaps pre-eminently, British literature.

The reconciliation of English and Scottish nationalism in British national sentiment was epitomised in a poem of 1803, 'The Harp of Old Ossian':

> Now united with England, our int'rests are joined
> And from Caithness to Cornwall our strength is combin'd,
> All equally Britons, all equally brave,
> All detesting the Tyrant that dares to enslave.
> Thus runs Our New Charter, by Heav'ns first decree,
> Britannia shall conquer, and Britons be free.[26]

Two years later Sir Walter Scott, in his stunningly successful *Lay of the Last Minstrel*, wrote lines which can still stir patriotic sentiment. Though sung in the original by a Scot, they could be equally fervently sung by the English and the Welsh, and in a choir by Britons.

> Breathes there the man, with soul so dead,
> Who never to himself hath said,
> This is my own, my native land!
> Whose heart hath ne'er within him burn'd,
> As home his footsteps he hath turn'd,
> From wandering on a foreign strand!

As Robert Crawford puts it, the *Lay of the Last Minstrel* is 'a poem about the possibility of Britishness'.[27]

---

24. Ibid, p. 60.   25. Ibid, pp. 99, 16.   26. Ibid, pp. 540–1.
27. Ibid, p. 118.

PART ONE

The First Age of Party: 1680–1720

CHAPTER ONE

The First Age of Party

The late Geoffrey Holmes coined the phrase 'the first Age of Party' to refer to the period between the emergence of whigs and tories around 1680 and the relegation of the tory party to permanent opposition after the accession of George I in 1714. Before the late 1670s there had been rival groupings of politicians in parliament along lines which contemporaries called Court and Country, which was roughly equivalent to the modern terms of government and opposition. But these had rarely solidified long enough to be called parties. Nor could they effectively appeal to the electorate since there was no general election between 1661 and 1679. Then there was a sudden spate of three contests in three years, in which politicians appealed to the voters for support. It was during the election campaigns that the terms 'tory' and 'whig' first came into general use to describe political parties. Tory was a name given to Catholic bandits in Ireland. It was applied to those who stood by the Crown's insistence that it ruled by divine, indefeasible hereditary right. Whig was a term used to describe radical Scottish Covenanters, rebellious Presbyterians north of the border. It was similarly transferred to those who denied the divine right of the king's brother to succeed him. Both labels were therefore originally terms of abuse. It is significant that they also had religious connotations, tories being identified with Catholics and whigs with radical Protestant sectarians. For the vast majority of members of both houses of parliament were in fact Anglicans. The second Test Act of 1678 specifically excluded Roman Catholics from the legislature. While dissenters from the Chuch of England were not similarly proscribed, nevertheless few nonconformists sat in the Lords or were returned to the Commons. The party labels were therefore originally associating the peers and MPs to whom they were affixed with extremists at either edge of the religious spectrum in order to discredit them. Tories were alleged to subscribe to views summed up in the contemporary slogan 'Popery and arbitrary power'. Whigs were accused of sympathising with radical sectarianism which had triumphed in the civil wars during the mid-seventeenth century when monarchy had been abolished and a republic had been established. The pejorative origin of the party labels, however, tended to be lost sight of as they continued to be used to describe rival parties well into the eighteenth century.

Although the degree to which the tories were marginalised following the death of Queen Anne has been challenged, her demise indisputably also brought to an end an era in which the parties had alternated in power to such an extent that something like a two-party system seemed to be emerging. Thus there was a whig government between 1708 and 1710, followed by a tory government from 1710 to 1714. The development of a two-party system was cut short with the triumph of the whigs at Court and at the polls in 1715, after which they retained their hold on power so firmly that Britain almost became a one-party state under the first two Georges.

The ability of the tories to mount an effective electoral challenge to the whigs was severely restrained by the Septennial Act of 1716, which replaced the Triennial Act of 1694. This brought an end to an era when elections had taken place on average every two years, during which the electorate had played a major role in the party struggle. The main aim of the 1716 Act was to reduce the influence of the voters over the composition of the House of Commons. As the first duke of Dorset put it, 'triennial elections destroy all family interest and subject our excellent constitution to the caprice of the multitude.'[1] Extending the intervals between general elections to a maximum of seven years enabled family interests to become entrenched in many constituencies, making contests much less of an appeal to the people than they had been in the years 1695 to 1715. The results of this became clear in 1722 at the first septennial election, when the tories were trounced at the polls despite public opinion in the wake of the South Sea Bubble being in their favour. Thereafter, the tory party never came near to winning a majority of seats in the Commons under the first two Georges. The disintegration of the whig party into rival factions shortly afterwards further transformed the context in which the political struggle had been fought out in the first age of party.

1. *Dictionary of National Biography* sub Cranfield, Lionel, 1688–1765.

The emergence of the whig party during the Exclusion crisis of Charles II's reign was first thoroughly investigated by J. R. Jones.[2] He claimed that they brought together different elements which had previously formed the 'Country' opposition to the 'Court' into a party united on the single issue of preventing the king's brother, James, duke of York, from succeeding him. The duke became their target when the Popish Plot of 1678, allegedly a Catholic conspiracy to assassinate Charles, raised the issue of the succession. For James was a Roman Catholic, which was held to be incompatible with the exercise of a Protestant kingship and governorship of the Church of England. Worse yet, Catholics were regarded as potential traitors since their prime allegiance was to the Pope rather than to the constitution. In three successive parliaments held between 1679 and 1681 the whigs introduced bills to exclude James from the Crown. They passed the House of Commons, where they could command a majority, but failed to become law as the king prorogued parliament in 1679 and 1681 to prevent the further progress of the bill, while in 1680 it was actually defeated in the House of Lords.

According to Jones, the first whigs were held together by the leadership of the first earl of Shaftesbury. K. H. D. Haley essentially substantiated this thesis in his biography of Shaftesbury.[3] In Haley's view, Shaftesbury sought to make the king responsible to parliament. He did not commit himself to the duke of Monmouth, Charles II's illegitimate son, as a replacement for James. That would have alienated the duke's daughter, Mary, and her powerful Dutch husband, William, the Prince of Orange. Above all he did not wish to raise up a commonwealth, or republic, but wished to place parliamentary limitations on the monarchy. Hence the very term 'whig' was a libel fixed on the Exclusionists by their opponents in order to discredit them by association with the republicans of the Interregnum.

The picture of the first whigs painted by Jones and Haley remained the orthodoxy for a generation. Recently, however, it has come under heavy attack. The very idea that coherent parties emerged in the Exclusion crisis with programmes to implement and organisations to appeal to the electorate has been challenged by Mark Knights.[4] Knights investigates electoral activity in the period and sees very little evidence of party organisation in the constituencies. While conceding that parliament became increasingly polarised over the issue of Exclusion, he questions whether the alignments

2. J. R. Jones, *The First Whigs* (London, 1961).
3. K. H. D. Haley, *The First Earl of Shaftesbury* (London, 1968).
4. M. Knights, *Politics and Opinion in Crisis 1678–1681* (London, 1994).

of politicians at Westminster can be considered as parties in any modern sense.

The notion that the first whigs sought merely to exclude the duke of York from the throne and had no other constitutional objectives has been particularly criticised. One of the weightier attacks was launched by Richard Ashcraft.[5] Although primarily interested in the political theory of John Locke, he seeks to place this in the context of Restoration politics. For Locke was Shaftesbury's private secretary and, in Ashcraft's view, was much influenced by the earl in the formation of his radical political theory. Locke is principally remembered for his maxim that government exists to protect liberty and property. This became a respectable creed of the ruling classes in the eighteenth century. But they tended to play down the radical premises on which Locke based his liberal conclusion, which included the right of subjects to consent to laws, backed up ultimately by the right to resist a ruler who flouted their consent. Placed in the context of the Exclusion crisis, they advocated not so much parliamentary monarchy as republicanism. That the first whigs used parliament as a means to an end and not as an end in itself was demonstrated to Ashcraft's satisfaction by their involvement in the Rye House Plot in 1683. Where previous historians had written this off as being as fabricated as the Popish Plot in an attempt to 'frame' the whig leadership, revisionists maintain that it was a deadly serious conspiracy to kill both Charles and his brother. Ultimately, the whigs were a revolutionary party intent on setting up a commonwealth.

The notion that the first earl of Shaftesbury was the leader of the opposition to the Court in the parliaments held between 1679 and 1681 has also been challenged by Jonathan Scott. Like Ashcraft, he takes seriously the charge that republicanism was in the air during those years. But he sees the main republican threat coming not from John Locke and the whigs but from Algernon Sidney.[6] Scott is against the notion that these years were characterised by the Exclusion crisis. In his view, the attempt to exclude the duke of York was but one political campaign, and not the main one either. Charles II's opponents sought to limit him as well as his brother. They were intent on setting up a republic, hoping to succeed in the late 1670s and early 1680s where previous republicans had ultimately failed in the 1650s. In that sense it was the epilogue to the good old cause and not the prologue to the Glorious Revolution.

5. R. Ashcraft, *Revolutionary Politics and Locke's Two Treatises of Government* (London, 1986).
6. J. Scott, *Algernon Sidney and the Restoration Crisis, 1677–1683* (London, 1991).

Other historians, however, have questioned these assumptions, preferring to retain the notion of an Exclusion crisis.[7] Where Scott maintains that many 'whigs' of the early 1680s became 'tories' during the reaction of the mid-1680s, they see a continuity between the parties which emerged in the late 1670s and those which existed in the reigns of William and Anne. In particular, Tim Harris sees threads connecting the tories, whom Scott by and large ignores, right through from the later Stuart to the early Hanoverian eras.[8]

One thread was the succession and the divine indefeasible right of the Stuarts to it. The word 'tory' was first used as a political term to describe those who stood by the duke of York when he was under attack from the whigs. They upheld the hereditary principle and denied that subjects had any right to resist at all. On the contrary, they should practise passive obedience and nonresistance. These principles were constantly preached by the clergy of the Church of England from the Restoration into the eighteenth century. Unfortunately, in James II's reign, tories found that they had to choose between the king and the church. For the Catholic monarch proceeded to strip the established church of privileges which it had enjoyed since his brother's restoration. For example, he used the royal prerogative of dispensing with laws to issue dispensations to non-Anglicans, granting them immunity from the Test and Corporation Acts. These laws in theory confined offices under the Crown and in borough corporations to communicating members of the Church of England. James' use of the dispensing power thus threatened to break the Anglican monopoly of power.

Faced with a choice between Crown and church, most tories chose the latter. They wished to maintain the privileged position of the Church of England which had been the cornerstone of the Restoration of Charles II in 1660. The church was 'by law established' and in theory Anglican worship was the only form of religious observance legally allowed by the Act of Uniformity of 1662. Other denominations, Protestant as well as Catholic, far from being tolerated, were banned and prosecuted for holding separate congregations. James sought to remove the discrimination when he issued two Declarations of Indulgence which breached the Act of Uniformity. These edicts of toleration suspended the penal laws so that no non-Anglicans

---

7. See the essays on 'Order and Authority: Creating Party in Restoration England' in *Albion* vol. 25, no. 4, Winter 1993.

8. T. Harris, *Politics under the Later Stuarts: Party Conflict in a Divided Society 1660–1715* (London, 1993). This is by far the best overview of the current historiography, with seminal ideas from the author's own research.

could be prosecuted for being in breach of them. This use of the
royal suspending power particularly alarmed the Anglican clergy.
When on the second occasion the king insisted that the Declaration
should be read out in every church by the minister, it produced a
storm of protest, led by seven bishops, including the archbishop
of Canterbury. The Revolution of 1688 occurred in great measure
because tories were not prepared to put up with the king's attacks
on their beloved church. Religious differences were thus a constant
theme in the debate between the whigs and tories during the first
age of party.

The Glorious Revolution, however, gave rise to questions which
had not faced the parties under Charles II and James II. Thus, the
great issues raised by the first whigs and tories of the succession
and the relationship of the Anglican Church to dissenters had been
apparently resolved by the Bill of Rights and the Toleration Act.
The former placed the succession to the throne in the children of
William and Mary, failing which, Anne's children should succeed
and then, if that failed, any children William might have should
he remarry in the event of Mary's death. At the time it seemed as
though every eventuality had been anticipated. Because most tories
had come to place their devotion to the church before their allegiance to the Stuarts, only a minority continued to support the exiled
James II, being called Jacobites after the Latin form of the king's
name, Jacobus. An abortive attempt to assassinate William in 1696
and to restore James revealed how little support the Jacobite cause
had in England, even among the tories. The succession was no longer
a major issue between the parties. The Bill of Rights also placed
restrictions upon the royal prerogative which, in the opinion of its
framers, had been abused by James II. Most of these safeguarded
the Church of England from misuse of the suspending and dispensing powers by future monarchs. At the same time, the Toleration
Act removed the safegurd of the penal laws in the case of Protestant
dissenters. Those who believed in the Trinity were allowed to worship
separately from the established church in their own conventicles.

In the place of the succession and religion other issues arose,
mainly as a result of the outbreak of war with Louis XIV's France.
Outstanding among these was the sheer cost of the war. Where
under Charles II and James II the total permanent revenue granted
to the Crown by parliament amounted to £1,200,000 a year, under
William III the Commons voted on average £5,000,000 per annum
for the war effort. These unprecedented sums were raised by taxation, the most important being the land tax, which, in theory at

least, was a twenty per cent rate on landed incomes. The gentry, who bore the brunt of this, found it an increasingly intolerable burden. They were particularly incensed when those who lent to the state in anticipation of the yields of taxation seemed to be enjoying a good return on their loans. The gentry objected that the state's creditors were benefiting at their expense. They claimed that war finance had created a monied interest which was profiting at the expense of the landed interest. What they were objecting to was what historians have dubbed the military-fiscal state. Britain's rapid rise to great power status after the Glorious Revolution was achieved by the state's harnessing of resources to sustain a military and naval machine which enabled it successfully to challenge the hegemony of France – ultimately on three continents.

Objections to the creation of this financial-military complex took on a political aspect when the new machinery of public credit established to manage the national debt, which included the establishment of the Bank of England in 1694, was attributed to the whig ministers whom William had appointed in 1693. But the complaints did not come just from disgruntled tories. The most vociferous criticisms of the Junto, as the new ministers were known, came from fellow whigs led by Robert Harley. They joined with opposition tories to form what contemporaries called the Country party.

One of the planks in the Country platform was the campaign to remove placemen from parliament. Placemen were those members of parliament who had 'places' under the Crown. They might have Cabinet posts such as that of Chancellor of the Exchequer, whose presence in the Commons was regarded by the government as essential for the effective management of its business in the lower house. But they also included sinecurists such as the farmers of the green wax or the clerks comptrollers of the green cloth. These posts had long since ceased to serve any administrative purpose and were used purely to reward MPs for their support of the government's measures. It was this function which raised alarm among the Country members. They argued that the Court was systematically promoting MPs to places which were little more than bribes for services rendered, and that, if this process continued, the Commons would become a mere mouthpiece of the government. These fears were expressed in *The Danger of Mercenary Parliaments*, published in 1696. It complained that debates in the Commons had been orchestrated by the Court, reducing it to an organ where the little squeaking trebles and the great humming basses were blown with one blast of wind from the same source. The campaign against placemen made some striking progress in William's reign. In 1700 Acts of parliament excluded excise officers from the Commons, declaring membership to be incompatible with a place in the excise service. In 1701 the Act of Settlement was passed, containing a clause that no member should be allowed to accept an office of profit under the Crown.

The Country opposition also criticised the standing army on the grounds that it was a threat to liberty. They pointed out that professional troops had been used by absolute monarchs on the continent, such as Louis XIV of France, to crush representative institutions. Liberty was best secured by a citizen militia. England did not need a standing army since the navy could protect its shores. The Bill of Rights actually contained a clause which made illegal the maintenance of a standing army in time of peace without consent of parliament. Since William was at war with France from 1689 until 1697 this restriction upon his prerogative did not come into operation immediately.

When the nine years' war ended in 1697, however, the Country elements in the Commons objected to the maintenance of a standing army in time of peace. The king, realising that the treaty of Ryswick was merely a truce, wished to keep on foot at least 30,000 men in anticipation of renewed hostilities. His tory and whig opponents joined to defeat him, reducing the armed forces to 10,000 before the general election in 1698, and to 7,000 after their success at the polls. The election polarised the electorate as well as the politicians more along the lines of Court and Country than whig and tory.

Although historians used to call the opposition to the emerging fiscal-military state the Country party, recently David Hayton has convincingly refuted this concept.[9] He has shown that most of the Court's opponents were, in fact, tories. Moreover, the whigs who opposed it were far from being typical Country members of parliament. Although Country propaganda appealed to independent gentry living on their own estates, most so-called Country whigs were professional men, army officers, lawyers and the like. Their criticism of the Court was partly inspired by careerist ambitions. Certainly, their careers showed that they were not against joining the government benches when it suited them. While the issues raised by the war cut across those which divided tory from whig, therefore, they did not similarly polarise parliament into permanent parties. The main division remained that separating tories from whigs.

9. D. Hayton, 'The "Country" interest and the party system, 1689–c1720', in C. Jones (ed.), *Party and Management in Parliament, 1660–1784* (London, 1984), pp. 37–86.

This became abundantly clear in Anne's reign. For while Country issues survived William's death, finding expression in campaigns to exclude placemen from parliament, they did not assume the significance that they had done in the 1690s. Above all, they did not lead to the formation of a Country party, even in contemporary parlance. The biggest attack on placemen occurred in the session of 1705–6 when whigs opposed to the Court actually adopted a different stance from that taken up by the tories. The place clause in the Act of Settlement, had it come into effect, would have eliminated all placemen from the Commons – Cabinet ministers as well as sinecurists. This would effectively have nipped Cabinet government in the bud, and the Court was determined to amend, if not repeal, it. Fortunately for the Court, there was a breathing space provided by the fact that the Act was not to come into operation until the death of Anne. In 1705 an opportunity was created by the passage of a Regency Act, making arrangements for the smooth transference of government to her successor, to alter the blanket proscription of placemen. The tories still insisted on their complete elimination from the Commons. But opposition whigs appreciated the need for key government ministers to be in the house, and tried to exempt them from the general ban. In the end a compromise was struck whereby certain offices were declared incompatible with membership of parliament, including any post created after the passage of the Act, while all MPs appointed to positions under the Crown had to seek re-election from their constituencies. The holding of by-elections after a placeman had been appointed to office aimed at obtaining the endorsement of his constituents that he could serve both them and the Crown.

The Country whigs' appreciation of the need to have ministers in the Commons stemmed from their concern that the ministry should not be weakened in parliament at the time of the transference of the Crown to the House of Hanover and thus play into the hands of the exiled Stuarts. Critics of the tories accused them of secretly abetting the Jacobite cause by their intransigence over the issue. This demonstrated that the succession had again come to the foreground of the political scene.

The re-emergence of the succession problem arose from the fact that all the arrangements made in the Bill of Rights to secure it had failed. Mary had died childless in 1694. It was clear that William would never marry again. Then, in 1700, the duke of Gloucester, the only one of Anne's children to survive babyhood, died at the age of eleven. Fresh statutory provision had therefore to be made for the queen's successor. In 1701 the Act of Settlement placed the succession in the House of Hanover, but many tories had misgivings over an arrangement which broke the hereditary principle in order to ensure a Protestant successor to such an extent that some fifty Catholic claimants were overlooked.

The religious questions apparently resolved in the Revolution settlement were also re-opened towards the end of William's reign. The so-called Toleration Act of 1689, granting the right to Protestants to worship separately in their own conventicles, led to the emergence of rival congregations of Presbyterians, Baptists, Independents and Quakers. The legal challenge to their care of souls alarmed the Anglican clergy. They saw their congregations falling as their parishioners left the established church to attend conventicles, or even stopped going to church altogether. For although the Toleration Act did not remove the statutory requirement that people attend their compulsory devotions on Sundays, there was little that could be done to enforce it now that the Church of England had been partially disestablished. The Toleration Act also specifically upheld the duty of every subject to pay tithes to the established church. But many dissenters, especially Quakers, objected to doing so. Those who obstinately refused to pay had to be sued by Anglican vicars, a hazardous and contentious process from which many shrank. Even those who were determined to secure their dues, whatever the hazard to relations with their parishioners, were thwarted by the weakening of the powers of the ecclesiastical courts, and the recourse of men sued for nonpayment of tithes to have their cases transferred to the lay courts where ministers were less sympathetically treated. Little wonder that the bulk of the Anglican clergy felt that the church was in danger during the 1690s.

Many sought to turn the clock back by demanding that Convocation should meet to clamp down on dissent. Convocation was a body which represented the clergy of the diocese of Canterbury, bishops being returned directly to an upper house, while representatives of the inferior clergy were elected to a lower house. It had not met since 1689, which some clergymen felt was a deliberate conspiracy to silence them. Led by Francis Atterbury, who published *A Letter to a Convocation Man* in 1696, they demanded that it should meet. When it eventually met in 1701, however, it showed itself to be violently divided between the two houses. The upper house was reluctant to antagonise dissenters, as nonconformists were called, while the lower house demanded action to uphold Anglican privileges. The majority in the upper house were dubbed 'low church' while that in the lower was known as 'high church'. The low and high church parties were the clerical equivalents of the lay whigs and tories.

The latter sought in parliament to retrieve the monopoly of power held by Anglicans before the Revolution. This had been breached in practice because some dissenters, mainly Presbyterians, had no scruples about taking communion in the established church in order to qualify for office, especially in borough corporations, then attending their own conventicles. Tories were determined to stamp out this 'occasional conformity' as it was called, and tried to pass statutes to penalise it. Though bills passed the House of Commons three times in the first three years of Anne's reign, they were prevented from becoming law by opposition in the Lords. Thus, Anne's first parliament reflected the situation in Convocation, with a whig upper house and a tory lower house. An occasional conformity bill eventually reached the statute book in 1711 only because for the first time in the reign the measure obtained a majority in both houses. The tories wrested control of the Commons from the whigs in the general election of 1710. This reversal of the outcome of the previous election (held as recently as 1708) was partly due to the raising of the cry 'the church in danger' by tories alarmed at the impeachment of Dr Sacheverell by the whig-dominated parliament. This signalised a reversal of fortune for the whigs. The tories sustained a petitioning campaign over the summer of 1710, assuring the queen that, were she to dissolve parliament, a tory majority would emerge from the subsequent polls. Anne eventually proclaimed a dissolution in September and the result, as predicted, was a defeat for the whigs and a victory for their rivals.

When the tories met in parliament they revived the clamour over occasional conformity which had been raised in Anne's first parliament. But this time the whigs in the upper house did not renew their resistance to passing a bill to outlaw the practice. Although they were criticised for deserting their dissenting allies, they justified their apparent apostasy on the grounds that their opposition to the peace terms which the tory ministry was negotiating with France was a higher priority, and they needed the support of renegade tories to defeat them. Acquiescence in the passage of the Occasional Conformity Act was the price paid for that support.

Certainly, the ending of the War of the Spanish Succession became the greatest issue in the last four years of Anne's reign. Swift even asserted in his history of them

> by this time ... all disputes which used originally to divide whig
> and tory were wholly dropped; and those fantastical words ought in
> justice to have been so too, provided we could have found out more
> convenient terms whereby to distinguish lovers of peace from lovers
> of war.[10]

Swift thereby summed up a theme which he himself had developed
since becoming the tory ministry's main propagandist after 1710.
In the pages of *The Examiner*, a weekly paper supporting government policy, and in *The Conduct of the Allies* he accused the whigs
of being warmongers, asserting that they, in alliance with the duke
of Marlborough, had sought to perpetuate the war in order to
aggrandise themselves and to ruin tory country gentlemen who paid
heavily in direct taxes to sustain the war effort.

Although this was an exaggeration, there was some truth in it.
Tories had all along expressed reservations about the commitment
to the war aims of the Grand Alliance. These necessitated massive
military involvement in continental Europe. To the tory mentality
England's natural element was the sea rather than land, and naval
warfare was more appropriate than military campaigns on the continent. This so-called 'blue water policy' had caused tory ministers
to clash with the duke of Marlborough in Cabinet discussions about
strategy earlier in the reign. One reason why the Captain General
persuaded the queen to get rid of her tory advisers and to turn to
the whigs was that the whig party was much more solidly in favour
of backing his continental campaigns. These paid dividends in his
great victories at Blenheim, Ramillies and Oudenarde, but seemed
to be committing the country to endless hostilities with France after
the battle of Malplaquet. War weariness as much as fear that the
church was in danger accounted for the success of tories at the polls
in 1710. Thereafter, there were other signs that the war had come
to eclipse the religious and dynastic issues which had previously been
the main bones of contention between the parties. Whig acceptance
of a bill against occasional conformity seemed to mark a diminution
of the religious antagonisms which divided them, while the acceptance of the Hanoverian succession by the bulk of the tory party also
marked a diminution of the importance of the dynastic question.
But the making of the treaty of Utrecht kept up the rage of party.
The tories, backed by a war-weary gentry protesting against the burden of the land tax, sought peace at almost any price. The whigs
still held out for placing the Habsburg candidate on the throne of

10. J. Swift, *The History of the Four last Years of the Queen* (London, 1758), p. 7.

Spain, even to the point of insisting that Louis XIV should help the allies to prise his grandson the Bourbon claimant from it. Their intransigence, summed up in the slogan 'no peace without Spain', led their opponents to claim that they were deliberately prolonging the war for their own advantage, being the party of military and monied men who profited from the war.

As we shall see, there was a serious discrepancy between the image and the social reality in this dispute.[11] But though there were many whig gentry and not a few tory military and monied men, this does not mean that the claims should be totally discarded. Party ideology is a political reality which is a significant historical phenomenon regardless of its objective validity. In recent times the Conservative and Labour parties in Britain claimed to be protecting the interests of distinct classes. The fact that many middle-class voters voted Labour and many more working class voters polled for the Conservatives is really beside the point. Partisans on both sides believed that their party best upheld the interests of the classes they claimed to espouse. Similarly, the tories and whigs of Anne's reign claimed that they best maintained the landed and the monied interests respectively. Tories waxed lyrical over the merits of the country gentry. 'The gentry of England', claimed a tory writer, 'are the Treasury of the nation, the support of the Crown, the safety of the Kingdom, the walls of the Church, the pillars of the state.'[12] Francis Atterbury described the landed interest as 'the political blood of the nation'. Whig writers extolled the contribution of merchants to the economy. In *The Spectator* Addison and Steele could paint a sympathetic portrait of a country gentleman in the figure of Sir Roger de Coverley, but their main sympathies clearly lay with Sir Andrew Freeport, the merchant member of the Club. They also defended public credit, the money market and the Bank of England.

The alleged clash of interests thus exacerbated the debate over the ending of the War of the Spanish Succession. Although the tories upheld the peace preliminaries in the House of Commons, the whigs in the Lords, with assistance from a small group of tories led by the earl of Nottingham, managed to defeat them in December 1711. The leading minister, Robert Harley, solved the political dilemma this provoked by persuading the queen to create twelve new peers in January 1712. This controversial move meant that there was a

---

11. See below.
12. *The Character of a Whig under Several Denominations* (London, 1700), p. 132. After castigating whigs of all kinds the author of the tract turned to depict 'a true English country gentleman'.

tory majority in both houses for the first and only time in the early
eighteenth century.

The creation of a dozen peers demonstrated in the starkest
possible way that the Crown was still a major force in politics. The
influence of the Crown offset the tendency towards a two-party
system.[13] For although the alternation in power of the whigs, from
1708 to 1710, with the tories, from 1710 to 1714, seemed to demonstrate that such a system had emerged, in the last analysis no
party completely monopolised power under Anne. While the Cabinet
consisted overwhelmingly of one party between 1708 and 1710, and
again from 1712 to 1714, there were junior officers and placemen
from the other party in post in both periods. This was because the
Crown was determined that no one party should be in complete
control of the ministry. Both William and Anne sought to keep
themselves out of the hands of 'the merciless men of both parties'
by forming mixed ministries. It was only when George I was persuaded to proscribe the tories from office completely at all levels
of the administration, including even the commissions of the peace,
that one party began to enjoy a monopoly of power. With that
development the first age of party came to an end.

13. W. A. Speck, *The Birth of Britain: A New Nation 1700–1710* (London, 1994)
attempts to establish this from a narrative of the politics of the first decade of the
eighteenth century.

CHAPTER TWO

Poems on Affairs of State

A characteristic literary work of the late Stuart age was the poem on affairs of state. Topical verse satires of the Court and prominent politicians were written by poets as eminent as John Dryden, Andrew Marvell, the earl of Rochester and Jonathan Swift, as well as by anonymous Grub Street hacks, with Daniel Defoe's doggerel verses lying somewhere in between. They began to appear in the 1660s, but gathered momentum towards the end of the 1670s under the stimulus of the Popish Plot and Exclusion crisis.[1] After the Glorious Revolution anthologies of them were published with such titles as *Wit and Mirth: or, Pills to Purge Melancholy, Political Merriment* and *Poems on Affairs of State*. Such compilations were produced regularly under Queen Anne. But shortly after her death the seam suddenly expired. To be sure, there were political poems aplenty thereafter. Much of Pope's output was political, while Johnson's first poem, 'London', was charged with politics. Poets continued to discuss the state of affairs down to Shelley's 'The Mask of Anarchy' and beyond. But they did not address affairs of state in the same way as their predecessors had done under the later Stuarts.

What characterised the genre was an assumption by the poet of familiarity with the private lives of kings, queens and politicians. For instance, their sexual activities are related often in startling detail, which makes some of the poems not just suggestive but quite explicitly pornographic. The aim of such scandalous assertions was not merely to titillate or shock the reader. It was to insinuate that infidelity to a spouse implied disloyalty to public duties too. Thus,

1. Thus in the edition of *Poems on Affairs of State: Augustan Satirical Verse 1660–1714* under the general editorship of George deForest Lord, published by Yale University Press (7 volumes, 1962–75) [hereafter *POAS*] one volume sufficed for the years 1660–78, while the second volume dealt with the years 1678–81.

31

the divine right of kings claimed by Charles and James II contrasted starkly with their flagrant immorality. Hence the stress in
the poems on their promiscuity. John Wilmot, earl of Rochester,
represented the king as a debauchee in 'A satyr on Charles II'.

> Peace is his aim, his gentleness is such
> And love he loves, for he loves fucking much
> Nor are his high desires above his strength
> His sceptre and his prick are of a length;
> And she may sway the one who plays with th'other
> And make him little wiser than his brother.[2]

Charles' brother James was not renowned for his wisdom. 'Oh sacred
James!' implored a poem after he became king himself, 'may thy
dread noddle be, as free from danger as from wit 'tis free.' Like Charles before him he was known for his lechery, though as one poet
put it, 'in his mistresses kind James loves ugliness in its extremes.'[3]
Their looks allegedly led Charles to say that they were imposed on
James as a penance by his priests. William III's homosexuality was
taken for granted in satirical verse of the 1690s.[4] As a ballad on the
coronation delicately put it

> . . . buggering of Benting doth please to the life
> A dainty fine King indeed.[5]

It enabled Jacobite poets to satirise his conduct as unnatural both
in his sexual relations with favourites such as the earl of Portland
and in his political relations with his father-in-law James II. It also
gave rise to speculation about his physical relations with his wife
Mary. The satire on the coronation claimed that

> He is not qualified for his wife
> Because of the cruel midwife's knife.

Early in their reign a poet imagined Mary

> At dead of night after an evening ball
> In her own father's lodgings at Whitehall

2. *The Complete Poems of John Wilmot, earl of Rochester*, ed. David M. Vieth (London,
1968), p. 61. Cf. *POAS*, i, 424.
3. *POAS*, iv, 154, 193.
4. W. A. Speck, 'William – and Mary?', in Lois G. Schwoerer (ed.), *The Revolution
of 1688–1689: changing perspectives* (Cambridge, 1992), p. 143.
5. *POAS*, v, 41–2.

lying unregarded by 'a dull lump of Netherlandish clay'

> Whose frozen veins not all her charms could move
> (The hero is uncapable of love
> Thanks to a secret gripe he got when young . . .
> Neglected thus the longing wishing queen
> Contemplates on the gallant youths she'd seen
> Whose brisk ideas feed her warm desire
> And fancy adds more fuel to the fire . . .[6]

As for Anne, her relationship with Abigail Masham inspired a whig poet to write

> Whenas Queen Anne of great renown
> Great Britain's scepter swayed
> Besides the church she dearly loved
> A dirty chambermaid . . .[7]

The sex lives of politicians were given a similar treatment. The earl of Dorset lambasted a host of them in *A faithful catalogue of our most eminent ninnies*:

> Go on my muse and with bold voice proclaim
> The vicious lives and long detested fame
> Of scoundrel lords and their lewd wives' amours
> Pimp-statesmen, buggr'ing priests, court bawds and whores.[8]

The poets assumed that their readers were familiar with the private lives of eminent persons too, which implies a restricted readership of initiates. High politics was still a game with relatively few players, and verse satires circulated, often in manuscript, among a small circle of interested parties. Thus the *Catalogue of ninnies* was never printed, being 'written for those among the gentry and court who could understand the numerous allusions to contemporary scandal'.[9] Among the poems inspired by the trial of Dr Sacheverell in 1710, one, 'Dr Sacheverell and Benjamin Hoadly . . . survives in a printed copy and ten manuscripts', another, 'The Thanksgiving . . . survives in 16 manuscript copies and two printed anthologies', and a third, 'Found on the Queen's Toilet . . . survives in the copy text and 13 collateral manuscripts'.[10] All these manuscript copies indicate that the poems were distributed among a number of prominent peers and politicians. There is even evidence for the existence of scriptoria which employed amanuenses to make multiple copies

6. *Anthology of Poems on Affairs of State*, ed. George deForest Lord (London, 1975), p. 528.

7. Ibid, pp. 706–7.   8. *POAS*, iv, 190.   9. *POAS*, iv, 190.

10. *POAS*, vii, 653, 661, 663, 665.

of poems for distribution. Most poems on affairs of state clearly appealed to the elite more than to the plebs. It is this exclusive audience as much as the distance in time which makes the poems so allusive that they require extensive annotation in modern editions, such as the seven volumes of *Poems on Affairs of State* which Yale University Press published between 1962 and 1975. These were felt to need so much elucidation that at times the texts of the poems become thin rivulets of verse trickling through fertile meadows of footnotes. Contemporaries outside the charmed circle familiar with Court and parliament would have been as baffled as today's students by the allusions, and have needed almost as much explanation.

The limited readership of such poems is an important clue to their target audiences. This can be illustrated from the most celebrated example of the genre, Dryden's 'Absalom and Achitophel'. It has been suggested that the satire was intended to influence the Middlesex grand jury, which was about to hear charges of treason against the first earl of Shaftesbury, the 'false Achitophel' of the poem, shortly after it first appeared on 17 November 1681. But this is highly improbable. That they would return an answer of 'ignoramus' to the charges, meaning that Shaftesbury had no case to answer and was therefore acquitted, was a foregone conclusion. The jury had been handpicked by sheriffs who were political associates of Shaftesbury.

Who, then, was 'the reader' whom Dryden addressed in the preface to the poem? 'He who draws his pen for one party', he there asserts, 'must expect to make enemies of the other.' The two parties he had in mind are indicated when he continues 'For Wit and Fool are consequences of Whig and Tory.' A whig was the pejorative name given to anybody who wished to exclude James duke of York, the king's brother, from the succession to the Crown. A tory was the riposte of those who stood by his indefeasible divine hereditary right to succeed. Dryden, who supported James's claim to the throne, is usually identified as a tory. But it is not clear that he identifies himself with that party in the poem. On the contrary he says of an 'Anti-Bromingham', another abusive name for a tory, that 'their manifest prejudice to my Cause will render their Judgment of less Authority against me.' What was his 'cause' that the tories opposed? It was not 'the good old cause' of the 'commonwealthsmen', or republicans, whom he also criticises. In doing so he draws attention to the anonymity of the poem's publication. 'You cannot be so unconscionable as to charge me for not subscribing of my own name, for that would reflect too grossly upon your own party, who never dare.' Dryden published the poem anonymously in order to impersonate a moderate politician: 'they are not the violent whom I desire to please.' Moreover, the moderation he personified was that of a moderate whig rather than of a tory. 'If I happen to please the more moderate sort', he asserts, 'I shall be sure of an Honest party.' It was the whigs who called themselves the 'honest party' by contrast with the tories, whom they dubbed 'the faction'.

Dryden's target, therefore, is the moderate whig politicians, whom he hopes to persuade to repudiate Shaftesbury and the extremists with whom he is allegedly in league to bring about a quasi-republic under a puppet king, the duke of Monmouth. One such moderate is Monmouth himself, whom 'the author' hopes will be reconciled with his father. 'Were I the Inventor, who am only the Historian, I should certainly conclude the Piece with the Reconcilement of Absalom to David.' By impersonating one of them, Dryden attempted to reconcile moderate whigs with the king too. In this he was following royal policy, for Charles II dreaded a violent outcome of the crisis, and tried to avert one by appealing to the same elements to rally to his side.

Dryden's impersonation of a whig is evident from the opening line of the poem: 'in pious times e'er Priestcraft did begin'. For 'priestcraft' was a term employed by anti-clerical whigs at the time.[11] The unflattering view of the king 'scattering his Maker's image through the land' is scarcely that of a believer in his divine right. Yet the résumé of recent English history in the poem stresses a lesson which the Court's appeal to moderate whigs stressed endlessly: the danger of civil war erupting again. Earlier crises in Charles' reign had been resolved when 'moderate men', 'looking backward with a wise affright . . . curst the memory of civil wars' and 'inclined the ballance to the better side'. What made the Exclusion crisis potentially different was the Popish Plot which preceded it and to some extent precipitated it. This had provided Shaftesbury with an opportunity which he had exploited for his own ends.

> The wish'd occasion of the Plot he takes
> Some circumstances finds but more he makes.

That there was a genuine plot the moderate whig 'author' believes, though Dryden himself did not: 'some truth there was, but dash'd and brewed with lies.' It was the unscrupulous exploitation of it

---

11. Mark Goldie, 'Priestcraft and the birth of whiggism', in N. Phillipson and Q. Skinner (eds), *Political Discourse in Early Modern Britain* (London, 1993), pp. 209–31.

which betrayed 'Achitophel' as an extremist: 'the good old cause reviv'd a Plot requires'.

How far the first earl of Shaftesbury was committed to 'the good old cause', that of the Republicans in the Interregnum, is debated by historians.[12] To the earl's biographer and to the historian of 'the first whigs' he was a consistent parliamentary monarchist who simply wanted to make kings accountable to parliament. Dryden was therefore guilty of flagrant tory propaganda when he associated them with the 'good old cause'. To recent revisionist historians, however, Shaftesbury was bent on reducing the Crown to a cipher. Dryden therefore was saying no more than the truth when he wrote that

> Plots true or false are necessary things
> To raise up Commonwealths and ruin Kings.

Dryden, however, is speaking here not directly but through the mouth of a moderate whig who regards the earl as a crypto-republican. He accuses him of seducing Monmouth to his side in order to make him a puppet king

> That kingly power thus ebbing out might be
> Drawn to the dregs of a Democracy.

For the poem to be effective it had to convince men who had been opposed to the accession of the duke of York that Shaftesbury had been using them for his own sinister ends. These were those whigs the 'author' describes as

> The Best, and of the princes some were such
> Who thought the power of Monarchy too much:
> Mistaken men, and patriots in their hearts
> Not wicked but seduc'd by impious arts.

The 'impious arts' were the attempts made to persuade them that, since sovereignty rests with the people, they 'have a right supreme to make their kings'. To convince them otherwise Dryden could not simply reiterate the tory view expressed in Filmer's *Patriarcha* that the hereditary right of kings derived from the Old Testament, and give James

> A successive title, long and dark,
> Drawn from the mouldy rolls of Noah's ark.[13]

---

12. See above pp. 19–20.

13. Michael McKeon notes that the poem does not uphold divine right kingship, but attributes this to Dryden's own view rather than to that of his target audience, the moderate whigs. 'Historicizing "Absalom and Achitophel", in Felicity Nussbaum and Laura Brown (eds), *The New Eighteenth Century* (London, 1987), p. 31.

That might appeal to tories, but scarcely to whigs, even moderate ones. Instead he gets the moderate whig 'author' to ask the rhetorical question 'What shall we think?' The answer reinforces moderate whiggism. Sovereignty indeed lies with the people, but, having delegated power to the king, they could not resume it at will. Otherwise, if they could arbitrarily take away the Crown,

> then kings are slaves to those whom they command
> and tenants to their people's pleasure stand.

It was a shrewd thrust to equate kings with the people's tenants since many of the moderate whigs were men of property which could be threatened if 'the power for property' was 'mischievously seated in the crowd'.

> For who could be secure of private right
> If Sovereign sway may be dissolved by might?

Again, Dryden plays on memories of the civil wars, when the Crown was taken away by men speaking in the names of the sovereign people and private property was jeopardised by Levellers. Had they not then run down a 'faultless king', Charles I, and had not the Rump parliament 'infected with this publick lunacy' murdered him 'for imagin'd crimes'?[14] The people had the right to mend abuses:

> If ancient fabricks nod, and threat to fall
> To patch the flaws and buttress up the wall
> Thus far 'tis duty.

'But here fix the mark': they could not change the system of government.

> To change Foundations, cast the Frame anew
> is work for rebels who base ends pursue.

Reform is one thing, revolution another. Moderate whigs were reformers, but Shaftesbury was a revolutionary. This was Dryden's message in 'Absalom and Achitophel'. It helped prepare the way – not for a conviction of Shaftesbury, for he was bound to be acquitted – but for the acquiescence of the body of the whigs when their leaders were implicated in the Rye House Plot in 1683. The fact that a whig revolution failed in the years of the tory reaction was partly due to the effectiveness of appeals to their moderate elements, of which Dryden's poem was the most prominent.

14. Cf. Steven N. Zwicker, *Lines of Authority: Politics and Literary Culture 1649–1689* (London, 1993), p. 136.

They were relatively few in number, possibly confined to moderate whigs who had been members of the Exclusion parliaments or aldermen and common councilmen in the City of London. Such men Dryden assumed would know the leading figures at Court, in both houses and in the City. The vignettes of the duke of Buckingham and Slingsby Bethel, for instance, take it for granted that allusions to their eccentricities would be immediately recognised. The lines wherein Zimri's characteristics were exposed fitted Buckingham so perfectly that Dryden himself felt they were the finest in the whole poem, and his critics agree.

> A man so various, that he seem'd to be
> Not one, but all Mankinds Epitome.
> Stiff in Opinions, always in the wrong;
> Was every thing by starts, and nothing long:
> But, in the course of one revolving Moon,
> Was Chymist, Fidler, States – man, and Buffoon;
> Then all for Women, Painting, Rhiming, Drinking . . .

Shimei would be identified as Bethel with the lines

> His business was by writing to persuade
> That kings were useless and a clog to trade

only by readers familiar with his pamphlets such as *The Interest of Princes and States* published in 1680.

This close association between the 'real' politicians and their representation in poems on affairs of state is crucial to the way that this form of satirical verse works. The fact that Charles II had a libertine reputation was an essential ingredient of Dryden's poem. Rochester had already claimed that 'restless he rolls around from whore to whore' before Dryden maintained that 'his vigorous warmth' was variously imparted 'to wives and slaves'.[15]

Much personal comment on politicians depended on relating real or alleged traits in an individual to characteristics of a political stereotype. Archetypal tory and whig 'characters' were constructed from distortions of genuinely held attitudes and beliefs.[16] Thus, Tory commitment to divine right monarchy and the Church of England was represented as a hankering for absolute power, religious bigotry and even Jacobitism. Similarly, whig advocacy of limited monarchy

15. *The Complete Poems of John Wimot, earl of Rochester*, ed. David M. Vieth (London, 1968), p. 61.

16. T. N. Corns, W. A. Speck and J. A. Downie, 'Archetypal Mystification: Polemic and Reality in English Political Literature, 1640–1750', *Eighteenth-Century Life* (London, 1982), vii, 1–27.

and religious toleration was transmuted into republicanism, nonconformity and even atheism. The stock whig 'character' was thus a 'fanatic' who aimed at replacing monarchy with a republic and the Church of England with a general toleration of all creeds, including atheism.

The most celebrated of all poems on state affairs was surely 'Lilliburlero', the author of which boasted that he had 'sung a deluded prince out of three kingdoms'. When Henry Purcell adapted the song to the celebrated march rhythm, then, in Burnet's words, 'the whole army and at last the people, both in city and country, were singing it perpetually.' The appointment of Tyrconnel as Lord Deputy presented an opportunity to develop a tory stereotype, the good Talbot, a mock Catholic Irishman threatening to hang Protestant Englishmen. This archetypal tory 'character' was developed by poets and pamphleteers during the first age of party. 'We have Tory priests as well as tory laymen', claimed one whig writer. 'One designs the enslaving of the soul as the other does the enslaving of the body.'[17] Tories were said to 'trample upon all laws' and to 'make a jest of liberty and property'.[18] They were also alleged to 'drink healths, sometimes to the Pretender, sometimes to the Pope, and sometimes to the Devil several times in an hour'.[19]

A real politician whose characteristics were made to conform with this stereotype was William Bromley, the tory candidate for the Speaker's chair in 1705. Bromley features in a 'Declaration without Doors', a poem in which his high church toryism, exemplified by his advocacy of an occasional conformity bill, is distorted into crypto-Catholicism and Jacobitism. Bromley led the high church tory campaign to outlaw the practice whereby dissenters took communion in the church of England in order to qualify for office in borough corporations, as required by the Corporation Act of 1661. Bills to penalise the practice were introduced into the House of Commons three times during Anne's first parliament. Because they were held up by the whig majority in the House of Lords on each occasion, he persuaded his supporters to 'tack' the third to the land tax bill. Had the 'tack' succeeded, it would have forced the measure through the upper house and onto the statute book, since the peers could

17. *The True Picture of an Ancient Tory, in a Dialogue between Vassal, a Tory, and Freeman a Whig* (London, 1702), pp. 9–10.
18. *A Dialogue between Whig and Tory alias Williamite and Jacobite* (London, 1693), p. 6.
19. *The Character of a Modern Tory; in a Letter to a Friend. By which it is evident that he is the most unnatural and destructive monster (both in religion and politicks) that hath yet appear'd in any community in the world* (London, 1713), p. 18.

not amend money bills and the government could not afford to lose the main source of direct taxation. Fortunately for the Court, the attempt was defeated by 151 votes to 134, the minority being distinguished as tackers. There can be no doubt of Bromley's sincere abhorrence of occasional conformity, which he denounced as 'abominable hypocrisy' and 'inexcusable immorality'. At the same time, the bills to outlaw it and above all the Tack could be regarded as the purest political expediency, since the effect of outlawing the practice would be to eliminate the dissenting vote in several constituencies, thereby reducing the electoral support for the whigs. Bromley's motives could therefore be depicted as cynical ploys to improve his party's prospects at the polls. But the anonymous whig author of the 'Declaration Without Doors' went further than this, getting the high church tory leader to say

> The Occasional Bill
> Was fram'd in our Mill,
> Of true Catholick Preparation;
> The Warp and the Woof
> Look'd like Protestant Stuff,
> But the Devil was in the Fashion.

> I huzza'd for the Tack,
> For I was always a Jack,
> And was fond of *Jure Divino* . . .

The tackers, whom Bromley led, could even be depicted as abetting the French war effort, for, had the tactic succeeded, a major prop of war finance, and with it the war effort, would have been jeopardised. Another poem, by the whig John Tutchin, imagined the king of France, Louis XIV, taking comfort from the attempt of the 134 high church tories to reverse the blow dealt to him shortly before in the duke of Marlborough's victory at the battle of Blenheim.

> When my Troops from *Bavaria* were Packing,
> No *Plaister* so fitted my Sore
> As the *brawling* and *wrangling* and TACKING
> *Of the One Hundred and Thirty Four.*

Again the high church men are portrayed as Jacks or Jacobites:

> The *Cub* that I've Nourished so long,
> In Time will pay off his Score,
> For I find his Party is Strong
> 'Tis *One Hundred and Thirty Four.*

I'll send him Home to his Throne,
Which his *Father* abandon'd before,
Where he'll be Supported and own'd
By the One Hundred and Thirty Four.

The whig archetype was also applied to particular politicians. The most libelled of the second-generation whigs was Thomas, Lord Wharton. Swift was merely joining in a popular sport when he savaged him in *A Short Character of his Ex[cellency] T[homas] E[arl] of W[harton]*. About the time that Swift's tract was published there also appeared *An Acrostick on Wharton*.

Whig's the first Letter of his odious Name;
Hypocrisy's the second of the same;
Anarchy's his Darling; and his Aim
Rebellion, Discord, Mutiny, and Faction;
Tom, Captain of the Mob in Soul and Action;
O'ergrown in Sin, cornuted, old, in Debt,
Noll's Soul and *Ireton's* live within him yet.

The Jacobite William Shippen excoriated the whig leaders in *Faction Display'd*.[20] He imagined them meeting in 1704 to plot against Anne as their predecessors, likewise inspired by the spirit of faction, had done against Charles I and James II. They meet in 'an antique pile', the refuge of Faction, whose owner, 'Moro', was 'a stamm'ring Hot, Conceited Laughing Lord'. Most contemporaries as well as modern readers would need a gloss on these lines to identify Faction's refuge with Northumberland House and the owner as the duke of Somerset. Only those familiar with his Grace's speech impediment would identify 'Moro' immediately.

Among the cabal he has invited is Ario

A *Scotch*, Seditious, Unbelieving Priest
The Brawny Chaplain of the *Calves-head-Feast.*

This was the standard tory caricature of Gilbert Burnet, the whig bishop of Salisbury. It associates him with republicanism, since the Calve's Head Club allegedly met on 30 January, the anniversary of the execution of Charles I, to drink wine from a calf's skull, toasting the king's executioner. He is also alluded to in the lines condemning those bishops who the established church's 'ancient Truths with Modern Glosses blend'. This is an allusion to Burnet's *Exposition of the Thirty-Nine Articles of the Church of England* which had been published in 1699 and condemned by high church clergymen in

20. *POAS*, vi, 648–73.

Convocation in 1701. They insisted that all the articles had a clear meaning in conformity with their views, whereas Burnet had glossed some, claiming that they were deliberately ambiguous and could bear more than one interpretation. Shippen depicts this as deliberate destruction of the church's creed.

Two other bishops are also present, 'Patriarcho' and 'Mysterio'. That the first is Tenison, archbishop of Canterbury, might be deduced from his pseudonym, but the second can only be identified as Bishop Lloyd of Worcester if it is known that in his dotage he took to prophesying. This enables Shippen to claim that Lloyd identified Queen Anne with the Beast in Revelation. 'Unhappy Church by such Usurpers sway'd', he concludes, castigating them for supporting 'Schism and Toleration'. Tenison is even accused of maintaining the cause of 'Atheists and Socinians'.

Just as the clerical leaders of the whig party are associated with irreligion, so the lay politicians are shown to be republicans. The first to be mentioned in the poem is 'Clodio, the chief of all the Rebel-Race'. To tory initiates this would immediately identify the most libelled of all the whig leaders, Thomas, marquis of Wharton. Shippen has him deliver the keynote speech to the plotters assembled in Northumberland House.

> Tho *Nassau's* Death has all our Measures broke
> Yet never will we bend to *Anna's* Yoke.
> The glorious *Revolution* was in vain
> If Monarchy once more its Rights regain.

Shippen imagines Wharton subscribing to the view that William III had sought to eliminate Anne from the line of succession laid down in the Act of Settlement. But there is no evidence that the king seriously contemplated this step, let alone that Wharton approved of it. On the contrary, a commission set up to investigate the rumour of William's intentions concluded that it was 'groundless, false, villanous and scandalous'. But that goes for naught in a poem on state affairs. It is part and parcel of the libel that any rumour, however spurious, will serve to develop the stereotype of the poet's opponents.

One of the attributes of the rival tory and whig 'characters' was that the tories were alleged to be admirers of France and detractors of the Dutch, whereas their rivals reversed these attitudes. Sure enough 'Clodio' runs true to form:

> We may the Praises of the *Dutch* advance,
> Rail at the Arbitrary Rule of *France.*

Usually whig partiality for the Dutch was attributed to their admiration of Holland's religious pluriformity and commercial success. Here it is derived from the United Provinces being a republic, which the whigs are accused of desiring instead of monarchy. The accusation of republicanism is also hurled at 'Sigillo', the pseudonym for Lord Somers, who is summed up as 'Deist, Republican, Adulterer'. The first and last charges rested on innuendo or scurrilous rumours. Somers undoubtedly knew the deists Matthew Tindal and John Toland, and might have written the preface to the former's *Rights of the Christian Church*. This was enough for Shippen to damn him as a deist too, though he significantly failed to mention Somers' acquaintance with the non-juror George Hickes. The allegation that Somers was an adulterer was based on the bachelor's association with a Mrs Blount. It was even said that in his capacity as a judge he kept her husband in jail 'while he lay with his wife'.[21] While this accusation is impossible to prove or disprove, enough mud stuck to Somers to sully his reputation. Thus his Victorian biographer in the *Dictionary of National Biography* acknowledged that 'his domestic life did not escape the breath of scandal', while his modern biographer concedes that 'there is reason to believe that he was "something of a libertine"'.[22] But there is no evidence whatsoever that he entertained republican principles. Yet Shippen probably held against him his leading role in the committee which drew up the Bill of Rights in 1689, and argued from a Jacobite viewpoint that restrictions on the royal prerogative smacked of republicanism. His role in the plot hatched in Northumberland House was to organise whig propaganda justifying rebellion and accusing the tories of Jacobitism, and to spread the message through the county constituencies, the City and every coffee house.

The whig publicity machine was seen by Shippen as a formidable weapon in the party's armoury. Thus, he depicts the earl of Halifax as a modern Maecenas co-ordinating the efforts of a team of writers who allegedly 'write as I Command, as I inspire'. These included Joseph Addison, William Congreve, Samuel Garth, Nicholas Rowe, John Vanbrugh and William Walsh. Halifax, 'Bathillo' in the poem, concludes his contribution to the conclave with a boast that Anne 'shall feel the vengeance of the Poet's Pen'. This was in many ways the most empty of the prophecies in *Faction Display'd*. For in fact all these writers became identified with the Court as it turned more

21. *POAS*, vi, 16.
22. W. Sachse, *Lord Somers: A Political Portrait* (London, 1975), pp. 67–8.

and more to the whigs, and rather sang the queen's praises than plotted her downfall.

Four of them, indeed, wrote verses celebrating Marlborough's great victories at Blenheim, Ramillies and Oudenarde. Addison's 'The Campaign' was one of the more fulsome tributes to the battle of Blenheim. It portrayed the duke of Marlborough as an avenging angel, flying over the battlefield as a great storm had flown over England the previous November:

> So when an angel by divine command
> With rising tempests shakes a guilty land;
> Such as of late o'er pale Britannia past
> Calm and serene he drives the furious blast;
> And, pleas'd the Almighty's orders to perform,
> Rides in the whirlwind and directs the storm.

Both Rowe and Walsh wrote poems on the victory at Ramillies which heaped praise on Anne as well as Marlborough. Rowe's contained the lines

> To Heav'n, the Royal ANNA owes, alone,
> The Virtues which adorn and guard her Throne;
> Thence is her Justice Wretches to redress,
> Thence is her Mercy and Her Love of Peace;
> Thence is Her Pow'r, Her Scepter uncontrol'd
> To bend the Stubborn, and repress the Bold;
> Her peaceful Arts, fierce Factions to assuage,
> To heal their Breaches, and to sooth their Rage;
> Thence is that happy Prudence, which presides
> In each Design, and ev'ry Action guides;
> Thence is She taught Her shining Court to grace,
> And fix the Worthiest in the worthiest Place.

Walsh was even more fulsome, urging Anne to

> Go on, Great QUEEN, with like success!
> Just Heav'n will still that Monarch bless,
>   That injur'd Kingdoms serves:
> Belov'd by all! Serene and Calm in Mind! . . .
>   'Tis ANNA fires each Breast:
> 'Tis ANNA's Glory that inspires the Muse,
> 'Tis ANNA's Glory ev'ry Chief pursue,
> She chains th' Oppressor, and She frees th' Opprest.

Congreve responded in verse, 'Jack Frenchman's Defeat', to another of the duke's victories, the battle of Oudenarde in 1708.

> Ye Commons and Peers,
> Pray lend me your Ears,
> I'll sing you a Song if I can;
> How *Louis le Grand*
> Was put to a Stand
> By the Arms of our Gracious Queen *Anne*.

He applauded the role of the son of the elector of Hanover, the future George II, in the battle, concluding that

> This Gallant Young Man
> Being kin to Queen *Anne*,
> Did as were she a Man, she wou'd do.

The literally fantastic and incredible aspects of *Faction Display'd* suggest one reason why the genre of poems on affairs of state petered out in the early eighteenth century. As we have seen, they depend upon extracting characteristics from living politicians and projecting them onto political archetypes. The more closely the poet could make the victim identify with the character the better. There is evidence that towards the end of Anne's reign the archetypal characters had 'passed their sell-by date', at least as far as the elite was concerned. They might have survived for electoral and other purposes below the level of the peers and MPs well into the eighteenth century. But the notion that their political rivals really did seek either to restore Stuart absolutism and religious intolerance or a republic and religious anarchy gradually became more and more absurd. The absurdity was captured beautifully by Jonathan Swift in 'Toland's invitation to Dismal to dine at the Calves' head club'. This was inspired by the alliance forged between the high church tory earl of Nottingham and the whig Junto against the peace preliminaries in 1711. John Toland, the deist, and secretary of the imaginary club, issues an invitation to Nottingham, who was known as 'dismal' to join its members on 30 January 1712.

> If, dearest *Dismal*, you for once can dine
> Upon a single Dish, and Tavern Wine
> *Toland* to you this Invitation sends,
> To eat the *CALVES – HEAD* with your Trusty Friends . . .
> To morrow We our *Mystick Feast* prepare,
> Where Thou, our latest *Proselyte*, shalt share:
> When we, by proper Signs and Symbols tell,
> How, by *Brave Hands*, the *Royal TRAYTOR* fell;
> The Meat shall represent the *TYRANT*'s Head,
> The Wine, his Blood, *our Predecessors* shed:

> Whilst an *alluding* Hymn some Artist sings,
> We toast Confusion to the Race of Kings:
> At Monarchy we nobly shew our Spight,
> And talk *what Fools call Treason* all the Night.

The joke of a staunch humourless high churchman supping and dining with rakes and sots only works if the whole scenario is dismissed as fantastic. If the whigs really had met on 30 January to celebrate the execution of Charles I in this fashion it would have been an exercise in black comedy rather than bantering humour.

Over the years the stock political characters became less and less credible. It was possible to believe that Shaftesbury was plotting to revive the good old cause, or that James II was bent on imposing Catholicism on the country. But it became more and more difficult to accuse the second generation of whig leaders of aiming at the same ends as the first, or the tories of seeking those of James. William Bromley was not working for the overthrow of Queen Anne and her replacement by the self-styled James III. Wharton was not bent on anarchy. Although there were republicans in whig ranks, and rather more Jacobites among the tories, the bulk of both parties became committed to preserving the constitution in church and state as it had been settled at the Revolution of 1688–9. This consensus made nonsense of the basic premises of poems on affairs of state.

While this in itself did not stop propagandists from depicting their political opponents as extremists, another trend made it more and more difficult to relate the behaviour of specific individuals to the traditional stereotypes. This was the growth of the readership for political propaganda. In the reign of Charles II poems on affairs of state, as we have seen, circulated amongst a few elite readers who could be presumed to know personally the personalities who were being satirised. Their foibles and eccentricities provided the raw materials on which the satirists worked. During the Exclusion crisis, however, and especially after the Glorious Revolution and the passage of the Triennial Act, the electorate at large was drawn into the debate. This added a potential readership of between 200,000 and 250,000 voters to the audience for polemical writing. This audience was hard to address by manuscript productions, although there were handwritten newsletters, such as Dyer's, which still employed numerous amanuenses to make multiple copies, perhaps as many as a thousand at a time. Clearly, though, the higher the number of readers the more sense it made to resort to print.

More to the point, an expanded readership could not be expected to be familiar with the personal characteristics of particular politicians. References to the malodorous duke of Kent as 'his stinkingness' or 'the bug', for example, would be lost on those who did not have to be in his company. Prints could bring home the essential attributes of a few well-known individuals better than poems. Walpole's obesity, for example, could be used to symbolise the great man more readily in a print than in verse. Hence, perhaps, the increased output of satirical prints as the vogue for poems on affairs of state came to a close, along with the first age of party, shortly after the death of Queen Anne.

CHAPTER THREE

Party Ideology and Society

In addition to the political archetypes, such as tory Jacobite and whig republican, there were social stereotypes onto which alleged party characteristics were projected. For example, whig writers depicted tories as backwoods country gentlemen, while tory authors represented whigs as upstarts, rising in society from humble and even obscure origins.

Whig dramatists developed the character of a booby squire, a familiar feature of the Restoration stage, into a grotesque tory caricature. Sir John Vanbrugh portrayed Sir Tunbelly Clumsy in *The Relapse*, Polidorus Hogstye of Beast County in *Aesop* and Sir Francis Wronghead in *The Provok'd Husband: or A Journey to London*. Their very names betray their bucolic beastliness. Sir Francis, MP for Guzzledown in Yorkshire, comes on stage 'drunk in a riding dress . . . gaping and stumping about the streets in his dirty boots'. Sir Richard Steele's *The Tender Husband* had Sir Harry Gubbin, a 'rough-country knight' among its *dramatis personae*. The best-known fictional country gentleman of the period was undoubtedly Sir Roger de Coverley, who appeared in the pages of *The Spectator*. Sir Roger does not display the cruder characteristics of the stage squire, however, since his creator, Joseph Addison, although a whig himself, was anxious not to turn the periodical into a party polemic. Its whiggery was more subtle than that of newspapers such as George Ridpath's rabidly anti-clerical *Flying Post*, for example. Whilst *The Spectator* subscribed to whig causes, lending its support to the party's candidates in the elections to the governing body of the Bank of England in 1711, it did not portray the tories as ignorant reactionaries. Instead, it upheld whig values by juxtaposing the views of Sir Andrew Freeport, the merchant member of the Spectator club, with those of Sir Roger, the Worcestershire baronet. While Sir Andrew's views on the economy are displayed as hard-headed and realistic, Sir Roger's toryism is nevertheless represented sympathetically as a sentimental paternalism. It is even suggested that he exaggerates it for electoral purposes, since he whispered in Mr Spectator's ear that he was a much stauncher tory in the country than he was in London, 'which was absolutely necessary for keeping up his interest'. The most explicit representation of a backwoods tory squire in Addison's political writing was not Sir Roger de Coverley but his portrayal of Foxhunter in *The Freeholder,* a paper he produced during the Jacobite rebellion of 1715. 'Freeholder' encounters 'Foxhunter' in 'a remote part of the country', thereby stressing the provincial nature of the tory gentry. In the course of their conversation 'Foxhunter' exhibits a host of bigoted opinions. He is rabidly xenophobic, fulminating against foreigners, and shows a violent dislike of dissenters. Above all, he inveighs against merchants in general and London and foreign merchants in particular, 'not forgetting the Directors of the Bank'.

Tory satirists developed a whig character of low birth who rose above his station in life. Thus *The Character of a Whig under Several Denominations* described 'senceless upstart whig country gentlemen' as being 'like mushrooms' since 'they grew up in a night of rebellion by plundering the royal party'. The notion that the whigs were upstarts who rose in the world by being totally unscrupulous was most brilliantly exploited by Charles Davenant, who created the whig character Tom Double in his *The True Picture of a Modern Whig.* Double twice improves his condition by fraudulent practices in the revenue service. Thus, in James II's reign he goes from shoemaking to being a customs official thanks to a legacy left him by his grandmother, 'who sold barley broth and firmity by Fleetditch'. He is subsequently convicted of fraud and dismissed from the service, so that on the eve of the Revolution he is reduced to being a proof corrector in a garret. During November 1688 he goes into an alehouse where he has credit for a pint of beer and a black pudding. There he encounters an Essex gentleman well into his cups, from whom he learns that William of Orange has landed in Devon and aims to march on London. Double takes advantage of the gentleman's drunken condition to cheat him out of some money, which he uses to travel down to the West Country, where he introduces himself to the prince as an influential supporter in the capital. This image enables him to benefit from the new regime after the Revolution, when he profits from the machinery of public credit set up to finance the war against France. Thus, as receiver of taxes he manages to hold on to £30,000, enabling him to acquire a country seat, a town house and a coach and six.

In 1711, by which time Davenant had 'knighted' Tom, Swift could argue that the whole whig party consisted of Sir Thomas Doubles. 'Let any man observe the equipages in this town', he asserted in *The Examiner*, 'he shall find the greater number of those who make a figure to be a species of men quite different from any that were ever known before the Revolution; consisting either of generals or colonels or of such whose whole Fortunes lie in funds and stocks.' The notion that there was a financial-military complex which profited from the war was further elaborated in Swift's *The Conduct of the Allies and of the late Ministry in beginning and carrying on the Present War.* 'A set of upstarts', he claimed, referring to the whigs of William's reign, 'finding that the gentlemen of estates were not willing to come into their measures, fell upon these new schemes of raising money, in order to create a money'd interest that might in time vie with the landed.'

These social stereotypes represented society as being polarised between tory backwoods gentry and whig military and monied men. The social assumptions behind these symbolic characters reflect the prejudices of their target audiences. The whig readership at which the character of ignorant, bigoted tory squire was aimed was presumed to be largely urban and cosmopolitan, educated and even sophisticated, tolerant of divergent Christian beliefs and even of foreigners and non-Christians. The tories who read of upwardly mobile careerists rising by devious means to the ranks of the elite were presumed to believe in a stable social hierarchy where people knew and kept their place. These were the very reverse of modern assumptions that there is something noble about merit being rewarded by upward mobility. The virtue of moving from log cabin to White House would have been lost on this audience. Quite the contrary, the more humble the social origins of their political adversaries could be represented, the more effective the propaganda. Even whigs felt uncomfortable about being associated with the mob. Both parties vied to claim not the quantity but the quality of their supporters. In reporting election contests, both tory and whig newspapers tended to boast that the 'quality' voted for their candidates, whereas the rabble was recruited by their opponents.

The actual relationship between these ideological constructs and the social reality was complex. Thirty years ago it seemed that the distinction between a tory landed interest and a monied whig interest was in very broad terms valid.[1] War finance, it was claimed, drove a wedge between those who paid direct taxes – principally country gentlemen, whose estates bore the burden of the land tax – and those who lent money to the government – principally investors in the stock of the Bank of England, and the East India and South Sea companies. Taxation crippled many of the lesser gentry, who lived entirely off their rents and were therefore unable to generate alternative sources of income. Interest on loans to the government, by contrast, reaped handsome rewards for those with surplus capital to invest in 'the funds'. These were by and large distinct communities, since relatively few landowners invested in such stock, while the state's creditors rarely bought land. There was therefore a transfer of income from the landed to the financial sector during the war years 1689 to 1697 and again from 1702 to 1713. This exacerbated the party conflict, for as one contemporary observed, 'the majority of the gentry upon a poll will be found Tories', while at the same time the stockholders in the City companies were mainly whigs. War weariness from tory gentry bled white by taxation led to demands for peace in the general election of 1710. The Bank of England, on the other hand, stood by the whig ministry's determination to fight on until France was brought to its knees. When Lord Treasurer Godolphin protested to the Governor that they were criticised every day for prolonging the war for their own benefit he replied that those who made such claims were 'a company of rotten rogues'. This nexus between the whig government and the whig city seemed to symbolise the political dichotomy between the landed and the monied interests.

Reviewing this thesis in 1987, however, Geoffrey Holmes concluded that it had not survived unscathed after closer scrutiny of the social and economic assumptions upon which it was based.[2] Confident generalisations about the state of the landed economy and the impact of the land tax upon estates, based largely on conclusions reached from a handful of counties, mainly in the south of England, could no longer be used to sustain the argument. Investigations of other regions had shown that there was great regional variety in the land market and in the incidence of direct taxation upon rental incomes. Away from the Home Counties the actual

---

1. G. Holmes, *British Politics in the Age of Anne* (London, 1967), chapter five, 'The Clash of Interests'; W. A. Speck, 'Conflict in Society', in G. Holmes (ed.), *Britain after the Glorious Revolution* (London, 1969).

2. G. Holmes, *British Politics in the Age of Anne* (revised edn., London, 1987), p. xlv.

burden of the land tax, so far from being four shillings in the pound, could sink below one shilling. Further analysis of the stock market had shown that the distinction drawn by some contemporaries between monied men who lent to the government and other businessmen who engaged in trade was artificial. Most of the state's creditors were involved in other business enterprises too. Moreover, although the analysis of poll books by and large confirmed the impression that most country gentlemen voted tory, there were also a significant number of tories among the smaller investors in the 'funds' as well as whigs.

Nevertheless, some of the argument survives this scrutiny. The high taxation and credit squeeze on landowners in areas where the land tax really was implemented at the wartime rate of four shillings in the pound did cause hardship for many of them. And the big investors in the stock of the City companies, those who purchased enough to vote for Directors, by and large were resident in London or the Home Counties and were rentiers living off the returns on their investments. Moreover, a surprisingly high number of them were Jews or Protestant immigrants. This lent some credence to the complaint made to Robert Harley in 1702 that the system of public credit had enriched 'Dutch, Jews, French and other foreigners, scoundrel stock-jobbers and tally-jobbers who have been sucking our vitals for many years'. The high profile of non-Anglicans among the plutocrats of the City was highlighted by the fact that some forty-three per cent of Bank Directors between 1694 and 1715 were Presbyterians, Independents and Baptists. Such considerations led Holmes to add to the clash of interests 'the religious dimension'. As he concludes, 'the monied men aggravated all their other sins with the most unforgivable sin of all (in Tory eyes, at least) the stigma of religious Dissent'.[3]

There was a religious dimension, too, to the stereotypes of the high and low church parties. These parties came about as a result of divisions among the Anglican clergy which were exposed in the Convocation of 1701, arising from different solutions to the perceived problems of dissent. The bulk of the inferior clergy in the lower house saw it as an immediate and considerable threat. They were in the front line in the struggle for the cure of souls, many having to compete with a nonconformist rival in their own parish, thanks to the Toleration Act which allowed dissenters to worship in their own conventicles. Their response was to raise the war cry 'the church

3. Ibid, pp. xlix–l.

in danger' and seek help to deal with it. Their approach, to try to use institutions like Convocation and parliament to suppress nonconformity, led them to be labelled 'high church'. The majority of bishops in the upper house were no less concerned about the problem, but adopted a different strategy. In their view, persecution merely strengthened dissent. Nonconformity throve when it was proscribed. Moreover, the Presbyterians, who constituted the great majority of nonconformists, were fellow Protestants whose views were very close to Anglicanism. They mainly objected to the authority of bishops and to three or four of the Thirty-nine Articles. There had, after all, been attempts in 1689 to accommodate the Anglican liturgy to their scruples. Had it succeeded they would have been comprehended within the established church. The failure of comprehension, largely due to Anglican intransigence on such issues as episcopal ordination and subscription to all of the Articles, had resulted in the Presbyterians having to take advantage of the Toleration Act, which was really meant to allow separate worship for sects such as the Baptists, who could not contemplate union with the Church of England. Some accommodation between Anglicanism and Presbyterianism was still a goal to pursue. Cracking down on nonconformity with the full rigour of the law, however, was no way to achieve it. Instead, a milder approach, treating Presbyterians as fellow Christians who were in error rather than in schism, would be a better policy. This moderate approach was the low church solution to the problem of dissent.

These divergent attitudes towards dissent were distorted in the stereotypes of propaganda. The high church 'character' was portrayed as a bigot, sympathetic to Catholicism, but breathing fire and brimstone on dissenters. The low church 'character' was depicted as a 'fanatic', a radical dissenter sympathetic to freethinkers, deists and even atheists, but antagonistic towards Anglicans and 'priestcraft'. 'The Body of Papists, Jacobites and Non-Jurors, are all link'd together with that Gang which call themselves HIGH-CHURCH,' asserted a whig pamphleteer in the general election of 1702. At the next election the Tackers were calumniated as 'carrying two shapes in one body, like a centaur, or the Irish Virgin with a fish in her tail, half Protestant, half Papist'.[4] 'His profession (I cannot call it religion) is of the Genevan stamp', maintained *The Character of a Modern*

---

4. *Some Plain Observations, Recommended to the Consideration of every Honest English-man* and *The Character of a Tacker* quoted in A. Downie, 'The Character of a Tory', *Eighteenth-Century Life* (London, 1982), vii, 22.

Whig,[5] 'his father begetting him in the hot zeal of this persuasion, and his dam all that while fixing her teeming fancy with adulterous lust on their able Holder – forth he was moulded a strong Presbyterian in the very womb and so proves a rank Phanatick.' 'His religion consists in railing against all Governments but Oliver's', asserted *The Character of a Whig*

> and cursing the whore of Babylon worse than the street crack that clap'd him. He would be a Presbyterian but for fear of the close stool of repentance. An Independent but that he has neither Gifts nor Graces, and thinks himself nor fool nor madman enough yet to be a Quaker . . .'[6]

Acknowledging that some whigs were Anglicans, it characterised them as 'Church whigs'. A Church whig 'is externally a Church of England man, but inwardly a phanatique'. Thus he 'leaves nothing unattempted that may shew his respects to the dissenting party'.[7]

Such crude representations of the religious views of one's party's opponents help to explain why Defoe's *The Shortest Way with the Dissenters* was taken so seriously. For they were mostly written in a flagrantly partisan manner as an attack upon a perceived enemy. Thus tories lambasted dissenters, while whigs railed against high church Anglicans. It was relatively rare for an anonymous author to be a persona created by the real author in order to attack his views. Swift pulled off the feat in *A Tale of a Tub*, when he put on the mask of a Grub Street hack sympathetic to religious enthusiasm. But that, too, was misread by contemporaries and even by later scholars. Readers in Anne's reign were shocked by the bantering nature of the satire and lost sight of the positive qualities of Martin, the representative of the Anglican Church, in the ridicule poured on his two brothers, Peter and Jack, representing Catholicism and Dissent respectively. Swift was accused of ridiculing religion itself, and, so far from fostering his ecclesiastical career, the *Tale* hindered his advancement in the church. Some later critics so confused Swift with the hack that they even used the 'digression concerning madness' as evidence that the Dean was insane!

So when *The Shortest Way with the Dissenters* appeared on 1 December 1702 readers would anticipate, not a whig send-up of high church views, but another tory diatribe against nonconformists. It is often

---

5. 'The Character of a Modern Whig: or an Alamode True Loyal Protestant' (London, 1681), *Clarendon Historical Society Reprints* (1884–86), series 11, p. 358.
6. *The Character of a Whig under Several Denominations* (London, 1700), pp. 67–8.
7. Ibid, p. 75.

claimed that Defoe was inspired to publish his tract by the introduction into the House of Lords on 2 December of a bill to penalise occasional conformity which had just pass the tory-dominated lower house. But he himself denied this, saying that he wrote it

> without the least retrospect to, or concern in the public Bills in Parliament now depending, or any other proceedings of either House, or of the Government relating to the Dissenters, whose occasional conformity the author has constantly opposed.

This was strictly true. Defoe, in common with other dissenters, disliked occasional conformity, calling it 'playing Bo-peep with God Almighty'. Yet the appearance of the pamphlet the day before the peers considered the bill seems more than a coincidence. According to Defoe, *The Shortest Way* had 'its immediate original from the virulent spirits of some men who have thought fit to express themselves to the same effect in their printed books, tho' not in words so plain'. One of these 'originals' was Dr Henry Sacheverell's sermon preached in Oxford the previous June, which, as Alan Downie points out, scarcely seems to be an 'immediate' occasion.[8] Nevertheless, Defoe can scarcely have expected his arguments to sway the outcome of the debate in parliament. He could, however, have legitimately hoped to persuade people that the occasional conformity bill was the thin end of a sinister wedge. Even if they succeeded in getting it onto the statute book, the high church tories would not have been content to rest there. They had a hidden agenda, which Defoe sought to expose in *The Shortest Way*. Ultimately, they wanted to eradicate dissent altogether. One of the main devices in the tract was to dehumanise dissenters so that their elimination could be more readily advocated. This is a stock device of extremists who advocate treating minorities as less than human. Thus, Jews have been compared to parasites in anti-semitic literature throughout the ages. Similarly, dissenters were compared to insects in genuine high church rhetoric. In his Oxford sermon, Sacheverell had distinguished the established church from 'that confused swarm of sectarists that gather about its body, not to partake of its communion, but to disturb its peace'.[9]

8. Defoe, *An Enquiry into the Occasional Conformity of Dissenters* (London, 1697), p. 17. Alan Downie maintains that *The Shortest Way* was meant to influence debates in the House of Lords on the occasional conformity bill, pointing out that it was published the day before it was introduced into the upper house. J. A. Downie, 'Defoe's *Shortest Way with the Dissenters: Irony, Intention and Reader Response*', in T. N. Corns (ed.), *The Literature of Controversy: Polemical Strategy from Milton to Junius* (London, 1987), pp. 136–7.

9. Henry Sacheverell, *The Political Union* (London, 1702), p. 48.

Defoe merely went a stage further when he compared them to toads and vipers.

> 'Tis cruelty to kill a snake or a toad in cold blood, but the poyson of their nature makes it a charity to our neighbours, to destroy those creatures, not for any personal injury receive'd, but for prevention; not for the Evil they have done, but the evil they might do.
>
> Serpents, toads, vipers etc. are noxious to the body, and poyson their sensative life; these poyson the soul, corrupt our posterity, ensnare our children, destroy the vitals of our happiness, our future felicity, and contaminate the whole mass.
>
> Shall any law be given to such wild creatures? Some beasts are for sport, and the huntsmen give them advantages of the ground; but some are knock'd on the head by all possible ways of violence and surprise.

This seems to be advocating mass murder, but the 'author' denies that he is prescribing 'fire and faggot'; instead, he urges that the dissenters should be 'rooted out of this nation'.

> If one severe law were made, and punctually executed, that whoever was found at a Conventicle, should be banish'd the nation, and the preacher be hang'd, we should soon see an end of the Tale, they would all come to Church, and one Age would make us all one again.

There had, in fact, been a law in Charles II's time – the Conventicle Act of 1663 – which had prescribed transportation for seven years as the penalty for the third offence of attending a conventicle. What the high church men wanted was to turn the clock back to a time before the Revolution and the reign of James II, to good King Charley's golden days. Then they had ruled the roost and the dissenters had been persecuted.

What Defoe's high church persona did, therefore, was to take the violent language of clergymen like Sacheverell and make it more explicit. He touched a chord he had perhaps not anticipated, articulating sentiments which were shared by the more extreme high flyers, but which they dared not utter in public. He actually tapped into the paranoid mentality of the high church clergyman who felt that the church was in danger from dissent and that something should be done about it. As he himself expostulated, 'a poor author has ventur'd to have all mankind call him villain and traitor to his country and friends, for making other people's thoughts speak in his words'. It seemed that one high church man had been courageous enough to make their real feelings known.

Defoe claimed to be appalled that his hoax had backfired. He wrote 'a brief explanation' to a second edition, the title page of which added 'taken from Dr Sach—ll's sermon and others' after *The Shortest Way with the Dissenters*. In it he protested that 'if any man take the pains seriously to reflect upon the contents, the nature of the thing, and the manner of the stile, it seems impossible to imagine it should pass for any thing but a banter upon the high-flying Church-men'.[10] It is, in fact, not that easy to prove from internal evidence alone that *The Shortest Way* is ironic. The opening paragraphs depict the dissenters as ruling the roost for fourteen years under William III, but of having been knocked off their perch with the accession of Queen Anne. This was axiomatic in tory circles. Francis Atterbury had penned a *Letter to a Convocation Man* in 1697 in which he had argued precisely that the church was in danger from dissent. The Toleration Act, the failure to convene Convocation, the relaxation of the control of the press following the lapsing of the Licensing Act in 1695, the rise of occasional conformity, had all brought the established church into the greatest peril. When Anne came to the throne, tories rejoiced that the 'Golden Age' had returned, so that

> With its own Lustre now the Church appears
> As one year makes amends for fourteen years[11]

'You have butcher'd one King, depos'd another King, and made a mock King of a third', rants Defoe's high church man. Assertions that the dissenters were the descendants of the regicides of 1641 were commonplace in tory propaganda. The whole conceit that there was a Calves' Head Club which commemorated the anniversary of Charles I's execution rested on this association. The sympathy shown for James II, however, was unusual. It is taken even further when the claim is made that James began his reign by showing mercy to the dissenters: 'nor could their joining with the Duke of *Monmouth* against him, move him to do himself Justice upon them'. This is truly a breathtaking claim, as Defoe, who had himself taken part in the duke of Monmouth's rebellion, well knew. Alan Downie observes that 'it is as if Judge Jeffrey's Bloody Assizes had never

10. This was his immediate explanation, when he was trying to avert prosecution. But, as Alan Downie has pointed out, he later claimed to have anticipated that it would be taken seriously, not only to smoke out high-flying bigots but to embarrass the tory government. J. A. Downie, 'Defoe's *Shortest Way with the Dissenters*', p. 123.
11. 'The Golden Age', in George deforest Lord (ed.), *Poems on Affairs of State: Augustan Satirical Verse 1660–1774* (Yale University Press, 1962–75), vi, 453.

taken place.'[12] Defoe's mask slips here to reveal a Jacobite, or non-
juror who, having taken the oaths of allegiance to James, refused to
take them to William. This is a clue to moderate readers that his
intention is ironic, and that he is impersonating a high church
bigot. But it is only a fleeting clue. For the denigration of William III
for his subservience to the whigs and dissenters was a stock in trade
of tory writers.

The succession question is raised again, however, in the context
of Scotland and the prospects of a Union. After a standard tory
denunciation of the Presbyterians north of the border for their
treatment of the episcopalians, the high church 'author' picks up
the possibility, already hinted at by some Scots, that they might
settle the succession differently from the settlement of the English
crown in the House of Hanover by the Act of Settlement. 'The
Crowns of these kingdoms have not so far disown'd the Right of
Succession but they may retrieve it again', he argues, 'and if Scotland thinks to come off from a successive, to an elective State of
Government, England has not promis'd not to assist the right heir,
and putting them into possession.' Again this indicates a commitment to restoring the exiled Stuarts. Defoe here was drawing on
the non-juror Charles Leslie, who expressed similar sentiments in
a tract *The New Association of those called moderate church men with the
modern whigs and fanatics to undermine and blow up the present Church
and Government*. As he explained with clear exasperation in the
'brief explanation',

> Any gentlemen who have patience to peruse the Author of the *New
> Association* will find gallows, gallies, persecution, and destruction of
> the dissenters, are directly pointed at, as fairly intended, and design'd,
> as in this shortest way, as had it been real, can be pretended; there
> is as much virulence against a Union with Scotland, against King
> William's Government, and against the line of Hanover.

But the implied Jacobitism revealed in these slips of the high church
mask were explicitly denied by the 'author' in other passages. 'What
may be the consequence of a neglect of such opportunities?' he
asked.

> The succession of the Crown has but a dark prospect; another Dutch
> turn may make the hopes of it ridiculous, and the practice imposs-
> ible: Be the House of our future Princes never so well inclin'd, they
> will be foreigners; and many years will be spent in suiting the Genious
> of Strangers to this Crown and the Interests of the Nation; and how

12. J. A. Downie, 'Defoe's *Shortest Way with the Dissenters*', p. 135.

many ages it may be before the English throne be fill'd with so much zeal and candour, so much tenderness and hearty affection to the Church, as we see it now cover'd with, who can imagine?

It was therefore not surprising that Defoe's purpose was misconstrued. He paid the hard way for impersonating people like Leslie and Sacheverell. When he was tracked down as the author he was prosecuted for seditious libel, made to stand in the pillory three times, fined and imprisoned. He never again ran the risk of parodying a high church man and non-jurors so closely.

Just how close his parody was can be seen from a notorious sermon which Sacheverell delivered in St Paul's cathedral in 1709 on 'the danger of false brethren'. In it he claimed that 'false brethren in our Government' tolerated atheism, deism and socinianism. 'Certainly the Toleration was never intended to indulge and cherish such monsters and vipers in our bosom', he thundered, 'that scatter their pestilence at noon-day.' The direct comparison of his opponents with vipers was the same as Defoe's high church man's likening of dissenters to serpents.

Sacheverell's sermon was so incendiary that the whig government could not ignore it. Since passages in it called in question the validity of the Revolution settlement, it was determined to impeach him in parliament. The Commons appointed managers to bring four articles of impeachment against him before the House of Lords. The first and most important claimed that he had maintained 'that the necessary means used to bring about the ... Revolution were odious and unjustifiable'. The second accused him of attacking the Toleration Act. The third and fourth asserted that he preached that the church and the constitution were in danger under her Majesty's government. After a trial lasting several weeks he was found guilty by the Lords, but sentenced to the mild punishment of being barred from preaching for three years. Since the ministry had wanted him barred from preaching and preferment for seven years, and imprisoned for three months, this was a virtual acquittal. Sacheverell suffered far more lightly for his inflammatory sermon than Defoe did for his ironical tract.

The Sacheverell affair heralded the tory reaction of the four last years of Anne's reign. High church tories consolidated their triumphs at the polls in 1710 and 1713 by passing measures designed to secure the church from the perceived threats posed by dissenters. Not only was an Occasional Conformity Act finally passed in 1711 but in 1714 a Schism Act was put on the statute book, aimed at closing down dissenting schools and academies. Sacheverell had earmarked these as a particular danger to the doctrines of the established church in his 1709 sermon, calling them 'seminaries wherein Atheism, Deism, Tritheism, Socinianism with all the hellish principles of fanaticism, regicide and anarchy are openly profess'd and taught to corrupt and debauch the youth of the nation'. The dehumanising of dissenters helped to foment the violence against them witnessed in the destruction of chapels in London during 'the night of fire' in 1710 at the time of Sacheverell's trial, and again in 1715, following the coronation of George I. The extent and scale of the attacks upon conventicles led to the hasty passing of the Riot Act in 1715 to protect nonconformists from high church mobs.

That was the high-water mark of anti-dissenting sentiment. Thereafter, the animosity against dissenters appears to have subsided. It is significant that apparently no prosecutions were brought against Presbyterians who became Unitarians in the second decade of the eighteenth century, even though technically the Toleration Act only covered Protestants who believed in the Trinity. At the same time, the close ties between the whigs and the dissenters, already loosened by the party's acceptance of the Occasional Conformity Act, were further relaxed. During the whig schism from 1717 to 1720, when Robert Walpole went into opposition, those who followed him were reluctant to repeal the Act in 1718. After Walpole came to power he resisted attempts by dissenters and whig allies to repeal the Test Act, being content to grant them immunity from prosecution by annual Indemnity Acts. These developments made the stereotype of the whig as a 'fanatic' less credible.

But perhaps more important in the gradual fading of the image was the fact that the next controversy to break out in the Church of England, after the Sacheverell affair, did not polarise the parties along the lines of high church tories and non-jurors on one side, and low church whigs and dissenters on the other. Instead, the Bangorian controversy of 1717 divided Erastians, who argued that the church was subordinate to the state, from those who insisted that it was an equal partner. While high church clergymen had previously been so insistent, the blatant Erastianism of the low church bishop of Bangor, Benjamin Hoadly, alienated whig clergymen like Bishop Gibson of London. These emphasised a moderate churchmanship which, while not lacking in Anne's reign, had nevertheless been overwhelmed by the vehemence of the quarrels between high and low church. The emergence of moderation as a dominant force in ecclesiastical politics after the accession of the House of Hanover made the religious stereotypes of the first age of party increasingly inappropriate.[13]

The conflict of interests also subsided after reaching a climax in the South Sea Bubble. In the first half of 1720, the orgy of speculation in South Sea Company stock led many who had previously criticised the funds as shady whig finance to speculate in them. Even Oxford colleges and tory country gentlemen played the market that summer. There were more potential investors since the ending of the War of the Spanish Succession reduced the burden of the land tax and gave landlords previously strapped for cash to pay it spare capital to invest. When the crash came many were ruined, including whig investors who had previously been staunch advocates of the money market. One result was a panic flight from paper securities to safer investments in land. Another was that the stock market no longer polarised the parties. Where the severest critics of the Bank and the stock exchange had previously been tories like Swift, in 1720 even more stringent criticisms were made of the City's financial institutions by whigs like Thomas Gordon and John Trenchard, who called in *Cato's Letters* for exemplary punishments of the perpetrators of the swindle. The Bank, the East India Company and the South Sea Company came to be regarded not so much as whig as Court institutions. This was another indication that the first age of party had come to a close.

13. John Walsh, Colin Haydon and Stephen Taylor (eds), *The Church of England c.1689–c.1833: From Toleration to Tractarianism* (Cambridge, 1993), p. 53.

PART TWO

The Classical Age of the Constitution: 1720–1788

CHAPTER FOUR

The Classical Age of the Constitution

In 1938 D. Lindsay Keir published a constitutional history of Britain in which he devoted a chapter to 'the Classical Age of the Constitution 1714 to 1782'. It still repays reading, since its opening paragraphs sum up the state of historiography before the war, which, in its essentials, was not changed by subsequent research until surprisingly recently. 'For three quarters of a century before 1714,' begins the first sentence, 'England had been a byword for political instability.' After discussing the civil wars and revolutions and their consequent constitutional changes, he continued by asserting that the accession of the House of Hanover 'ushered in an age of almost unbroken internal tranquillity and external progress'. This political stability produced a constitutional equilibrium which was not to be disturbed until 'in the disasters of the American Revolution the eighteenth-century constitution sustained its death blow'.[1] Keir thus anticipated in some respects the thesis put forward by Professor J. H. Plumb in his Ford lectures of 1965 that the rage of party was followed by an age of political stability.[2]

One reason for this alleged development was that the tories were eclipsed as a party actively competing for power with the whigs. In Plumb's words 'the Tory party was destroyed'; England became 'a single party state'.[3] Geoffrey Holmes appeared to endorse this view when, in 1969, he published an essay on 'the death of the tory party'.[4] It followed that it was inappropriate to discuss the politics

---

1. D. Lindsay Keir, *The Constitutional History of Modern Britain 1485–1937* (2nd edn., London, 1943), pp. 289, 299.
2. J. H. Plumb, *The Growth of Political Stability 1675–1725* (London, 1967).
3. Ibid, p. 172.
4. G. Holmes, 'Harley, St John and the death of the Tory Party', in G. Holmes (ed.), *Britain after the Glorious Revolution* (London, 1969), pp. 216–37.

of the early Hanoverian era in terms of the two parties of the late Stuart period. Instead, historians took seriously the contention of some opposition politicians that the division into tory and whig parties had been superseded by a polarisation between Court and Country. It seemed to them that the political discourse of the time also marked a change from that which had characterised 'the first age of party'. The great issues which had divided tories from whigs – the succession, the status of dissent and the wars against Louis XIV – had been resolved. In their place other issues came to dominate politics, especially the argument over the preservation of the Revolution settlement. Debates over the constitution divided Court from Country rather than whig from tory.

There was a widespread agreement that the constitutional arrangements effected during the Glorious Revolution were the best that could be devised. They had produced a balanced constitution, wherein the three powers of the Crown, the Lords and the Commons had been brought into equilibrium. Thereby the pure classical forms of polity, monarchy, aristocracy and democracy, were each represented in the constitution. Furthermore, the balance ensured that the disadvantages of each could be avoided. The tendency of monarchy to degenerate into tyranny could be offset by the Lords and Commons combined, that of aristocracy towards oligarchy by the Crown and Commons, and that of democracy towards anarchy by the Crown and Lords. William Blackstone summed up the consensus on the constitution in his celebrated *Commentaries upon the laws of England*:

> herein indeed consists the true excellence of the English government, that all the parts of it form a mutual check upon each other. In the legislature, the people are a check upon the nobility, and the nobility a check upon the people . . . while the king is a check upon both, which preserves the executive power from encroachments. And this very executive power is again checked and kept within due bounds by the two houses . . .[5]

There was no agreement, however, about how this process would work in practice. Although Blackstone argued that the constitutional equilibrium was a self-regulating mechanism, others disagreed. The Court sought to expand the Crown's influence over the two houses of parliament, while the Country strove to reduce it. Country writers argued that the Court sought constantly to increase its

---

5. W. Blackstone, *Commentaries upon the Laws of England* (4 vols, London, 1765–69), i, 154.

influence over the legislature, and that it was the duty of the virtuous citizen to maintain constant vigilance to detect and disarm these attempts.

Thus there was a revival of the concern over placemen which had emerged during the Country agitation against the Court in the 1690s. *The Danger of Mercenary Parliaments*, first published in 1696, was republished in 1722.

Another notorious example of the Court's aspiration to reduce the independence of the Commons was the Septennial Act of 1716. This replaced the Triennial Act of 1694, which had required general elections to be held at least once every three years. Now the maximum interval between dissolutions of parliament was extended to seven years. The measure provoked fierce opposition, not only from tories but also from Country whigs. The latter argued that it was a betrayal of whig principles to weaken the link between parliament and the people in this way, and that the Triennial Act had been reluctantly accepted by William III only because of pressure from whigs. After it was passed, repeal of the Septennial Act became a plank in the Country platform.

The extension of the statutory interval between elections from three to seven years had a profound impact on the politics of the period. During the years of the Triennial Act, between 1694 and 1716, there were no fewer than ten general elections – one nearly every two years. Between 1716 and 1783 there were a further ten – one every six and a half years. This produced an expectation that parliaments would run more or less their full course. Hence the furore when George III dissolved parliament in 1784, a full three years before a dissolution was required by the Septennial Act. This led to the general election of that year being one of the most contentious in the entire century, providing another reason for considering the 1780s as a watershed in constitutional and political history.

The long intervals between elections helped to consolidate the grip of oligarchy in the constituencies. Borough patrons had much more time to build up their interests, and tended to invest more money in returning members since the return on their investments was much more durable. The resulting inflation of election expenses played into the hands of the wealthier landlords and impoverished the lesser gentry. Since the more affluent peers and country gentlemen gravitated into the whig orbit, while the Court gave financial backing exclusively to whig candidates, then the growth of oligarchy was held to have squeezed tories out of electoral contests altogether. This abetted the process whereby they became so marginalised as not to count in the political world of the early Hanoverians.

The notion that Court and Country parties largely replaced the whig and tory parties under the first two Georges became the conventional wisdom during the 1970s. Meanwhile, however, it was being undermined by investigations of the tories during their reigns. One published as early as 1970 documented that, so far from being killed off after Anne's death, they survived in significant numbers in the parliaments of her successors.[6] Although their ranks fell below 200 in 1722, and eventually were reduced to just over 100 in 1754, after most general elections held under George II they numbered between 120 and 150. These findings did not have an immediate impact on the prevailing historiography, largely because they were accompanied by the claim that the majority of tories were Jacobites actively seeking a Stuart restoration, which was greeted with incredulity by the then leading authorities in the field. Thus, Plumb had confidently asserted in his Ford lectures that 'the vast bulk of the Tory party, of course, never had been and never was Jacobite.'[7] Linda Colley's investigation of the tory party between 1714 and 1760, however, was taken more seriously, not least because she maintained that most tories were loyal Hanoverians.[8] She also showed that the traditional depiction of eighteenth-century tories as backbenchers returned as knights of the shires or for their own pocket boroughs was at odds with the reality. Many represented large urban constituencies and had trading or professional interests. Further investigations of tory activity and beliefs led other scholars to endorse the conclusion that Jacobitism was rife in their ranks and indeed throughout the country.[9]

These contributions raise serious doubts about the acceptability of Plumb's concept of political stability. He partly defined it as 'the acceptance by society of its political institutions'. Yet if large numbers of English men and women did not accept the Protestant succession in the House of Hanover, and yearned for the restoration of the Stuarts, then 'society' did not accept the key institution of parliamentary monarchy. Even if the tories were not Jacobites, their survival through the early Georgian era ensured that England did not become completely a one-party state.

The extent of Jacobitism will never be satisfactorily gauged because by its very nature it did not leave behind the kind of documentation

6. R. Sedgwick (ed.), *The History of Parliament: The Commons 1715–1754* (2 vols, London, 1970). The introductory survey on 'The Tories' was written by Eveline Cruickshanks.

7. Plumb, *The Growth of Political Stability*, p. 168.

8. L. Colley, *In Defiance of Oligarchy: The Tory Party 1714–1760* (London, 1982).

9. The literature on Jacobitism is enormous. For a synthesis with an extensive bibliography see Daniel Szechi, *The Jacobites* (London, 1994).

historians would agree to accept. Government and Stuart estimates of it were both inclined to exaggerate, though for different reasons. Walpole used the smear that all tories were potential Jacobites in an attempt to prevent dissident whigs making common cause with them. The Pretender's own agents were keen to persuade him that the potential support in the event of his invading the country to regain his crown was substantial. Any analysis based on these sources will therefore never command universal acceptance. Yet there are few cases of individuals whose papers document their adherence to the Stuarts. This is not surprising since they ran the terrible risk of being found guilty of treason. One cannot, however, argue from silence that this points to suspicion of Jacobitism. All that can be done is to investigate alleged instances of allegiance to the Stuarts by testing them against other evidence. So far this has shown that several claims to the effect that particular politicians were Jacobites cannot be substantiated. Further investigations will probably endorse B. W. Hill's view that 'the great majority of the Tory party had better hopes to pursue than the will-o'-the-wisp of Stuart restoration.'[10]

What those hopes were, beyond the mirage of relaxing their proscription from office, was expressed in *The Weekly Miscellany*.[11] Its author, William Webster, was a staunch Hanoverian who later wrote *A Vindication of his Majesty's Title to the Crown*. He dedicated the *Weekly Miscellany* to the earl of Anglesey. 'When we see such noblemen as the earls of Anglesey, Abingdon and Nottingham, with the excellent archbishop of York, uniting their interests for the security of the Hanover succession', he observed, with reference to their conduct on the death of Queen Anne, 'we must be convinc'd that the heartiest friends to the Church are always the loyalest subjects to the King.' Hanoverian churchmanship thus informed the work.

> It is the business of that paper to defend Revelation against the objections of the Deists, the Church of England from the dangerous attempts of a powerful confederacy; to encourage useful literature as the truest friend to both; to preserve some common principles of morality and a sense of duty without which no society can survive.

The 'powerful confederacy' Webster feared was the combination of dissenters and dissident whigs to repeal the Test and Corporation Acts. Religion was still the acid test of party allegiance. Ironically, the dissident whigs who opposed Walpole were more marked by their

10. B. W. Hill, *The Early Parties and Politics in Britain 1688–1832* (London, 1995), p. 75.
11. *The Weekly Miscellany, giving an Account of the Religion, Morality and Learning of the Present Times* began publication in December 1732 and was published in a collected edition in two volumes in 1736 and 1738.

sympathy for dissent and their antipathy to the Church of England than were the prime minister's supporters. In the event, the move to repeal the Acts was defeated with government support. Some of the anti-Anglican sentiment amongst the opposition whigs can be detected from *The Old Whig*, a weekly newspaper which ran from March 1735 to March 1738.[12] This supported the campaign for repeal. It particularly attacked the *Weekly Miscellany*: 'Inquisitions, purgations, priestly powers and the like are the goodly group of doctrines now openly avowed and publickly pleaded for.' The anti-clerical sentiment hinted at in 'priestly power' was one of the main reasons why the dissident whigs failed to combine with the tories into an effective Country party, despite all the exhortations of *The Craftsman* that they should bury their differences.

Yet although there never was a Country party under the first two Georges, there was an opposition rhetoric which transcended the tory and whig parties to transform the ideological debate which had informed the first age of party. In some respects this was a continuation of the 'Country' campaigns of the 1690s and 1700s against standing armies and placemen. And indeed there was a connexion between them and the opposition propaganda of the 1720s in the person of John Trenchard, who wrote the most celebrated tract to the standing army controversy of William's reign and contributed to the most effective critique of the Court of George I, *Cato's Letters*. But the letters Trenchard wrote with Thomas Gordon for *The London Journal* in 1720, and later reprinted in four volumes, were far more influential than his *Argument Shewing that a Standing Army is Inconsistent with a Free Government*, published in 1697. The standing army affair, serious though it was at the time, was a nine days' wonder in comparison with the impact of the South Sea Bubble, which provoked *Cato's Letters*.

The South Sea Bubble sent shock waves through the political system as severe as the Exclusion crisis or the Sacheverell affair. 'Enthusiasm in different shapes returns often upon this poor nation,' observed the bishop of Peterborough, 'we have had religious enthusiasm, political enthusiasm and this was merely secular enthusiasm.'[13] That fraudulent practices had been used by the directors of the South Sea Company to raise the value of the stock it was allowed to issue for taking over a share of the national debt was one thing. That it involved leading politicians, courtiers and perhaps

12. *The Old Whig: or the Consistent Protestant* (2 vols, London, 1739).
13. Bodleian Library Ballard MS 7, f. 151. White Kennett to Arthur Charlett, 20 Oct 1720.

even members of the royal household made it far worse. When the bubble burst, and the market value of shares tumbled, many were ruined. They cried out for culprits. Trenchard and Gordon answered the call. 'Whether the Directors and their Masters shall be punish'd or no', they wrote as 'Cato', 'is to me one and the same question, as to ask, whether you will preserve your Constitution or no, or whether you will have any Constitution at all?' The constitutional implications of the bubble were that the balance established at the Revolution would be completely disturbed, and the Crown would acquire control of parliament, if corruption on such a colossal scale went unchecked. *Cato's Letters* thus became key texts in the development of an ideology of civic humanism which informed political rhetoric on both sides of the Atlantic from the South Sea Bubble to the American Revolution.

The leading historian of this ideology is Professor J. G. A. Pocock. In a number of works, outstanding among which is his *The Machiavellian Moment*, he has elaborated the concept of civic humanism.[14] He traces its pedigree to Machiavelli's cynical exposure of the motives of politicians, and how men in power constantly endeavour to become more powerful. Virtuous citizens must therefore be perpetually vigilant to resist moves by those in authority to undermine their liberty. These machiavellian notions were transmitted into English political discourse in the eighteenth century through the medium of James Harrington's *Oceana*. For Harrington in the 1650s had wrestled with the problem of how to preserve a virtuous republic. His investigation of English history in the previous two centuries led him to conclude that power was ultimately based on landed property. Thus he argued that, before the advent of the Tudors, there had been what he termed a Gothic constitution in which the power of the Crown, the Lords and the Commons had been more or less equal. This was because the Crown, the nobility, and the gentry had each owned roughly the same amount of land. Between 1485 and 1640, however, the Crown and the nobility had alienated land to the Commons. This shift in landed wealth caused an accompanying shift in the balance of power, from the Crown and the Lords to the Commons. The readjustment resulted in the civil war. As Harrington put it, the dissolution of the Gothic constitution caused the war, not the war the dissolution of the constitution. He was concerned to prevent a similar seismic movement which would cause the

14. J. G. A. Pocock, *The Machiavellian Moment: Florentine Political Thought and the Atlantic Revolution* (London, 1975).

Commonwealth to collapse, and proposed an agrarian law which would stop men from acquiring enough landed property to threaten the stability of the republic.

With the Restoration the Gothic constitution was restored, and the disturbance to its balance during the 1680s was rectified in the Glorious Revolution. Harrington's prescription for preserving the republic was thereby rendered anachronistic. But his equation of power with land remained axiomatic among political theorists such as Gordon and Trenchard, whom Pocock dubs 'neo-Harringtonians'. Their theories, however, were threatened by the development of the fiscal-military state and the emergence of a machinery of public credit. The state's creditors manipulated a new form of property – liquid rather than fixed assets, which could be sold on the stock market. The rise of this monied interest threatened to undermine the stability of the constitutional balance. In the South Sea Bubble this threat seemed to become a reality. The neo-Harringtonian advocates of civic humanism therefore deplored the emergence of finance capitalism and sought to restrain it in much the same way as Harrington himself had sought to prevent the accumulation of landed property.

In this sense, therefore, the Country advocates of public virtue were doomed to defeat as a capitalist economy developed, and took refuge in what has been termed a 'politics of nostalgia'.[15] There were, however, Court whig writers who welcomed, or at least accepted as inevitable, the economic trends of post-Revolution England, and sought to relate virtuous citizenship to them. The third earl of Shaftesbury was not nostalgic for the reign of Elizabeth, finding his own times better. In his profoundly influential *Characteristics* he sought to inculcate public virtue in the form of politeness. Polite whiggism was an essential alternative to tory stress on church and Court as agents of civic virtue. He replaced godly and courtly agencies with the ideal of the public gentleman. Gentility and good manners thus took over from religion and the Court the task of what Norbert Elias called 'the civilising process'.[16]

A direct response to this programme was Bernard Mandeville's *Fable of the Bees.* Where Shaftesbury's proposals implied that public

15. I. Kramnick, *Bolingbroke and his Circle: the Politics of Nostalgia in the Age of Walpole* (London, 1968).
16. Lawrence E. Klein, *Shaftesbury and the culture of politeness* (London, 1994). As Klein observes, 'the study of politeness helps delineate both the continuity and the break between the courtly world explored by Norbert Elias and the public sphere described by Jurgen Habermas'. (p. 14) For abortive attempts to develop private virtue, see Shelley Burtt, *Virtue Transformed: Political Argument in England, 1688–1740* (London, 1992).

virtues could be public benefits, Mandeville made quite explicit the contrary proposition that 'private vices' could be 'public benefits'. Where previous whig writers had tried to reconcile virtue with the rapidly changing economy of post-Revolution England, Mandeville pointed out that they were ultimately incompatible. In the earliest version of his thesis, a crude poem 'The Grumbling Hive or knaves turned honest', he argued that to maintain the status of a great power and at the same time to preserve a virtuous society was 'a vain Eutopia seated in the brain'. He showed how the new fiscal-military state, which he represented as a flourishing beehive, depended for its existence upon the accumulation of wealth based on conspicuous consumption. When the bees hypocritically ask Jove to make them virtuous, he answers their request. The result is to turn an affluent society and expanding economy into a primitive state. In the *Fable of the Bees* Mandeville drew on an alternative moral tradition, developed by continental thinkers, to substitute different sanctions on human behaviour.[17] These were the manipulations of 'skilful politicians' whose 'dextrous management' could transform private vices into public benefits. Their intentions are often overlooked by critics who deplore Mandeville's paradox as an attack upon morality without noting how he resolves it. They were certainly ignored by many of his contemporaries, whose reactions to the *Fable* were knee-jerk responses in favour of traditional Christian morality. The skilful politicians could exploit all seven of the deadly sins to turn them into public benefits. Thus pride, based on self-love, could be transformed into an aristocratic code of honour and this, by a 'civilising process', subsequently transmuted into polished civility. By a very different route, therefore, Mandeville arrived at a similar conclusion to Shaftesbury. Where the third earl assumed, following John Locke, that man was an altruistic, sociable creature, Mandeville, more a disciple of Thomas Hobbes, considered him to be an egoistical solitary being. Good manners arose in the first from enlightened self-interest and in the second from the cynical exploitation of egoistic hedonism by skilful politicians. Mandeville at least had the virtue of coming to terms with the economic changes attendant upon the Revolution of 1688.

Mandeville's views were regarded as so extreme that some Court whigs as well as opposition politicians found them repugnant. They offered the example of Cicero in response to that of Cato. The 'Ciceronian Vision' was especially appealing because his works could

---

17. E. G. Hundert, *The Enlightenment's Fable: Bernard Mandeville and the Discovery of Society* (London, 1994).

be used in praise of the balanced constitution. This it had in common with the Catonic vision of the Country mentality, since there was a consensus that the constitutional equilibrium was theoretically the best that could be devised. However, it differed sharply from the Country analysis of the working of the constitution in practice, since that deplored the economic trends consequent upon the Revolution, arguing that they threatened to displace the balance. The Court whigs, by contrast, argued that the Revolution settlement established a polity which was conducive to economic growth. The prosperity which the opposition denounced as luxury was a blessing which flowed from the polity established after 1688.[18]

The division in the ranks of the Court whigs in 1733, which led several to go into opposition to Walpole over his Excise scheme, brought into being a group of self-styled 'patriots' who did not share the pessimism of earlier Country whigs. On the contrary, they continued to applaud the economic advances made since the Revolution, and began to blame Walpole for impeding it. Thus they accused his ministry of surrendering the interests of merchants trading with the Spanish empire in America to those of Spain. Criticism of his alleged pusillanimity over the attacks on British merchant shipping by Spanish coast guards in the Caribbean reached a climax with the incident of Jenkins' ear. 'There's now no insolence that Spain can offer', lamented a character in George Lillo's play *Fatal Curiosity*, 'but to the shame of this pacifick reign poor England must submit to.'[19] Walpole reluctantly gave in to the clamour and went to war with Spain in 1739. After an initial success at Porto Bello, the naval engagements in Spanish America resulted in costly defeat at Cartagena in 1741. Tobias Smollett, who was a ship's surgeon on the Cartagena expedition, wrote a scathing critique of its mishandling by the British commanders in *Roderick Random*.

'Patriotism' in this context arose basically because the Court was associated with the foreign dynasty of the House of Hanover, which was alleged to be giving priority to the interests of its German possessions over those of Britain. But it was also inspired by the apparent preference of the aristocracy for French culture. The dom-

---

18. Reed Browning, *Political and Constitutional Ideas of the Court Whigs* (London, 1982). Browning, in common with most recent commentators on political theory in the eighteenth century, plays down the significance of John Locke's *Two Treatises of Government*. Yet one of his 'Court whig' writers was Benjamin Hoadly, whose political essays drew very much on Locke's views. The reaction to the tradition which made Locke the major political theorist of the eighteenth century seems to have gone too far, and a reassessment is desirable.

19. G. Lillo, *Fatal Curiosity* (London, 1737), p. 6.

inant tastes amongst the country's rulers seemed to be for alien influences. Much of the drive behind the 'patriot' critique of the Court and aristocracy came from a bourgeois belief that the interests of Britain, a 'trading nation', were being sacrificed to continental concerns.

This trend was exacerbated by the widening gulf between two different political spheres. There was the sphere of influence of the whig oligarchy, based on its landed estates, which enabled the Court whigs to exercise an increasingly firm grip on small constituencies. The pocket and rotten boroughs gave them a majority in the House of Commons. Alongside this was the sphere of influence of such cities as London, Westminster, Southwark, Bristol, Newcastle-upon-Tyne and other urban constituencies where the local mercantile community, rather than the aristocracy and gentry, exerted the paramount interest. The gulf between them was exposed in the general election of 1741 when Admiral Vernon, the hero of Porto Bello, represented the 'patriot' opposition to the Walpolian whigs. He was not only returned for several urban constituencies, including London, but his exploits were used for electoral purposes in others, including Coventry, Liverpool, Newcastle and York. Demonstrations on his behalf took place even in unenfranchised towns like Birmingham and Leeds.[20] He was also a truly 'patriotic' figure in having support in Scotland as well as in England. 'Vernon was hailed repeatedly as the ultimate "Free-born *Briton*".'[21]

The fall of Walpole and the consequent unseemly scrambling for posts in the reconstructed ministry damaged the claims of the 'patriots' to be high-minded independents, concerned only for their country's interests and not for their own. Patriotism became a pejorative word in the political vocabulary of the 1740s. As Henry Fielding put it in the second issue of his weekly paper *The True Patriot* on 14 November 1745:

> I had the misfortune . . . to find it [the title] opposed by many of my friends; one of whom, a pretty true-speaker, advised me rather to appear under the character of *The Pickpocket*. A Title, he said, which would as effectually recommend me to my country as that which I have chosen.
>
> It must be confessed, indeed, that this word *Patriot* hath of late years been very scandalously abused by some persons, who, from their Actions as well public as private, appear to have a much juster

20. Kathleen Wilson, *The Sense of the People* (London, 1995), pp. 150–1.
21. Ibid, p. 161.

claim to that appellation which my humorous Friend above recommended. Ambition, Avarice, Revenge, Envy, Malice, every bad Passion in the Mind of Man, have cloaked themselves under this amiable character, and have misrepresented Persons and Things in unjust colours to the Public. We have now Men among us, who have stiled themselves Patriots, while they have pushed their own Preferment, and the Ruin of their Enemies, at the manifest Hazard of the Ruin of their country.

By the 1750s, however, the term 'patriotism' was again being used by critics of the Court, including the elder Pitt, who, when he came to power in 1756, was known as the 'Patriot minister'. It was also adopted by radicals in the reign of George III. Thus John Wilkes was praised as 'the Beloved Patriot'.[22] Wilkes exploited the 'alternative structure of politics', which Admiral Vernon had first exposed in 1741. His support was strong in the metropolis and in many provincial towns. A study of its social origins established that the Wilkites were predominantly bourgeois.[23] The same constituency expressed sympathy for the colonial cause in the form of petitions and addresses for conciliation on the eve of the War of American Independence.[24]

During the war, however, 'patriotism' became an embarrassingly inappropriate stance for radical 'friends of America' to adopt. Instead, the attribute was appropriated more by supporters of the government's policy of confronting the rebellion with force. There was thus a sea change in the political application of the term 'patriot' in the 1770s from the opposition to the Court. This prefigured the distinction between 'Jacobins' and 'loyalists' which emerged in the 1790s.[25]

Nevertheless, the consensus on the constitution survived even the rise of radical politics in the 1760s. Although the American colonists challenged the sovereignty of parliament, few English politicians agreed with them. Even those sympathetic to the American cause, such as the Rockinghamites, upheld it. When the Stamp Act was repealed by the Rockingham administration, it passed the Declaratory Act to declare the right of parliament to legislate for

22. Linda Colley, 'Radical Patriotism in eighteenth-century England', in R. Samuel (ed.), *Patriotism* (3 vols, London, 1989), i, p. 170.

23. J. Brewer, 'English Radicalism in the Age of George III', in J. G. A. Pocock (ed.), *Three British Revolutions* (London, 1980).

24. J. R. Bradley, *Popular Politics and the American Revolution in England: Petitions, the Crown and Public Opinion* (London, 1986).

25. Ibid, pp. 183–4.

the colonies 'in all cases whatsoever'. The Wilkesite movement might have appeared more of a challenge to the balanced constitution with its demands for parliamentary reform, but these were still couched in the language of restoring an allegedly disturbed equilibrium.[26] Not for nothing was its main organisation called the Society of Supporters of the Bill of Rights.

Lindsay Keir ended what he called the classical age of the constitution in 1782. For it was in that year that the ministry of Lord North, reeling from the impact of the battle of Yorktown, fell, to be replaced by the marquis of Rockingham's second administration. Rockingham was not only determined to end the War of American Independence by recognising the United States, he was also committed to measures of reform which undermined the ability of the Crown to influence proceedings in parliament. One of his supporters, Dunning, had put forward the celebrated motion in 1780 that 'the influence of the Crown has increased, is increasing and ought to be diminished.' At the time nothing could be done in practice to follow up the motion, since on routine business North could command a majority of the Commons. When he was replaced by Rockingham, however, measures of so-called 'economical reform' were passed which abolished many posts which had previously been used to reward MPs. Among them was an Act which disqualified customs officers from voting in parliamentary elections, significantly reducing the Crown's interest in ports which returned members to parliament.

The fact that the government led by the younger Pitt secured a substantial majority at the subsequent general election held in 1784 has been taken to indicate that the measures were largely ineffectual. However, the outcome of the election was due not so much to the Crown's influence as to the genuine popularity of the ministry, which romped home in the larger constituencies. This wrong-footed Pitt's main rival, Charles James Fox, who had campaigned on the issue of the king's influence in parliament only to find that his championing of the people against the prerogative was paradoxically unpopular. The issue also gave the electors a choice between two parties for the first time since the reign of George I.

At this juncture the Foxites and the Pittites were not polarised entirely along ideological lines. Pitt, for instance, favoured electoral reform, and actually introduced a bill to effect it in 1785. It was

26. See John Brewer, *Party Ideology and Popular Politics at the Accession of George III* (London, 1976), pp. 240–64.

defeated since he supported it as a private and not as a government bill. The dissenting vote, too, was divided at the polls in 1784, though dissenters united to petition for the repeal of the Test and Corporation Acts in the years 1787 to 1790. The ideological fissure opened up by the French Revolution was thus already discernible as a fault line in British politics before the 1790s.

CHAPTER FIVE

Jacobitism and Patriotism

It has become a truism that the outstanding writers of the early Hanoverian era were almost all critics of the government. Walpole became known as the 'poet's foe', while those authors the prime minister patronised were dismissed as 'dunces'.[1] Although some of his critics were not averse from seeking his patronage for themselves, disappointed ambition alone does not explain their opposition. Instead, explanation has been sought in their ideological stance against the ministry. Until recently this was discussed in terms of Country rhetoric against the Court. With the recent reappraisal of the fortunes of the tory party, however, there has been an increasing insistence that many opposition writers were motivated by toryism and even by Jacobitism. Three in particular have been identified as harbouring sympathy for the Pretender: Swift, Pope and Johnson.

Ian Higgins has advanced the view that Swift 'may have had, from time to time, conditional Jacobite sympathies and perhaps would have gone over to the Jacobite side if circumstances had been right'.[2] This cautious thesis is supported by the circumstantial evidence of the known Jacobitism of some of Swift's friends, such as Bishop Atterbury, and a reading of his works looking for clues to his susceptibility to Jacobitism. Although he accepts that 'if in fact [Swift] was a Jacobite he did not commit explicit incriminating evidence to paper', Higgins nevertheless, not surprisingly, finds what he

---

1. See A. J. Downie, 'Walpole,"the poet's foe"', in J. Black (ed.), *Britain in the Age of Walpole* (London, 1984). One of the few poets patronised by the prime minister was Joseph Mitchell, who became known as 'Walpole's poet'. In 'The Sinecure' he pleaded with his patron to

> Hear me, thou Atlas of our leaning State
> Consent at least to make one poet great ...

2. Ian Higgins, *Swift's Politics: A Study in Disaffection* (Cambridge, 1994), p. 45.

seeks.[3] Thus, he notes the ambiguity of the early Odes to the king and to Archbishop Sancroft, and makes much of Swift's marginalia to such publications as Burnet's *History of his own Time* and Addison's *The Freeholders*.

Indeed, he makes rather too much of Swift's marginal comments. For instance, Burnet, discussing the proposals made in the Convention parliament of 1689 by the Lords for settling the Crown, observed that there were several distinct attitudes. Some argued that there was an original contract between the monarch and his subjects, that James II had broken it, and that the people had thereby been freed to make another with William and Mary. Others maintained that there was no precedent for such a procedure in English law, and indeed no such contract. In a hereditary monarchy the only remedy when a king was incapacitated from ruling, for instance, by being a minor, or mad, was to set up a regency. The advocates of this solution included some who wished to restore James, realised that an immediate restoration was impractical, and sought to keep the option open by setting up regents to rule in his stead. Alongside this passage Swift noted that he was of the party that subscribed to the contract theory and yet would have been for a regency. Previously, scholars had stressed Swift's subscription to a contractual political theory, and deduced from it that this indicated his support of the whig position in the Convention. Higgins rightly points out that they overlooked his support of the regency proposal, and uses this to suggest that Swift agreed with those who saw in it a substitute for an overtly Jacobite solution.[4] Yet there were peers who voted for the regency who were far from being Jacobites, but genuinely believed that the proposal was more consistent with the constitution. These included the high church earls of Nottingham and Rochester, who played a key role in the Convention. Swift's marginal comment therefore did not necessarily document a Jacobite position. What it does record is Swift's fondness for antithesis. Burnet was wrong to imply that the two positions were incompatible, Swift seems to be saying. As was often the case, on this issue Swift was by intellect a whig and by instinct a high church tory. He himself explained this rather curious combination in conversations with Lord Somers thus:

> that, having been long conversant with the Greek and Roman authors and therefore a lover of liberty, I found myself much inclined to be what they called a Whig in politics; and that, besides, I thought

3. Ibid, p. 74.   4. Ibid, p. 75.

it impossible, upon any other principle, to defend or submit to the Revolution; but as to religion, I confessed myself to be an High-churchman, and that I did not conceive how any one, who wore the habit of a clergyman, could be otherwise . . .[5]

Higgins plays down Swift's whig credentials and plays up his high churchmanship in his determination to associate the dean with Jacobitism. It is in his observation on Swift's marginalia to the *Freeholder* that he shows most clearly his inclination to find what he is looking for. Alongside one passage of Addison's paper Swift wrote 'suppose a King grows a Beast, or a Tyrant, after I have taken an oath; a 'prentice takes an oath, but if his master useth him barbarously, the lad may be excused if he wishes for a better.' Higgins uses this as an example of 'Swift's pro-Tory marginalia in Addison's *Freeholder*'.[6] In fact, the proposition that the behaviour of the king could nullify an oath of allegiance was a whig notion, and tories who took the oaths to the post-Revolution regime were vilified for betraying their principles by the non-jurors in their midst.

'The representation of William III in Swift's marginalia in *Bishop Burnet's History of His Own Time*,' according to Higgins, 'strongly implies Jacobite sympathies.'[7] This is to make the same erroneous assumption that the Pretender's agents made when they interpreted criticism of the post-Revolution regimes as support for the exiled House of Stuart. It cannot be stressed too much that disparaging remarks about the regime did not imply support for the alternative dynasty. Swift made clear his attitude to the House of Hanover in a tract written in the summer of 1714, when some of his acquaintance were desperately canvassing the possibility of restoring the Stuart line. Swift was quite emphatically opposed to this policy. 'There are two Points of the highest importance', he wrote, 'wherein a very great majority of the Kingdom appear perfectly hearty and unanimous.' The first was that the privileged position of the Church of England should be maintained. 'The other Point of great Importance', he

---

5. *The Prose Works of Jonathan Swift*, ed. Herbert Davis (16 volumes, Oxford, 1939–75) [hereafter *Prose Works*], viii, 120. Swift's relationship with Somers was complex. He defended him along with other whig lords in his first published tract *A Discourse of the Contests and Dissensions in Athens and Rome* (London, 1701). *A Tale of a Tub* contained the bookseller's dedication to Somers, which has been taken as genuine, though Higgins argues persuasively that it was ironic (*Swift's Politics*, pp. 122–8). Certainly, when he began to write for the tory ministry after 1710, Swift savaged Somers in *The Examiner*. Yet in 1733 he could observe, 'I allow him to have possessed all excellent Qualifications except Virtue. He had violent passion(s), and hardly subdued them by his great Prudence.' *Prose Works*, v, 258.

6. Higgins, *Swift's Politics*, p. 17.   7. Ibid, p. 77.

continued, 'is the Security of the Protestant Succession in the House of Hannover.'[8]

Howard Erskine-Hill similarly deduces from the young Alexander Pope's criticisms of William III that he too was a crypto-Jacobite.[9] Certainly, in 1705 Pope published a 'scathing lampoon on the "Dutch Prince" who conquered neither in love nor war'. Yet, as the footnote acknowledges, this is included in an epitaph on Queen Mary.[10] Many contemporaries who could not bring themselves to accept William were reconciled to the Revolution by his wife.[11] Erskine-Hill even reads condemnation of the Glorious Revolution into *The Rape of the Lock*![12] Yet it is good-natured in its attitude to Queen Anne, who 'sometimes counsel takes – and sometimes *tea*'. Like Mary, Anne reconciled many to the Revolution settlement who had never recognised William.

Anne indeed is given more reverential treatment in *Windsor Forest*, written to celebrate the treaty of Utrecht in 1713:

> At length great ANNA said – Let Discord cease!
> She said, the World obey'd, and all was *Peace*!

The passage which concludes 'And peace and plenty tell, a Stuart reigns', has been read as expressing Jacobite sympathy.[13] Yet Pope had no great regard for the Stuarts in private, dismissing James I's as 'absolutely the worst reign we ever had – except perhaps that of James the Second'.[14] He did, however, again contrast Queen Anne with her predecessor, to William's detriment. He is even compared to William the Conqueror. Under them, so far from there being peace and plenty in the forest, it appeared 'a dreary desert and a gloomy waste', because the kings 'dispeopled air and floods'. 'Succeeding

---

8. 'Some free thoughts upon the present state of affairs', *Prose Works*, viii, 88, 90. It is worth noting that Higgins nowhere deals with this tract.

9. Howard Erskine-Hill, 'Literature and the Jacobite Cause: was there a rhetoric of Jacobitism?', in Eveline Cruickshanks (ed.), *Ideology and Conspiracy: Aspects of Jacobitism 1689–1759* (Edinburgh, 1982), pp. 53–4.

10. Ibid, p. 65, note 56.

11. W. A. Speck, 'William – and Mary?', in Lois Schwoerer (ed.), *The Revolution of 1688–9: Changing Perspectives* (Cambridge, 1991), pp. 131–46.

12. Like Alan Downie 'I remain unconvinced . . . Pope's playful hyperbole fails to carry the emotional ring of Jacobitism'. J. A. Downie, '1688: Pope and the rhetoric of Jacobitism', in David Fairer (ed.), *Pope: New Contexts* (Oxford, 1986), p. 11.

13. J. A. Downie, *To Settle the Succession of the State: Literature and Politics 1678–1750* (London, 1994), pp. 88–9.

14. Carolyn D. Williams, *Pope, Homer and Manliness: Some Aspects of Eighteenth-Century Classical Learning* (London, 1993), p. 21, citing Spence's *Anecdotes*. Ms Williams also notes Pope's disparagement of Charles II.

monarchs' – apparently Stephen and Anne – adopted milder courses
until

> Fair *Liberty*, *Britannia*'s Goddess, rears
> Her cheerful Head, and leads the golden years.

Immediately after these lines in the 1712 edition appeared the
couplet:

> Oh may no more a foreign masters's rage
> With wrongs yet legal, curse a future age.

These were reduced to a footnote in later editions.

These passages in which Pope attributes the prosperity or dev-
astation of the forest to the policy of 'foreign' kings have been
taken by E. P. Thompson as implying that Pope must have objected
to the draconian application of forest laws under George I. Then
the idyllic harmony he describes under Anne was disturbed, and the
harsh suppression of customary rights like gathering firewood in
the interests of the magnates who hunted deer in the forest bred
a class antagonism. This found expression in the depredations of
the so-called Waltham Blacks, gangs of deer stealers whose activities
provoked the Black Act of 1723, the most notorious of all the capital statutes of the eighteenth century. It allegedly created some
fifty offences for which the penalty was death, one of which was to
black one's face to escape detection – hence the name. Among
those accused of being involved in the gangs were two kinsmen of
Alexander Pope, Charles and Michael Rackett. Thompson assumed
that Pope would have been sympathetic towards his relatives' activities, criminal though they were in the eyes of the government,
because they were a protest at the tyrannical regime introduced into
Windsor forest following Anne's death. Moreover, the ranger of the
forest was none other than the prime minister, Robert Walpole.
Pope had stood up for Bishop Atterbury when Walpole accused
him of Jacobite plotting at the very time of the outbreak of deer
stealing which led to the Waltham Black Act and the arrest of his
relatives. There is even some evidence that the Blacks were associated
with Jacobites, which, if Pope had been inclined towards that lost
cause, would have further endeared the Racketts to him. Thompson
claims that Walpole suspended proceedings against them in order
to have a hold over Pope, and that this succeeded, since for several
years the poet eschewed political verse.[15]

---

15. E. P. Thompson, *Whigs and Hunters* (London, 1977), p. 271.

Pat Rogers approaches the issue with entirely different assumptions. He regards the Waltham Blacks not as heroes but as thugs and bully boys. He cannot accept that Pope would have been anything but embarrassed by the involvement of the Racketts. That he identified himself with the suppression of blacking rather than the reverse Rogers deduces from his long friendship with and admiration for Lord Cobham, who was governor of Windsor castle until June 1723 and showed no sign of sympathy with the deer stealers. On the contrary, 'it was on his recommendation that the keeper Baptist Nunn, almost the arch-villain of *Whigs and Hunters*, was appointed as Porter of Windsor Castle on 25 June'.[16] As for Pope's not producing political verse, this is more than accounted for by his preoccupation with his editions of Homer and Shakespeare in the 1720s than with an alleged silence induced by Walpole's blackmailing him over the criminality of the Racketts. It can only be concluded that in this particular exchange it is game, set and match to Rogers.

H. T. Dickinson has pointed out that Pope was on curiously amicable terms with the prime minister, frequently dining with him in the late 1720s.[17] And Alan Downie has drawn attention to Pope's own description of himself as at least 'half a whig'.[18] By the 1730s, however, he became identified completely with the Opposition. The turning point was marked by the publication of *The Dunciad* in 1728, followed by the *Dunciad Variorum* the following year. Like his other works, this was regarded as a contribution to the Country critique of the Court until recently, when Douglas Brooks-Davies read it as 'a study in emotional Jacobitism'.[19] Some concern for the cogency of his argument arises, however, from an early example of his methodology. At the end of the *Dunciad Variorum* book two, Pope has the contestants in the games gradually fall asleep. Among them

> At last Centlivre felt her voice to fail
> Old James himself unfinished left his Tale
> Boyer the State, and Law the Stage gave o'er . . .

Susannah Centlivre, Abel Boyer and William Law are immediately recognisable contemporaries. 'Old James' poses problems, but is

16. Pat Rogers, *Eighteenth-Century Encounters: Studies in Literature and Society in the Age of Walpole* (London, 1985), p. 85.

17. H. T. Dickinson, 'The Politics of Pope', in Colin Nicholson (ed.), *Alexander Pope: Essays for the Tercentenary* (Aberdeen, 1988), p. 8.

18. Downie, '1688: Pope and the rhetoric of Jacobitism', pp. 13–14.

19. Douglas Brooks-Davies, *Pope's Dunciad and the Queen of Night* (Manchester, 1985).

identified by John Butt, the editor of the Twickenham edition of the poem, as James Pitt. Not so, claims Brooks-Davies, insisting that this line is a Jacobite allusion, for 'Old James is, surely, James II, who died in exile in 1701, leaving his tale as King of England "unfinish'd".'[20] Why Pope would resurrect the dead king to join the sleeping authors 'stretch'd on bulks, as usual' is not explained, and indeed is inexplicable. Suffice it to say that Old James is, surely, not James II, even if Butt did not satisfactorily identify him with a contemporary writer. Another dubious use of evidence is in his exposition of the Isis myth in *The Dunciad* book three. William Warburton explored the Egyptian cult of Isis in his *Divine Legation of Moses* published in 1738. Although he admits that Pope did not even know Warburton when he composed the original *Dunciad*, Brooks-Davies nevertheless maintains that it is 'not performing too much of an historical anachronism to use the 1738 part of *The Divine Legation* in order to help elucidate the political implications of the three-book *Dunciad*'![21]

The Egyptian allusions are crucial to Brooks-Davies' case. For it is a truism that *The Dunciad* was a devastating critique of the Hanoverian regime: 'Still Dunce the second reigns like Dunce the first.' But to read the poem as being not only anti-Hanoverian but also pro-Jacobite requires much ingenious wrestling with the Isis myth. Brooks-Davies insists that Pope is offering the Jacobite alternative to the Hanoverians through it. 'Book IV ends in darkness deeper and more terrible than the darkness that had concluded the three-book *Dunciad*', he writes, 'but the promise of Isis's restoration remains' (IV. 637–8).[22] The lines referred to read:

> As Argus' eyes by Hermes' wand opprest,
> Clos'd one by one to everlasting rest.

It is difficult to see how any contemporary, even after reading *The Divine Legation of Moses*, which was available when the four-book *Dunciad* appeared in 1743, could have interpreted these lines as offering the prospect of the restoration of the Stuarts.

Where Higgins suggests that Swift 'may have had . . . conditional Jacobite sympathies' and Brooks-Davies qualifies Pope's Jacobitism as being 'emotional', Jonathan Clark does not hedge his bets with Samuel Johnson, proclaiming boldly that 'Johnson was a Jacobite.'[23] Clark's familiarity with the history of the era enables him to put

20. Ibid, p. 34.   21. Ibid, p. 125.   22. Ibid, p. 127.
23. J. C. D. Clark, *Samuel Johnson: Literature. Religion and English Cultural Politics from the Restoration to Romanticism* (Cambridge, 1994), p. 7.

Johnson into a convincing context of Jacobite activity. He acknowledges that first- or even second-hand evidence that Johnson was a Jacobite before 1760 is hard to come by, and dismisses out of hand the Romantic nonsense that the Doctor was 'out' in Scotland in the '45. But there was a culture of Jacobitism which went far beyond a willingness to risk the axe or the rope for treasonable activity. Johnson associated closely with men who were imbued with that culture, such as Archibald Campbell, William Guthrie, William King, James Edward Oglethorpe, John, Earl of Orrery and Richard Savage. As Clark says, 'it would be realistic to infer . . . that Johnson's comments as expressed in private conversation with [such] men . . . were not restrained by any fundamental difference of orientation.'[24] While there is much to be said for judging a man by the company he keeps, a fellow traveller is not the same as a party member. In attempts to find evidence that Johnson carried a Jacobite card, Clark is reduced to methods no more convincing than the efforts of Higgins and Brooks-Davies to demonstrate that Swift and Pope were fully paid-up members. Thus, he interprets the line from Johnson's *London*: 'Give to St DAVID one *true Briton* more' as 'a clear allusion to the Jacobite periodical *The True Briton*'.[25] Why Johnson should refer in a poem published in 1738 to a newspaper which had ceased publication in 1724 is not all that clear. The expression 'true Briton' was apparently in common use at the time, for Clark quotes an anonymous review of William King's *Templum Libertatis* in 1742 which felt that 'it must be agreeable to every *True Briton*'. He does not, however, suggest that this, too, is a reference to the Jacobite journal of the early 1720s.[26]

The flyleaf of Clark's book claims that it 'offers the first analysis of the life and thought of the writer Samuel Johnson from an historian's viewpoint'. It is ironic that the year in which it appeared also saw the publication of John Cannon's *Samuel Johnson and the Politics of Hanoverian England*. This, too, deals with the problem of the Doctor's Jacobitism, albeit from a much more sceptical point of view. Cannon takes issue with close readings of Johnson's works in endeavours to document the Doctor's Jacobitism, but concurs with the judgement of Paul Monod that he was 'the "archetype" of the tippling and sentimental Jacobite' and therefore utterly harmless to the Hanoverian regime.[27]

---

24. Ibid, p. 9.   25. Ibid, p. 145.   26. Ibid, p. 169.
27. J. Cannon, *Samuel Johnson and the Politics of Hanoverian England* (Oxford, 1994), pp. 64, 66.

One close reading of a tract published in 1739, *Marmor Norfolciense*, led Howard Erskine-Hill to proclaim that it is 'a Jacobite tract if ever there was one'.[28] Even Cannon agrees that with it 'we come closest to a Jacobite Johnson'.[29] Yet Donald Greene claimed that 'Politically, *Marmor* is not very interesting; its targets are the commonplaces of opposition propaganda of the time', though he did concede that 'Johnson goes further than most of his contemporaries in insulting the king, and indeed kings in general.'[30] It is indeed an attack upon the Court, the main thrust being its upkeep of a standing army, not for an aggressive foreign policy, since the ministry was craven in its attitude towards Spain, but for domestic oppression. Greene is quite right in his claim that these were the principal objections of the opposition to the government in 1739. What gives rise to a more Jacobite reading of the tract, however, is a passage in which the anonymous author, 'probus Britannicus', a naive Court whig, deplores the anti-Hanoverian implications of the opposition's critique of the Court.

The conceit of *Marmor* is that an ancient prophecy 'in Monkish rhyme' has been unearthed on a stone in Norfolk. A gentleman of the county had translated the poem from Latin into English, and 'probus Britannicus' was commenting on the translation. His commentary is so laboured as to make the tract, in Pope's words, 'very humerous'. When he comes to a line foretelling that a horse would suck the blood of a lion, the commentator observes

> that a horse is born in the Arms of H——. But how then does the Horse suck the Lyon's Blood? Money is the Blood of the Body politick.
> – But my Zeal for the present happy Establishment will not suffer me to pursue a Train of Thought that leads to such shocking conclusions. The Idea is detestable, and such as, it ought to be hoped, can enter into the mind of none but a virulent Republican or bloody Jacobite.

To Clark and Erskine-Hill this is the smoking gun of Johnson's Jacobitism. Only a Jacobite could entertain such views, though, as Cannon observes, Johnson could also be called a Republican on the same basis, and indeed there is a curiously anti-monarchical strain to the tract, as Greene notes. But this is to fall into the same trap as Johnson has set for his naive commentator. The fact is that

28. Howard Erskine-Hill, 'The Political Character of Samuel Johnson: *The Lives of the Poets* and a further report on *The Vanity of Human Wishes*', in Eveline Cruickshanks (ed.), *The Jacobite Challenge* (Edinburgh, 1988), p. 161.
29. Cannon, *Samuel Johnson*, p. 51.
30. Donald Greene (ed.), *Samuel Johnson: Political Writings* (London, 1977), p. 21.

plenty of the Court's critics entertained such views of the Hanoverian connection without being either Jacobite or Republican. Tories and Country whigs alike subscribed to the view that Hanover was bleeding Britain white. Johnson almost rubs the reader's nose in this point when he gets 'probus Britannicus' to continue

> There is not one honest man in the Nation unconvinced how weak an Attempt it would be to endeavour to confute this Insinuation. An Insinuation which no Party will dare to abet, and of so fatal and destructive a tendency, that it may prove equally dangerous to the Author whether true or false.

The tract ends with a long suggestion from the commentator, who confesses his inadequacies at explicating the poem, as to how it could be more effectively analysed. He rejects the idea that the job might be done by the producers of the official *London Gazette*, allowing Johnson to score points off Walpole's publicity machine. He then proposes that a Society of Commentators should be set up consisting of thirty men, half of them lawyers and the other half army officers. When outlining the merits of the lawyers for the task he observes,

> It is well known to be the constant study of the lawyers to discover in Acts of Parliament meanings which escaped the Committees that drew them up and the Senates that pass'd them into Laws, and to explain wills into a sense wholly contrary to the Intention of the Testator. How easily may an Adept in these admirable and useful Arts, penetrate into the most hidden import of this Prediction.

The equivalent of the lawyers of 1739 are the modern commentators who look for overtly Jacobite sentiments in *Marmor Norfolciense*, and of course find what they are seeking.

This methodology is on a par with the anagrammatic techniques used by the academicians of Lagado, who could construe the message 'our brother Tom has just got the piles' as 'resist; a plot is brought home; the tower'. It could be applied to almost any contemporary writing which contained words like 'king', 'prince' and 'succession'. For example, Horace Walpole's Gothic novel *The Castle of Otranto* is susceptible to this treatment. Manfred, the tyrant of Otranto, is the grandson of a usurper who poisoned Alfonso, the legitimate prince, while they were on crusade in the Holy land. Manfred's plans to perpetuate the usurpation of his family are thwarted when his only son is crushed by a giant helmet. This heralds the fulfilment of the prophecy 'that the castle and lordship of Otranto should pass from the present family, whenever the real owner should be grown too large to inhabit it.' Manfred tries to evade the fateful results for his family by plotting to divorce his wife and marry the princess intended to have been his dead son's bride. But Alfonso's grandson turns up to thwart his plot and marry the princess himself. Here, surely, is a Jacobite novel extolling the hereditary principle and denouncing a ruling house which had set aside the legitimate line? It even fulfils the desires of the Jacobites in restoring the rightful dynasty. The only snags with this interpretation are that it was written by a staunch supporter of the Hanoverian succession in 1765, twenty years after any credence could be given to Stuart claims to the throne. Had it appeared anonymously in 1739, alongside Johnson's tract, it would no doubt be seized upon by scholars as yet another piece of crypto-Jacobite literature.

Two weeks after publishing *Marmor Norfolciense*, Johnson brought out *A Compleat Vindication of the Licensers of the Stage*. Like the former tract, this was a work in which Johnson created the persona of a Court whig ironically defending the government's actions – this time the decision to ban a performance of Henry Brooke's play *Gustavus Vasa*. Banned from the stage, the script appeared in print in a sumptuous edition supported by subscription. In a dedication to the subscribers, Brooke explained that 'Patriotism, or the love of country, is the great and single moral which I had in view thro' this play. This Love (so superior in its Nature to all other Interests and Affections) is personated in the character of Gustavus.' The Prologue embellished this theme.

> Britons! this night presents a State distress'd
> Tho' brave, yet vanquished; and tho' great, oppress'd;
> Vice, rav'ning Vulture, on her Vitals prey'd
> Her Peers, her Prelates, fell corruption sway'd . . .
> Truth, Justice, Honour fled th' infected Shore,
> For Freedom, sacred Freedom was no more

The plot concerned the uprising of Gustavus Adolphus to save Swedish liberties from the conqueror Cristiern, king of Denmark and Norway and usurper over Sweden, with the help of 'rustic sons of Liberty'. The fact that Gustavus had a stronger hereditary claim than Cristiern gave the play a Jacobite tinge which perhaps explains why among the subscribers were Sir William Wyndham, who gave a guinea, and Watkins Williams Wynn, who gave half a guinea. But then Gustavus is referred to in the Prologue as Sweden's 'Hero, her Deliverer', which has echoes of William of Orange rescuing England from tyranny in 1688. This possibly accounts for the earl of

Chesterfield's subscription of ten guineas. Either way it was a pro-foundly anti-Hanoverian play, which led to its suppression by the licensers of the stage, exercising powers given them by the Licensing Act of 1737.

This provoked Johnson to attack their high-handedness in the ironic *Vindication* of their actions. 'What is Power but the Liberty of acting without being accountable?' asks the anonymous defender of censorship. Clark hints, without stating it explicitly, that Johnson was defending the Jacobite implications of Brooke's play.[31] In Christine Gerrard's view, however, the *Vindication* was 'a work of undiluted Patriot Whiggery'.[32] Yet she accepts the argument that *Marmor* was Jacobite, and resolves the anomaly by referring to 'Johnson's unusual oscillation between Whig Patriot idealism and stubborn Jacobite resentment'.[33] She is so anxious to deny the concept of a Country ideology, shared by tories and dissident whigs, that she prefers to diagnose Johnson as suffering from a curious political schizophrenia rather than accept that he shared a common opposition mentality.

Gerrard does, however, identify a strain in opposition rhetoric which was largely whig – the stress on patriotism. The Patriots were overwhelmingly whigs. Those associated with Frederick, the Prince of Wales, after he went into opposition in 1737, included not only politicians like the earl of Chesterfield and Viscount Cobham but also poets such as Richard Glover and James Thomson. Perhaps their emphasis on the patriotic duty of Britons to defend liberty was more congenial to whigs than to tories, who tended to stress the liberties of Englishmen and to be suspicious of Scots like the Patriot politician Lord Marchmont and *the* Patriot poet, Thomson. Thomson's 'Rule, Britannia', first performed in 1740, became, as Gerrard points out, 'the unofficial national anthem'.[34]

Patriot poets of the late 1730s differed from previous Country writers, Gerrard insists, in many ways. Perhaps the most striking was that, where their predecessors had been pessimistic about social changes and fostered a 'politics of nostalgia' for a golden age when society and the economy had prospered under benevolent rulers, they were optimistic, and anticipated a brighter future under a Patriot king.

Certainly, the first decade of Walpole's ministry was overshadowed by the South Sea Bubble, which shattered faith in paper securities

---

31. Clark, *Samuel Johnson*, pp. 167–8.
32. Christine Gerrard, *The Patriot Opposition to Walpole: Politics, Poetry and National Myth 1725–1742* (Oxford, 1994), p. 231.
33. Ibid, p. 232.   34. Ibid, p. 3.

and restored confidence in land as an investment. The consequences of the Bubble were not merely economic. Money and land had acquired ideological values following the financial revolution, as we have seen.[35] In 1720 these were reinforced by the bursting of the Bubble. The very term 'bubble' carried with it the notion of a confidence trick – to be 'bubbled' was to be conned. The suspicions that there was a gigantic conspiracy between the Court and the City to ruin the landed interest now seemed to be confirmed. The result was that the Country writers of the 1720s and early 1730s, prominent amongst whom were Swift, Pope and Gay, upheld the alleged virtues of the traditional landed elite against the parvenus of the Walpolian era who had risen by shady transactions in the money market.

Colin Nicholson has demonstrated how many of the satires of the early eighteenth century were inspired by reactions to the South Sea Bubble.[36] Thus, he shows how *Gulliver's Travels* is at one level a satire on the shift from landed to monied values.[37] Lord Munodi is the epitome of the patriarchal landowner whose traditional methods of estate management work by sharp contrast with the innovations of the speculators. There is also a critique of trade, whereby, as Gulliver explains to the Houyhnhnms, 'in order to feed the Luxury and Intemperance of the Males, and the Vanity of the Females, we sent away the greatest Part of our necessary Things to other Countries, from whence in Return we brought the materials of Disease, Folly, and Vice, to spend among ourselves.' A similar contrast between a traditional landed patriarch and a nouveau riche patrician was made by Pope in the characters of the Man of Ross and Timon, while his representative merchant, Balaam, exemplifies the avarice, cheating and fraud of many in the commercial community as far as Country writers were concerned. Pope was particularly scathing in his attack on paper credit 'that lends Corruption lighter wings to fly'. The transition from a society upholding traditional landed values to one accepting new monetary values was nowhere better satirised than in *The Beggar's Opera*. As Nicholson puts it, Gay 'parodies a process of exchange that is accomplished through two metamorphoses of opposite yet mutually complementary character – the conversion

---

35. Above, pp. 51–2.
36. Colin Nicholson, *Writing and the Rise of Finance: Capital Satires of the Early Eighteenth Century* (Cambridge, 1994). He also shows how the reactions were ambiguous, since some writers also invested in South Sea stock and had their fingers burned – in Gay's case quite badly.
37. Ibid, pp. 91–122.

of commodities into money, and the reconversion of money into commodities'.[38] Friendship, Honour and Virtue are all commodities which can be exchanged for money, which, according to Peachum, 'is the true Fuller's earth for reputation, there is not a Spot or a Stain but what it can take out'. 'A man who loves money,' asserts Macheath, 'might as well be contented with one guinea as I with one woman.' As David Nokes observes, 'such satiric *bons mots* are only the tip of an iceberg of commercialising nouns and verbs which freeze-dries all relationships into market opportunities.'[39]

He further notes that 'the influence of Mandeville's *Fable of the Bees* is also evident in the opera.'[40] Mandeville had argued that man was not a social animal through love of his fellow creatures, as the third earl of Shaftesbury insisted. On the contrary, he was a beast of prey who exploited his fellows. Gay goes along with this cynical view of mankind. 'Lions, wolves and vultures don't live together in herds, droves and flocks,' Lockit soliloquises. 'Of all animals of prey, man is the only sociable one. Every one of us preys upon his neighbour, and yet we herd together.'

Mandeville, an unashamed apologist for the alleged benefits accruing to society from the pursuit of private advantage, was a target of Country satirists – not least because, as the protégé of the corrupt Lord Chancellor Macclesfield, he could be identified with the Court. Mandeville's *Fable* upheld the market economy as an engine of economic growth, even though he accepted that the conspicuous consumption which sustained it was based on all seven of the deadly sins. This shocked contemporaries who upheld traditional Christian values against the new doctrine of possessive individualism. One of Swift's prime targets in *Gulliver's Travels* was Pride, which Mandeville claimed employed a million of the poor. Pope attacked Timon's vanity, even though it created employment and thereby benefited the poor, providing indirectly a kind of charity which his hard heart denied giving directly. Gay displayed the corroding effects of avarice among courtiers and criminals alike.

The Country condemnation of commerce contrasts with the lavish praise heaped on it by the Patriot poet, Richard Glover, in *London: or the progress of commerce*, published in 1738. The poem describes the progress of Commerce from her birth, the result of a liaison between Neptune and Phonecia, to her arrival in London during the Interregnum of the 1650s. There

---

38. Ibid, pp. 136–7.   39. David Nokes, *John Gay* (London, 1995), p. 437.
40. Ibid, p. 440.

> grateful she bestow'd
> Th' unbounded empire of her father's floods
> And chose thee, London, for her chief abode . . .

Glover saw trade threatened by military rule, and advocated that defence should be confined to a citizen militia and the navy. Then

> liberty, security and fame
> Shall dwell for ever on our chosen plains.

James Thomson in *The Castle of Indolence* described how Industry 'quickened' towns 'by mechanic arts'

> And bade the fervent city glow with toil;
> Bade social commerce raise renowned marts,
> Join land to land, and marry soil to soil;
> Unite the poles, and without bloody spoil,
> Bring home of either Ind the gorgeous stores . . .

They were drawing on a whig tradition of esteeming trade and merchants which had found expression in Addison's Sir Andrew Freeport in *The Spectator* and Steele's Sealand in *The Conscious Lovers*. But where previous whig enthusiasts for commercial enterprise had also upheld the government, the Patriots were highly critical of it. Court supporters claimed that the balanced constitution established in the Revolution settlement was the best that could be devised, and was particularly conducive to economic growth. The Patriots agreed, but argued that the balance had been upset by the Court's undermining of the independence of the two houses of parliament by corruption, and that the restoration of the pristine equilibrium of 1689 was necessary to preserve liberty and with it prosperity. Thus Britain had to be rescued by the knight of Industry from the enervating effects of corruption by the wizard of Indolence. The knight is thereby represented, as John Barrell observes, 'as the ideal of a patriotic statesman who is "demanded" from his retirement to reanimate the public and private virtues of society'.[41]

The Patriot movement ran into the ground as a result of three developments in the decade 1742 to 1751. The first was the fall of Walpole, the second the Jacobite rebellion of 1745 and the third the death of Frederick himself in 1751, nine years before his father.

The fall of Walpole produced an unseemly struggle for power and place in which Patriot whigs appeared no more high-minded than the Old Corps who had supported the fallen prime minister.

---

41. John Barrell, *English Literature in History 1730–80* (London, 1983), p. 89.

On the contrary, they seemed worse to their disillusioned followers for having preached political virtue. The result was a cynical reaction to them. Among the cynics was Henry Fielding, who expressed his sense of betrayal in *The Opposition: a Vision* even before Walpole fell.[42] In it he pictured the minister's opponents on a waggon dragged by asses. Their luggage included 'a box with Public Spirit written in large golden characters on its outside'. Upon being opened it was found to be 'cramm'd with *Ambition, Malice, Envy, Avarice, Disaffection, Disappointment, Pride, Revenge* and many other heavy commodities'. When Fielding became reconciled to the subsequent ministry of Henry Pelham, he launched a weekly journal with the title *The True Patriot*. Where previously the opposition had attempted to deny the existence of parties, while the Court had maintained the continuance of tories and whigs, Fielding, writing a pro-ministerial paper, protested against 'this absurd and irrational distinction of parties' and even maintained that 'FACTION is no more . . . PARTY ANIMOSITIES are extinct.' 'It is now therefore that opposition is really and truly Faction; that the names of a Patriot and Courtier are not only compatible, but necessarily conjoined; and that none can be any longer enemies to the ministry, without being so to the public.'[43]

The True Patriot appeared during the Jacobite rebellion of 1745. This revealed that the ministerial accusation that the tories were crypto-Jacobites was untrue, and that the bulk of the tory party stayed loyal to the regime.[44] After the battle of Culloden, even those who might have hoped for its success realised that Jacobitism was a lost cause and rallied to the House of Hanover, or rather to the halfway house of the Prince of Wales' circle. Frederick remained in opposition until his sudden and unexpected death in 1751.

Patriotism, however, survived into the 1750s. It took the form of artistic and literary critiques of foreign influences, especially French, on English culture. In particular, the aristocracy were accused of aping continental models to the detriment of native traditions, employing French chefs, fashions and objets d'art. This insidious influence was eroding English manliness and weakening the country's ability to resist aggression. The gendered language was deliberate. Luxuria was a goddess and her baleful influence was emasculating the manliness of British males, rendering them unfit for manly

42. For a discussion of Fielding's politics see Speck, *Society and Literature in England 1700–1760* (London, 1983), pp. 140–50. Thomas R. Cleary, *Henry Fielding: Political Writer* (London, 1984).

43. *The True Patriot* nos. 14, 17, 18.

44. W. A. Speck, *The Butcher* (London, 1995).

exercise and martial virility. Consequently, Britain would be an easy prey for a foreign military power.

Thus, according to John Sekora, 'during the 1750s and early 1760s fear and anxiety brought forth by national and international conflict nourished the conventional criticism of luxury.'[45] It found expression in sermons and tracts as well as in novels. *The Tryal of the Lady Allurea Luxury*, published in 1763, made out the charges against the pernicious influence of luxury

> the prisoner, for near a century past, hath most wickedly and maliciously plotted and conspired the destruction of this land by corrupting the morals of our people, and endeavouring to the utmost of her power to eraze out of their hearts every sentiment of humanity and religion. That she hath promoted every folly, every impertinence, and every vice, that could debase human nature; and for that purpose hath made use of the most diabolical arts to bewitch the people to their ruin – to be base, venal, indolent and cowardly – to give themselves up entirely to empty amusements false pleasures and the lowest and most unworthy sensualities.[46]

Hogarth, Fielding and Smollett were in the vanguard of this attack upon the aristocratic penchant for French fripperies.[47] The warnings of the dire consequences which would result to national prestige seemed to be vindicated in the loss of Minorca in 1756.[48] Indeed, the inauspicious start to the war in North America, with the disastrous defeat of General Braddock's expedition to Fort Duquesne in 1755, seemed to justify the criticisms of Britain's degeneracy before it was apparently confirmed by Admiral Byng's disgrace.

Prominent among the Cassandras were John Brown and John Shebbeare. Brown's *Estimate of the manners and principles of the Times* attributed the degenerate state of the nation to the effeminacy of its ruling elite, brought about by its taste for French luxuries. Shebbeare's six Letters 'to the people of England' diagnosed a similar condition: 'That England has . . . sunk within the last fifty years into sloth, pusillanimity and dishonor, more precipitately than the other

---

45. John Sekora, *Luxury: the Concept in Western Thought, Eden to Smollett* (London, 1977), p. 90. Despite its title, this is primarily a study of Smollett's views on Luxury set in an eighteenth-century context.

46. *The Tryal of the Lady Allurea Luxury before the Lord Chief Justice Upright on an Information for a Conspiracy* (London, 1763).

47. Gerald Newman, *The Rise of English Nationalism* (London, 1987), pp. 63–9; Linda Colley, *Britons* (London, 1992), p. 88.

48. Kathleen Wilson, *The Sense of the People: Politics, Culture and Imperialism in England, 1715–1785* (London, 1995), pp. 178–85.

nations of Europe is alas! too fatally verified by the late conduct of affairs.' But he disagreed about the cause:

> That these flatigious effects have not so enormously prevailed from encreasing Luxury is certain, because in France it has been carried to a much greater excess than in this Kingdom, where such pernicious consequences have not followed; some other cause must then be searched after, which has operated to beget this degenerate and ruinous state of things in this country more effectually than in all others.[49]

His answer was that it was 'owing to the influence of Hanover on the Councils of England'.

Nevertheless, both authors agreed that the source of the problem was alien, France in the case of Brown, Hanover in that of Shebbeare. They both reflected and fuelled xenophobic sentiments in Britain which were the negative side of a growing sense of British nationalism which grew out of the Patriotism of mid-century politics. Victories over France in the Seven Years' War achieved by the British army and the Royal Navy boosted national pride. As William Robertson put it, 'by this juncture of its whole native force, Great Britain hath risen to an eminence and authority in Europe which England and Scotland could never have obtained.'[50]

During the 1760s, however, English national sentiment was nurtured by a perceived threat from another country, Scotland. Anti-Scottish sentiment found expression at almost every level of society in this decade. Wilkes led a scurrilous attack upon the Scottish favourite, Lord Bute, in the pages of *The North Briton*, the very title of which meant 'Scot'. For at the Union of 1707 the official names of 'Scotland' on the one hand, and 'England' and 'Wales' on the other, were supposed to be replaced by 'North' and 'South Britain' respectively. There was some attempt to use the expression 'North Britain' for Scotland, though 'South Britain' was relatively rarely used. The Scot Tobias Smollett was another target of Wilkes' spleen, since he edited a paper called *The Briton*. Radical charges that England was being swamped by Scots were pushed to extremes in an anonymous novel of 1769, *Private Letters from an American in England to his Friends in America*. This imagines a young American visitor to England in the late nineteenth century. 'The seat of government is

---

49. John Shebbeare, *A Sixth Letter to the People of England* (London, 1757), p. 6.
50. W. Robertson, *History of Scotland* (London, 1759), quoted in Howard Weinbrot, *Britannia's Issue: The Rise of British Literature from Dryden to Ossian* (Cambridge, 1993), p. 564.

transferred to America, and England is an almost deserted depopulated nation.' The main reason for the decadent state of England is ascribed to its being taken over by Scots. Thus a 'Scotch doctor ... pulled out a map of London – and, having turned to those streets which stretch away to Brentford and Uxbridge – said – not one house in all this quarter of the town is now inhabited by a South-Britain.'[51]

The main literary manifestation of the animosity which characterised Anglo-Scottish relations in the 1760s was the Ossian affair. In 1760 James Macpherson published *Fragments of Ancient Poetry Collected in the Highlands of Scotland, and Translated from the Gaelic or Erse language*. These impressed the antiquarian Hugh Blair of Edinburgh University, and he persuaded Macpherson to visit the Highlands in search of more Gaelic poetry. Macpherson's expedition resulted in the publication of *Fingal* in 1762, which he claimed was the translation of a complete epic poem by a third-century poet, Ossian. It recounted how Fingal, 'king of those Caledonians who inhabited the west coast of Scotland' went to help the kingdom of Ireland resist an invasion by Swaran from Scandinavia. Macpherson obligingly provided a precis of the poem in the introduction, before plunging the reader into the epic with the opening line: 'Cuchullin sat by Tura's wall; by the tree of the rustling leaf.' The poem was greeted with enthusiasm at the time, only a few expressing scepticism about its authenticity.

The appearance in 1763 of *Temora* in a volume along with other poems, however, did arouse suspicion, perhaps not least because they were dedicated to 'the earl of Bute, in obedience to whose commands they were translated from the original Galic of Ossian the son of Fingal'. Macpherson began to be widely suspected, at least in England, of counterfeiting Gaelic poetry. In Scotland he was stoutly defended as one who had genuinely recovered ancient verses recording the mythical origins of the nation. The fact that the myths were older than those surrounding the origins of England made some Scots even more tenacious about their authenticity. The debate split the English and Scottish literati (a word just coming into common usage). Among the former was the formidable figure of Dr Johnson, who made no bones about calling Macpherson a liar and a forger. Among the latter Blair continued to be Macpherson's most ardent supporter. The dispute really ranged over the authenticity

51. *Private Letters from an American in England to his Friends in America* (London, 1769), p. 100.

of Macpherson's sources. By and large the English insisted that these should be documentary, with original manuscript materials. Although Macpherson claimed that these existed, he did not help his case by not producing them, so that even the eminent Scottish scholar David Hume expressed scepticism about their provenance, though he did not publish his doubts. Blair and other Scottish men of letters, however, insisted that they had mainly descended by oral tradition from the Bards of the ancient clans.

The truth can never be known. That Macpherson collected some manuscripts for his fragments and for *Fingal*, if not for *Temora* seems to have been established.[52] At the same time it is generally agreed that he embellished fragmentary survivals to produce whole epics. The row was as much national as rational.

Yet one English scholar who was prepared initially to vouch for Macpherson's authenticity subsequently changed his mind, and provoked the most acrimonious exchange between the literati of the two nations. This was Thomas Percy, author of *Reliques of Ancient English Poetry*, a three-volume collection of songs and ballads published in 1765. Percy was a friend of Blair, and on a visit to Edinburgh was persuaded that Ossian was authentic. As he put it in a sentence added to the second edition of his *Reliques* in 1767,

> But no pieces of [the Irish bards'] poetry have been translated, unless their claim may be allowed to those beautiful pieces of ERSE POESY, which were lately given to the world in an English dress by Mr MACPHERSON: Several fragments of which the editor of this book has heard sung in the original language, and translated *viva voce*, by a native of the Highlands, who had, at the time, no opportunity of consulting Mr Macpherson's book.[53]

Percy left this sentence out of the third edition in 1775, having been persuaded in the meanwhile that he had been duped by his hosts in Edinburgh. Although he himself did not wish to score points by this omission, sceptics such as Johnson drew ammunition from it.

In the short run, the controversy by and large polarised Scottish and English men of letters and exacerbated relations between the two nations. But in the long run it did much to develop national feeling on both sides of the border, which ultimately fed into a British

52. Fiona J. Stafford, *The Sublime Savage: A Study of James Macpherson and the Poems of Ossian* (Edinburgh, 1988), p. 184.

53. Richard B. Sher, 'Percy, Shaw and the Ferguson "cheat": National Prejudice in the Ossian Wars', in Howard Gaskill (ed.), *Ossian Revisited* (Edinburgh, 1991), pp. 207–8.

identity. As Howard Weinbrot has chronicled, 'national self-esteem that came about through association with Southern classics, becomes national self-esteem through association with many native voices in one British chorus.'[54] Insofar as the term 'Augustan' is applicable to writers from Dryden to Johnson, it is justified by their use of classical models, especially the poetry of Horace and Juvenal for their verse satires. Macpherson and Percy pioneered the recourse to Anglo-Saxon and Celtic originals, giving a lead which was to inspire 'Romantic' poets, English and Scottish alike.

54. Howard Weinbrot, *Britannia's Issue*, p. 558.

CHAPTER SIX

The Emergence of the Novel

The reigns of George I and George II are generally agreed to have witnessed the emergence of the novel.[1] On the question of what caused it, however, there is general disagreement. Literary scholars even argue over the definition of a novel, disputing whether Swift's *Gulliver's Travels*, for example, really belongs to the genre.[2] While critical scepticism on that score is justifiable, from a historical point of view there is no reason to exclude it from a discussion of novels by such acknowledged novelists as Defoe, Richardson, Fielding, Smollett, Sterne, Burney and Goldsmith. The problem for the historian is to explain why the novel made its appearance in these years.

The starting point in any attempt to answer that question must be Ian Watt's *The Rise of the Novel*.[3] This was one of those truly seminal works which set the agenda for all future investigations, whether or not they accepted his thesis. That was basically that the novel appealed to a rising middle class who sought what Watt termed 'formal realism' as distinct from romance. An emergent bourgeoisie had the means and the leisure to form a new reading public. They sought not diversion from the real world, whether religious or romantic, but explorations of it. The autobiographical or biographical form of many early novels particularly appealed to them since they were motivated by possessive individualism. The fact that fictitious individuals included several women – Moll Flanders, Roxana, Pamela, Clarissa, for example – was significant since the new reading public

1. Cf. Margaret Anne Doody, *The True story of the Novel* (London, 1997), who argues that novels can be traced back to classical antiquity.

2. J. Paul Hunter, '*Gulliver's Travels* and the novel', in F. N. Smith (ed.), *The Genres of Gulliver's Travels* (London, 1990), pp. 56–73.

3. Ian Watt, *The Rise of the Novel* (London, 1957).

comprised especially bourgeois women who, above all, had the leisure to read novels.

Both parts of the argument have been criticised. Literary critics have shown that 'romances' were not replaced by novels but continued to flourish side by side with them.[4] Eliza Haywood wrote both, and published them together in four volumes as *Secret Histories [and] Novels* in 1725. Fielding's works exhibit elements of both, and Watt had problems accommodating them into his conceptual framework. Yet any explanation of the rise of the novel which fails to accommodate Fielding is seriously flawed. Social historians might also take issue with Watt's reliance on a rising middle class as an explanation for the popularity of novels. Some dispute the very phenomenon.[5] Others, while accepting it, would see coincidence rather than a causal relationship between it and the appearance of the novel. It is rare to find direct evidence of the impact of a novel on a particular urban audience. A letter from Philadelphia relating how *Pamela* helped the middle-class inhabitants to while away the winter months of 1741–2 is therefore worth quoting at length since it throws some light on the problem.

> If this pretty book of Pamela had not by some accident or other got into old Mrs Allen's hands and so into Mr Allen's even the man as well as the woman would have wanted subjects [of conversation] this long winter. But Pamela raised soon a most agreeable fund of discourse and reflection of the finest sort. Mr Allen ... when he had read the book spoke of it in the highest terms to the Governor and procured him the reading of it. He was more pleased if possible than Mr Allen and they too communicated such a fondness for the charming innocent that Pamela was in every one's mouth and happy that person who could procure a reading. To be sure no book ever yet penned in my opinion comes up to Pamela the model and envy of her sex.[6]

It is interesting that Mrs Allen first got hold of the novel, suggesting that women were more inclined to read them than the men. This seems to have been widely assumed by contemporaries. Thus, Burns implored the young girls of Mauchline to 'leave novels' since

4. Lennard J. Davis, *Factual Fictions: The Origins of the English Novel* (London, 1983). 'The romance is not usefully seen as a forbear of, a relative of, or an influence on the novel', p. 25.

5. See above pp. 9–10.

6. Historical Society of Pennsylvania: papers of Richard Peters, volume one, letter-book 'No. 5 Feb 1741 to June 1743': Peters to 'Mrs F', n.d. [February 1742].

> Such witching books are baited hooks
> For rakish rooks like Rob Mossgiel.
> Your fine Tom Jones and Grandisons
> They make your youthful fancies reel,
> They heat your brains and fire your veins,
> And then you're prey for Rob Mossgiel.[7]

It is also significant that Pamela was 'in every one's mouth', which suggests that all those whom the letter writer, the Secretary to the proprietors of the colony of Pennsylvania, knew were acquainted with the novel. This would be the circle of educated men and women who set up the Library Company of Philadelphia and launched the American Philosophical Society. Outstanding though these achievements were, there is no reason to believe that Philadelphia was any more sophisticated than other provincial towns of the British empire such as Dublin and Edinburgh, or for that matter Birmingham, Newcastle-upon-Tyne and York. Nor is there any reason to doubt Philip Skelton's claim, made in the 1780s, that novels 'for half a century have made the chief entertainment of that middle class which subsists between the Court and the spade'.[8]

Before that their chief entertainment had been provided by the newspaper press. Paul Hunter roots the new genre in the craving for news which characterised the opening years of the eighteenth century.[9] Journalism became a profession at that time. Defoe epitomised the link between journalists and novelists since he himself was both; his earlier journalism also spilled over into his novels. Thus the discussion of the hazards of the Yarmouth roads to shipping first appeared in the *Review* before it featured in *Robinson Crusoe.* The *Review* was but one of many journals which proliferated in Anne's reign. The most celebrated was undoubtedly *The Spectator.* The role of that periodical in the evolution of the novel was crucial. Addison and Steele created a fictional world, the Spectator club, whose members commented on the manners of the real world. The mixture of fact and fiction was used again by Addison when he developed the character of Foxhunter in *The Freeholder.* Macaulay was not far off the mark when he observed that 'this character is the original of Squire Western.'[10] Along with Sir Roger de Coverley

---

7. *Rhymer Rab: An Anthology of Poems and Prose by Robert Burns,* ed. Alan Bold (London, 1993), p. 113.

8. Quoted in Paul Langford, *A Polite and Commercial People: England 1727–1783* (London, 1989), p. 96.

9. J. Paul Hunter, *Before Novels: The Cultural Contexts of Eighteenth-century English Fiction* (London, 1990).

10. Lord Macaulay, *Essays* (London, 1893), p. 735.

and Sir Andrew Freeport, Addison demonstrated the existence of a middle-class readership for journalism which was not merely reporting or commenting on ephemeral events or gossip, but was creating imagined worlds which reflected the real world.

Watt saw a direct connexion between the rise of the middle class and the rise of the novel. This was a quasi-Marxist interpretation of the relationship. James Thompson puts forward an overtly Marxist explanation of the emergence of novels in the early eighteenth century.[11] He argues that changes in political economy were instrumental in bringing about changes in fictional writings which led to the rise of the novel.

As the financial revolution brought into being a machinery of public credit, so theoretical concepts were developed to explain the new phenomenon to bewildered contemporaries. For the creation of institutions like the Bank of England (established in 1694) to manage the national debt, brought into being, in Henry St John's words, 'a new interest almost equal to the terra firma of our island'.[12] The monied interest, which made money make money, baffled many observers. Swift was not alone in decrying the City in its new guise as 'a mystery of iniquity' with 'such an unintelligible jargon of terms to involve it in, as were never known in any other age or country in the world'.[13] Political economists tried to make sense of these innovations. As Thompson shows, they helped to develop the significant shift from seeing money as wealth to viewing it as capital, which facilitated the development of the financial market associated with the City ever since.

Side by side with the rise of the financial market rose a new marriage market. The portions brides brought with them to their husbands were regularly quoted in the press. For example, the following entries were inserted in Narcissus Luttrell's *Brief Historical Relation of State Affairs*, a series of newsletters, for the early months of 1706: 'a treaty of marriage is on foot between the duke of Beaufort and the lady Rachel Noell, daughter to the late earl of Gainsborough; her fortune above £60,000'; 'On Saturday Mr Harvey jun. of Coomb was married to Mrs Luttrell, worth £20,000'; 'On Thursday last the lord Bruce ... was married to the lady Ann Savil ... her fortune about £60,000'; 'On Thursday Mr Nevill member of parliament for Abingdon was married to Mr Butler's sister of Hartfordshire,

---

11. James Thompson, *Models of Value: Eighteenth-Century Political Economy and the Novel* (London, 1996).
12. Bodleian Library MS Eng. Misc. e. 180 f. 4: St John to Orrery, 9 July 1709.
13. *The Prose Works of Jonathan Swift*, ed. H. Davis (London, 1940), iii, pp. 6-7.

her fortune 8,000l'; 'Lord Scudamore is married to Mrs Digby . . . her fortune 10,000l'.[14]

Mercenary considerations were paramount in the selection of prospective partners. As Sir William Massingberd wrote to his cousin, a student at Cambridge,

> you are too well acquainted with the unfortunate circumstances of your family to stand in need of any information, and unless you marry a prudent person with a considerable fortune I fear you will let slip the most likely opportunity of retrieving it . . . A discreet wife with five or six thousand pound (and if she have more 'tis the better still) would put you in a condition to pay your brother and sisters' portions, clear the estate, furnish you wherewithal to build or repair, and give you a comfortable prospect of living easy in the world.[15]

Thompson draws attention to the way that fiction treated people, and especially women, as commodities with a value placed upon them. Thus, Moll Flanders and Roxana exploit the market value of their bodies to rise in the world from humble origins to affluence. Richardson attacked the degrading of marriage for mercenary motives in *Clarissa*. The heroine is right to object to her family's choice of the odious Solmes for her husband in order to benefit themselves financially. The Harlowes are a well-established landed family, whereas Solmes is merely a 'prosperous upstart, mushroomed into rank'. Ironically, the aristocratic Lovelace is socially a much more suitable match for Clarissa.

Nancy Armstrong has suggested that the novel appeared as a contribution to a discourse about the value of women not as financial so much as social assets. In her view 'a massive ideological struggle was underway' to redefine what made a woman desirable, and novels became an influential voice in the debate.[16] Thus, Richardson presented an exemplary domestic servant in his first heroine, Pamela. Female servants were generally regarded as fair game for the sexual gratification of their masters. Richardson was undoubtedly protesting against those crude sexual politics in the novel. But he was also, in Armstrong's view, concerned to make Pamela worth pursuing by her master, not as a sex object so much as a female desirable for her personal rather than her bodily charms. Pamela's personality and accomplishments made her the very model of femininity which conduct books strove to inculcate. As Armstrong puts it:

14. N. Luttrell, *A Brief Historical Relation of State Affairs* (London, 1857), vi, 3, 6, 14, 17, 23.

15. Lincolnshire Record Office Massingberd MSS 20/43.

16. Nancy Armstrong, *Desire and Domestic Fiction: A Political History of the Novel* (Oxford, 1987), p. 98.

Pamela's successful struggle against the sexual advances of Mr. B transformed the rules of an earlier model of kinship relations into a sexual contract that suppressed their difference in station. Rather than that of a master and servant, then, the relationship between the protagonists of these competing kinds of fiction may be understood as that of male and female. There can be no better illustration than this of how the discourse of sexuality worked and of what political goal was achieved as it suppressed the political categories that until then had dominated writing.[17]

By holding out against Mr B until he makes an honest woman of her, however, Pamela shows that virtue is not just its own reward. The fact that Richardson made her refusal to gratify Mr B's lust result in her marrying him prompted Fielding to protest in *Shamela* that the subtitle of *Pamela*, '*Virtue rewarded*', turned its heroine into little more than a whore. At the time it was almost unknown for a master to marry a servant. Richardson shows awareness of this when he has Pamela educated far above the normal level of female domestics. Where in reality these were the least literate of eighteenth-century adults, Pamela demonstrates her literacy on every page of the novel. Richardson explains this by making her the daughter of a schoolteacher who is further educated by Mr B's mother. But he does not explain it away. Mr B's sister is right to protest that Pamela is socially totally unsuited to be his wife.[18]

The early novel's obsession with the right choice of marriage partner coincided with the tensions within the bourgeois family, generated by desire on the part of parents to improve the family's standing in society through prudent marriages, especially for their daughters, and demands for freedom of choice by their children. Hogarth captured these in his series of paintings and prints *Marriage à la mode*. The dynastic ambitions of the London merchant overcome any concern for the wellbeing of his daughter when he marries her to the dissolute scion of an aristocratic family. The noble lord's main concern is to acquire a substantial dowry to remedy the insolvency he has brought on through imprudent building schemes. His son, too, is a victim of the arranged marriage. The plight of the doomed couple is symbolised by the yoking of the two dogs together in the first plate. Neither is given a choice of partner. The subsequent unhappy marriage and its tragic end are the inevitable consequence.

17. Ibid, p. 110.
18. Armstrong uses the disagreement between Richardson and Fielding to argue that Pamela represented thousands of females who had learned from conduct books to say 'no' to predatory males (ibid, p. 117). Maybe, but how many servants read them?

The theme is also at the heart of Richardson's *Clarissa*. The Harlowes are so intent on upward mobility that they are prepared to sacrifice the heroine to the odious Solmes, despite her objections and ultimate defiance. Yet her rejection of her father's choice and preference for Lovelace also leads to tragedy. The dilemma of duty and desire leads to irreconcilable conflict.

Insofar as this problem particularly affected the upwardly mobile middle-class family, then the early novel can still be seen as a bourgeois art form. It is perhaps significant that many novels addressed this issue, and that the canonical novelists – Defoe, Fielding, Richardson, Smollett and Sterne – were products of the bourgeoisie themselves and reflected its values in their novels. Defoe was a (failed) tradesman, Richardson a (successful) printer, while Fielding, Smollett and Sterne were professional men. The canon, however, has been much questioned of late for overlooking many minor authors, not least, as Janet Todd and Jane Spencer have pointed out, women.[19] If we extend the inquiry to include non-canonical authors, while many were of bourgeois origin, some were not. Eliza Haywood, the 'Juno of majestic size, with cow-like udders and with ox-like eyes' of Pope's *Dunciad*, was the daughter of a shopkeeper. But Horace Walpole was a substantial country gentleman who built the celebrated Gothic pile at Strawberry Hill and eventually became earl of Orford. Fanny Burney, daughter of a famous musicologist, became keeper of the queen's robes, then married a French army officer of modest means and lived mainly on her pension of £100 a year.

Eventually, however, Mrs d'Arblay, as Fanny Burney is quaintly referred to in the *Dictionary of National Biography*, was rescued from frugality by the receipt of £3,000 in royalties for her second novel, *Camilla*. Indeed, this was a bourgeois element which novelists had in common: they all made money from publishing novels. As Dr Johnson observed, only blockheads wrote for anything other than money. He himself paid off his mother's funeral expenses from sales of *Rasselas*. Defoe's *Robinson Crusoe* sold 5,000 copies at five shillings a copy, while Fielding's *Joseph Andrews* sold 6,000 at six shillings each. Eliza Haywood demonstrated, as Jane Spencer observes, 'that provided she was prolific and versatile, a woman could make her living by writing in the first half of the century'.[20]

19. Janet Todd, *The Sign of Angelica* (London, 1989); Jane Spencer, *The Rise of the Woman Novelist from Aphra Behn to Jane Austen* (London, 1986).
20. Jane Spencer, *The Rise of the Woman Novelist*, p. 9.

Although relatively few novelists were actually born in London, most gravitated to what Sir Walter Scott called 'the universal mart of talent'.[21] As Pat Rogers has observed of the period, 'few ages have known a more thoroughly metropolitan literary elite.'[22] The book trade was primarily based in the capital, where publishers like Robert Dodsley acted as middlemen between the producer and the consumer.[23] The novel was thus a new commodity in the urban market place, and in that sense, too, can be regarded as a bourgeois art form.

As Paul Hunter has observed, 'not all novels are set in London – though an astonishing number are either centred there or can hardly wait to get there.'[24] Defoe's *Journal of the Plague Year* is located in the City, while Moll Flanders spends much of her time there. Most of the action in Fielding's *Jonathan Wild the Great* also takes place in the capital, while episodes in *Amelia* and *Tom Jones* are located there. Smollett's Humphry Clinker and Roderick Random both pay visits to London, as does Burney's Evelina.

However, those episodes which do shift the scene to London scarcely sing its praises. On the contrary, many commentators have noted that whenever Fielding moves the action to the capital the tone becomes sombre and foreboding. In *Amelia* and *Tom Jones* the heroes and heroines find it infested with predatory creatures like Lady Bellaston and Lord Fellamar, while the Man on the Hill and Mr Wilson both experienced their downfalls in London. Roderick Random visits London three times and everywhere he goes, from jail to Court, from low alehouses to fashionable coffee houses, he encounters cunning, deception, hypocrisy, malice and treachery. This rather depressing reaction to London life seems curious if the novelists were reflecting bourgeois values.

The setting for these episodes, however, is not the City proper but Westminster. The novelists were satirising not the business district but the Court end of town. Tom Jones takes lodgings near Hanover Square and meets Lady Bellaston at a masquerade in the Haymarket. The Haymarket also features in *Amelia* while the heroine is invited to a masquerade at Ranelagh with potentially even more

21. Sir Walter Scott, *The Bride of Lammermoor* (Everyman, 1991), p. 20.

22. P. Rogers, *The Context of English Literature: The Eighteenth Century* (London, 1978), p. 21.

23. Alan Downie argues that publishers played a crucial role in 'The making of the English novel', *Eighteenth-Century Fiction* (London, 1997), ix, 249–66.

24. P. Hunter, 'The novel and social/cultural history', *The Cambridge Companion to the Eighteenth-century Novel* (Cambridge, 1996), p. 23.

107

.lts than Jones' encounter with Lady Bellaston.[25] Amelia's
Captain Booth, moves around the district of Grosvenor
Spring Gardens, Hyde Park, Monmouth Street and Gray's
.ne. Jonathan Wild also moves in with Count la Ruse into 'a
some house ready furnished in one of the new streets' around
Hanover Square. Heartfree, the jeweller whom they plot to cheat,
lives in the City proper and displays suitably bourgeois qualities of
integrity and probity. By contrast, the sharks who infest the other
end of town are identified with a corrupt Court and aristocracy.

The peers of the realm who appear in Fielding's novels are odious
parasites who exploit the people below them. For example, 'the
noble peer' in *Amelia* who pretends to be concerned for Captain
Booth's plight is really only interested in seducing his virtuous wife.
Ultimately, his insatiable womanising leads him to 'become so rotten
that he stunk above ground'. Smollet, too, expressed disdain for
aristocrats. Lord Struttwell, for instance, in *Roderick Random* not only
makes empty promises to the hero but also homosexual advances.

Although novelists attacked aristocrats, they rarely criticised
aristocracy itself, though Swift was not averse from doing so. One
of the greatest indictments of *Gulliver's Travels* is that of the English
peerage. In Brobdingnag Gulliver eulogises them, informing the king

> that they were persons of the noblest blood and of the most anci-
> ent and ample patrimonies . . . That these were the ornament and
> bulwark of the kingdom; worthy followers of their most renowned
> ancestors, whose honour had been the reward of their virtue; from
> which their posterity were never once known to degenerate.

In Glubdubdrib, however, Gulliver's admiration for the aristocracy
is considerably shaken when he is able to summon up the ancestors
of several 'counts, marquesses, dukes, earls and the like'. He then
discovers 'how cruelty falshood and cowardice grew to be characteristics, by which certain families are distinguished as much as by
their coats of arms'. Finally, he gives a very different account of the
aristocracy to his Houyhnhnm host from that which he gave to the
king of Brobdingnag:

> Our young noblemen are bred from their childhood in idleness and
> luxury; that as soon as years will permit they consume their vigour
> and contract odious diseases among lewd females, and when their

---

25. Masquerades were regarded as particularly corrosive of morality and social
hierarchy. See Eliza Haywood, *The Masqueraders, or Fatal Curiosity* (London, 1725);
Terry Castle, *Masquerade and Civilisation: the Carnivalesque in Eighteenth-century English
Culture and Fiction* (London, 1986).

fortunes are almost ruined, they marry some woman of mean birth, disagreeable person and unsound constitution, merely for the sake of money, whom they hate and despise. That the productions of such marriages are generally scrophulous, rickety or deformed children; by which means the family seldom continues above three generations, unless the wife take care to provide a healthy father among her neighbours, or domesticks, in order to improve and continue the breed.

This can be read as an indictment of the principle of an hereditary peerage as such. Yet Gulliver accepts and admires Houyhnhnm society, where there is an aristocracy based on race as well as upon birth. The bays, the dapple greys and the black Houyhnhnms were more intelligent than the white, the sorrel and the iron grey, which were kept as servants. What Gulliver objected to was that the aristocratic ideal which he outlined to the king of Brobdingnag was not being observed by contemporary English peers, so that instead of being the best they were among the worst of mankind.

These criticisms of the aristocracy could be seen as representing bourgeois condemnation of aristocratic decadence. For the derivation of the term aristocracy from the Greek meant literally 'the rule of the best'. Yet to Swift and other writers the present generation of aristocrats seemed to be 'the worst of mankind'. Michael McKeon has suggested that one of the concerns of the early novel was the contrast between the ideal, 'virtue' and the real, 'truth'.[26] One tension between truth and virtue which early novels investigated was that between the social and moral hierarchies. Contemporaries were acutely aware of the gradations of 'ranks, degrees and titles'. Gregory King in a well-known table distributed the population of England into no fewer than twenty-six rungs, with the temporal lords at the top and vagrants at the bottom. This implied a static hierarchy. But it appeared to observers that there was considerable movement up and down the ladder, and it concerned them not only that people were not prepared to accept their place in society but also that the undeserving were upwardly mobile. Thus, at one level, Defoe's *Robinson Crusoe* is a sermon on the sin of not accepting one's station in life. Crusoe's father warns him not to seek to rise 'in undertakings out of the common road', but to stay at home where he would enjoy 'the middle station of life, or what might be called the upper station of low life, which he had found by long experience was the best state in the world'. Disobedience leads to slavery in Morocco and solitude on the 'island of Despair' for twenty-eight years. Crusoe

26. M. McKeon, *The Origins of the English Novel 1600–1740* (London, 1987).

prospers in the end, but only after he literally deserves his fate by recognising his dependence upon divine providence.

The South Sea Bubble was the most spectacular example of how the traditional social hierarchy could be upset. As Charles Gildon observed of it, 'the world is now turned upside down, topsie turvy. Those who had plentiful fortunes are now in want, and those that were in want, have now got plentiful fortunes.'[27] The tensions between the ideal and the real social stratification exposed by the Bubble were developed by early novelists.

The idea that the peerage was degenerate was so widespread under the early Hanoverians that even John Cleland's Fanny Hill praises one of her lovers, the brother of an earl, for his

> firm texture of limbs, his square shoulders, broad chest, compact hard muscles, in short a system of manliness that might pass for no bad image of our ancient sturdy barons, when they wielded the battle-axe; whose race is now so thoroughly refin'd and frittered away into the more delicate and modern-built frame of our pap-nerv'd softlings, who are as pale, as pretty, and almost as masculine as their sisters.[28]

However, the aristocratic targets of these novels were not the peerage in general. They particularly charged the whig oligarchs of falling short of the aristocratic ideal. Smollett took the condemnation of them to extremes when he included a satirical depiction of the duke of Newcastle, the archetypal whig oligarch, in *Humphrey Clinker*. This reflects not so much bourgeois as Country ideology. The criticisms were aimed at the whig courtiers who presided over the nation under the first two Georges. As Squire Western puts it, 'I hate all lords; they are a parcel of Courtiers and Hanoverians.'

As ever, Fielding poses problems here. His novels might contain unsavoury noblemen, but he was a client of the fourth duke of Bedford, a leading Court whig, when he wrote them. There will always be difficulties in disentangling the conflicts between a Country mentality and a Court commitment in Fielding's works. Pat Rogers resolves the conflict by claiming that Fielding needed Court patronage to pay his bills. He literally sold out. But it was not quite so simple chronologically. His plays, written for the most part when he was not committed, for the most part adopt an opposition stance.

27. Charles Gildon, *All for the better; or, the world turned upside down; being the history of the headlongs and the long-heads* (London, 1720), p. 58. Gildon thought that the change was 'all for the better; it is plain that the side that is fallen made but very ill use of their riches'. But this was an untypical reaction to the crisis. Most commentators considered that it had rewarded the undeserving.

28. John Cleland, *Memoirs of a Woman of Pleasure* (London, 1993), p. 82.

His tracts, written when he was a Court client, support the government's position. But his novels, from *Jonathan Wild the Great* to *Amelia* uphold Country rather than Court values. This is apparent from Fielding's treatment of the gentry. His ideal is represented by Allworthy, the Somerset squire who lives in Paradise Hall. Its debasement is shown in the character of Squire Western. But even he has redeeming features by contrast with his sister, Di, the archetypal courtier. Similarly, Smollett juxtaposes Sir Timothy Thicket and Squires Bumper and Topehall in *Roderick Random* – country gentlemen brutalised by foxhunting and hard drinking like Western – with Roderick's father, Don Rodrigo, an Allworthy type. Mr Cringer, the Court MP, will do nothing without being bribed first.

By contrast, when Evelina makes her entrance into the world in 1775, it was in the Court end of London. She visits and enjoys such locations as Ranelagh which had threatened Amelia's virtue. Yet though her old-fashioned guardian expresses concern at her enjoyment of London's night life, and she has to learn how to fend off predatory males, ultimately Evelina comes to no harm there.[29] Far from it, she triumphantly scoops the jackpot in the marriage lottery by marrying a peer of the realm, Lord Orville. It is hard to imagine one of Fielding's heroines becoming a peeress.

Criticisms of effete aristocrats presiding over a decadent society reflected and informed a general feeling that the peers were not fulfilling their function in the reign of George II. Kathleen Wilson has drawn attention to a vein of anti-aristocratic sentiment in these years which accused the nobility of not providing a lead for the country's imperial ambitions.[30]

Such feelings were largely dispelled with the successes of Britain's armed forces against the French in India and North America during the Seven Years' War. A novel suffused with very different sentiments made its appearance in 'the wonderful year' of 1759 with the first two volumes of Sterne's *Tristram Shandy*. Sterne's own hero was William Pitt, who in his view had rescued Britain's reputation in Europe and the world. He dedicated the second edition of his novel to Pitt,

29. I cannot accept Judith Lowder Newton's feminist reading of the novel as 'a chronicle of assault' upon Evelina. *Women, Power and Subversion: Social Strategies in English Fiction 1778–1860* (London, 1981) p. 23. The preface to her book is one of the more overt statements of the kind of agenda some feminist literary critics address which is not so much ahistorical as anti-historical.

30. Kathleen Wilson, 'The good the bad and the impotent. Imperialism and the politics of identity in Georgian England', in Ann Bermingham and John Brewer (eds), *The Consumption of Culture 1600–1800: Image, Object, Text* (London, 1995), pp. 237–62.

claiming in the dedication 'if I am ever told it has made you smile; or can conceive it has beguiled you of one moment's pain, I shall think myself as happy as a minister of state.' The thought of Pitt laid up with one of his crippling attacks of gout seeking relief from pain in *Tristram Shandy* is itself a Shandean conceit. Although no aristocrat as such features in the novel, Walter Shandy, Tristram's father, 'was originally a Turkey merchant but had left off business for some years in order to retreat to, and die upon, his paternal estate in the county of ——'. This was a type of successful businessman turned landowner which previous writers had rather condemned than condoned. They had also been highly critical of Court whigs, but the occupants of Shandy hall share the ideology of the whig oligarchs. Uncle Toby and Corporal Trim spend their days re-enacting the sieges of King William's war in Walter Shandy's garden. Toby constantly whistles 'Lilliburlero', the whig anthem of 1688, and cannot hear of the treaty of Utrecht of 1713 without commenting that by it the tories had betrayed the allies and their country.

This sea change in the attitude towards the Court is discernible in Oliver Goldsmith's *The Vicar of Wakefield*. Charles Primrose's daughter, Sophia, marries the baronet, Sir William Thornhill, and his younger daughter, Olivia, marries Sir William's nephew. The two Thornhills exemplify the contrast between the ideal of a country gentleman and its debasement, for Sir William is in every way a deserving figure while Mr Thornhill is a dyed-in-the-wool villain. But where Sir William would probably have been presented as unsympathetic to the Court in earlier novels, Goldsmith assures us that he was 'a man of large fortune and great interest, to whom senates listened with applause, and whom party heard with conviction; who was the friend of his country but loyal to his king'.

There is, however, a curious passage in which the vicar expresses almost levelling opinions, and wishes all men were kings! He extols monarchy as acting as a bulwark to protect

> that order of men which subsists between the very rich and the very rabble; those men who are possessed of too large fortunes to submit to the neighbouring men in power and yet are too poor to set up for tyranny themselves. In this middle order of mankind are generally to be found all the arts, wisdom and virtues of society. This order alone is known to be the true preserver of freedom and may be called THE PEOPLE.

He considered that they were in danger of being crushed between the elite above and the electorate below them. The decline in the value of the property qualifications for voting had vastly expanded the number of voters 'and they, ever moving in the vortex of the great, will follow where greatness shall direct.' The only counter-weight to this alliance of the elite and the electorate was the Crown:

> In such a state, therefore, all that the middle order has left, is to preserve the prerogative and principles of the one principal governor with the most sacred circumspection. For he divides the power of the rich, and calls off the great from falling with tenfold weight on the middle order placed beneath them.

Primrose is not a republican, for in his view such republics as Holland, Genoa and Venice upheld the rich against the poor. He therefore concludes,

> I am, then, for, and would die for, monarchy, sacred monarchy; for if there be anything sacred amongst men, it must be the anointed sovereign of his people, and every diminution of his power, in war or in peace, is an infringement upon the real liberties of the subject. The sounds of liberty, patriotism, and Britons, have already done much; it is to be hoped that the true sons of freedom will prevent their ever doing more.

Such sentiments expressed in a novel published in 1766 reflect an ideological debate which has moved on from the dialogue between Court and Country which characterised the reign of George II. It is responding to the issues raised by the Wilkes controversy and the Stamp Act crisis. The Wilkites have been described as bourgeois, and the Society of Supporters of the Bill of Rights undoubtedly drew on middle-class support. But the middle classes were not united behind radical politics. There was substantial support for the monarch's stance too, as reactions to the War of American Independence and above all the French Revolution were to show. Goldsmith's novel documents a strain of middle-class conservatism which arose in response to the new issues of the 1760s.

CHAPTER SEVEN

Literature and Law and Order

At one time literature was used as a prime source for the history of crime. Social historians ransacked literary sources for easily accessible purple passages dealing with criminal activity. Thus, the *Newgate Calendar* and the novels of Defoe and Fielding were plundered to provide vivid illustrations of crime and vice in the eighteenth century. The result was to conjure up a vast underworld in which professional gangs terrorised the subjects of the first two Georges. Citizens especially went in fear of their lives from highwaymen, pickpockets, footpads and burglars. Some of the more flamboyant aspects of the fictitious characters seem to find confirmation in the real-life escapades of Jonathan Wild. Wild was compared to Al Capone, being represented as the mastermind at the centre of a vast network of gangs which dealt in stolen goods.[1]

Wild's particular forte was to employ thieves who deposited their takings in a so-called lost property office. These were then advertised as found, to be redeemed by their owners at a price, with no questions asked. Particularly 'hot' items were taken in a sloop to Holland to be sold abroad. The men Wild employed for these crimes were largely convicted felons who had been sentenced to transportation to the colonies and had returned illegally. They were therefore completely at his mercy since he could simply inform on them to a magistrate, and they would be automatically sentenced to death for having evaded the punishment for a capital crime. Fact and fiction seemed to reinforce each other, since Wild was the subject of a life by Defoe and a novel by Fielding. He also informs the character of Peachum in Gay's *The Beggar's Opera*, since the act of informing on convicts who had returned from penal servitude was known as impeaching them.

1. Gerald Howson, *Thief Taker General: The Life and Times of Jonathan Wild* (London, 1975).

Then serious work started on the evidence for actual criminal activity.[2] Several investigations of eighteenth-century court records substantially modified the lurid picture conjured up by the literary sources. The pattern of indictments, for instance, did not document the notion that England was experiencing a massive and uncontrollable crime wave. On the contrary, the trend in indictments for crimes such as assaults, and against property, appeared to be downward rather than upward. This trend could be reversed by sudden increases in food prices in rural areas, or by the ending of wars and the demobilisation of soldiers and sailors in ports, especially London, which could not absorb them quickly into the urban economy. But apart from such fluctuations, the incidence of indictments suggests a diminishing and controllable crime rate. Nor do the court records support the alleged existence of a vast criminal underworld. On the contrary, most crime appears to have been committed by amateurs, whose principal occupations were as servants, labourers and journeymen.

The relationship between rhetoric about law and order and the reality of crime is probably always remote. The debates at party political conferences about being tough on crime and on the causes of crime document ideological convictions rather than the complex motives behind the behaviour of criminals. They record perceptions of the levels of criminal activity rather than the actual incidence of crime. Similarly, literature, while a very suspect source for the crime rate in eighteenth-century England, documents a contemporary debate about how to deal with crime and criminals.

The equivalent of the 'tough on crime' school argued for ever more draconian laws and punishments. They considered individuals to be morally autonomous, so that crime was a conscious and free choice. It should be deterred by making the consequences as painful as possible. Those who advocated toughness against the causes of crime maintained that circumstances contributed to criminal behaviour. Poverty and ignorance were strong inducements to prostitution and theft. Society itself encouraged vice and crime if it turned a blind eye to duelling, drunkenness and gambling among the elite. For the lower orders allegedly looked to their social superiors for role models, and examples of good or bad behaviour trickled down from the top to the bottom rungs of the hierarchy. Above all, the Court

2. See especially John Beattie, *Crime and the Courts in England 1660–1800* (Oxford, 1986); Peter Linebaugh, *The London Hanged: Crime and Civil Society in the Eighteenth Century* (London, 1991); Robert B. Shoemaker, *Prosecution and Punishment: Petty Crime and the Law in London and Rural Middlesex* (London, 1991).

should set an example to the rest of society. A virtuous Court would improve the manners of the masses, while, by contrast, a vicious Court would ultimately lower the moral standards of the whole country.

Daniel Defoe sympathised with the view that social conditions contributed to the level of crime. He was fond of quoting the proverb 'Give me not poverty least I steal.' Crime and criminals are a major theme of such novels as *Moll Flanders* and *Colonel Jack.* In these he explores the problem of how far individuals have moral choices. Defoe loads the dice against his heroes and heroines. Moll is actually born in Newgate prison, while Colonel Jack is one of the urchins abandoned on the streets of London. Moll drifts into vice after being seduced by the son of a gentleman into whose service she had been placed. Colonel Jack similarly enters a criminal underworld through the circumstances in which he finds himself – in his case ignorance, so that he is unable to distinguish right from wrong. His lack of education is used by Defoe to advocate the provision of charity schools for the poor.

Bernard Mandeville had no truck with this solution. On the contrary, in his *Essay on charity schools* he insisted that they encouraged crime, since they educated poor children above their station in life. They would not be content to be hewers of wood and drawers of water once they could read and write. He was adamant that, so far from ignorance being conducive to crime, criminals were among the more intelligent of the lower orders, having a shrewd cunning which emboldened them to commit crime. Mandeville was a leading figure among the advocates of state suppression of crime by harsh measures. In his *Reflections on the Cause of the Frequent Executions at Tyburn* he asserted that the death penalty as it was currently being exacted was not deterrent enough. The convict became the hero of the day in the carnival atmosphere of the procession from Newgate to Tyburn. Fortified by alcohol, he could even contrive to go out of the world defiantly and make a good end. The executions of the most notorious criminals were, in Mandeville's view, examples which might inspire the onlooker to emulate rather than to avoid their careers. He therefore urged that capital punishment should be inflicted in private rather than in public, and that the condemned man should be allowed no alcohol before his execution. Everything should be contrived to induce in him feelings of dread and horror rather than of defiance and glory. Then the death penalty would truly deter.

Hogarth confirms Mandeville's criticism of the failure of Tyburn to deter in the plate of his series *Industry and Idleness* which depicts the execution of Tom Idle. It teems with crowd activity seemingly careless of the solemnity of the occasion. A small boy is actually picking a biscuit-seller's pocket. The whole series, like his *Harlot's Progress*, seems to point up the moral that vice and crime are conscious choices. Some scholars have suggested alternative readings of Hogarth's series. Thus Ronald Paulson and Ian Bell have urged that circumstances other than Idle's depravity led to his downfall.[3] That Hogarth's message was more complex than the simple moral that Idle and Goodchild chose their fates is undeniable. Plate ten is particularly ambiguous. Goodchild averts his gaze, apparently because he cannot face condemning his fellow apprentice to death. Yet this also prevents him seeing the perjury of a witness giving testimony which will send Idle to the gallows. If part of the complexity is that peer pressure is conducive to social behaviour, then where Idle's can be attributed to the low life in which he seeks diversion, so too must Goodchild's be conditioned by the company he keeps, which in the case of the guzzling aldermen at the Guildhall feast is not all edifying. But the bottom line is clearly that the Devil finds work for idle hands. There is no way that the plates can be read to reverse the conclusion that Hogarth is advocating industriousness and castigating idleness, or that these conditions are anything other than the choice of the idle and industrious.

Dr Johnson, however, had another explanation for the frequent executions at Tyburn. As he observed in *London*:

> A single jail in Alfred's golden reign
> Could half the nation's criminals contain

whereas in 1738

> Scarce can our fields, such crowds at Tyburn die
> With Hemp the gallows and the fleet supply.

Alfred's virtuous court had set a good example, so that there had been relatively little crime in his reign. By contrast, Walpole's vicious

3. Ronald Paulson, 'The simplicity of Hogarth's Industry and Idleness', *Journal of English Literary History* (London, 1974), **41**, 291–320; Ian A. Bell, *Literature and Crime in Augustan England* (London, 1991), pp. 28–46. Moll Hackabout is faced with a choice in plate one of *The Harlot's Progress*. Bell criticises me for reading into her mind an 'ability to understand what is going on' in the first plate (*Literature and Crime*, pp. 134–5). Yet he does not draw attention to the present for her cousin in Thames Street, which was presumably her original destination. It was only a short distance from Wood Street where the wagon had set her down. Though her cousin had not met her, Moll could have made some effort to find her. That she did not do so reinforces the view that Moll had a moral choice when she arrived in London.

administration set such a corrupt example that the country, and above all the capital, were experiencing an uncontrollable crime wave.

John Gay's *The Beggar's Opera* was built around much the same conceit. Peachum, Lockit and the gang are a mirror image of the ruling elite of aristocrats and gentry. They refer to each other as gentlemen and call their women ladies. Gay's gentlemen criminals protest that they are men of honour. When Peachum accuses Lockit of conning Ned Clincher, the jailor retorts, 'Mr Peachum this is the first time my honour was ever called in question', to which Peachum agrees 'business is at an end if once we act dishonourably.' This provokes Lockit to riposte 'he that attacks my honour attacks my livelihood.' They are even prepared to defend this debased honour by murder. As Peachum puts it, 'no gentleman is ever looked upon the worse for killing a man in his own defence.' This refers to the prevalent practice among the elite of duelling, which made a mockery of the law. As the beggar observes at the end of the Opera,

> Through the whole piece you may observe such a similitude of manner in high and low life, that it is difficult to determine whether (in the fashionable vices) the fine gentlemen imitate the gentlemen of the road, or the gentlemen of the road the fine gentlemen. Had the play remained as I at first intended, it would have carried a most excellent moral. 'Twould have shown that the lower sort of people have their vices in a degree as well as the rich, and that they are punished for them.

The original intention was to have Macheath executed. Before he is saved from the gallows, and the Opera from a tragic ending, by a timely reprieve he reflects on the moral in the condemned cell at Newgate.

> Since laws were made for every degree
> To curb vice in others as well as me
> I wonder we han't better company
>   Upon Tyburn tree.

> But gold from law can take out the sting
> And if rich men, like us, were to swing
> 'Twould thin the land such numbers to swing
>   Upon Tyburn tree.

This could be taken for a universal observation, as much a truism as the old saw 'it's the rich that get the pleasure, it's the poor that gets the blame.' But Gay makes it peculiarly pertinent to the contemporary scene. Throughout the Opera monetary values are assumed to be replacing moral values. Peachum makes this quite explicit when he asserts that 'money . . . is the true fuller's earth for reputation; there is not a spot or a stain but what it can take out. A rich rogue *nowadays* is fit company for any gentleman.' The elite have become corrupted by material considerations, until a man's creditworthiness is a better clue to his social standing than his moral worthiness.

The ultimate cause of this decline in morality is corruption at Court. There the subversion of honour by money is made clear in the song:

> The modes of the Court so common are grown
> That a true friend can hardly be met
> Friendship for interest is but a loan
> Which they let out for what they can get.

Even friendship has become a saleable commodity among the courtiers of George II's reign. And the most mercenary of them all is Walpole, with whom the criminals are openly compared. Thus, one is called 'Robin of Bagshot, alias Gorgon, alias Bluff Bob, alias Carbuncle, alias Bob Booty', a scarcely veiled reference to the prime minister. When Mrs Peachum says to Filch '[If] an unlucky session does not cut the rope of thy life . . . thou wilt be a great man in history' the reference to 'the Great Man', as Walpole was known, is not veiled at all. The ambiguous use of the word 'session', which could refer to the sitting of parliament as well as of a court, clinches the point. Walpole could preside over a Cabinet which connived at the concealment of gigantic frauds like the South Sea scandal and get away with it, while lesser fry like Wild who presided over 'a kind of corporation of thieves' went to the gallows.

Jonathan Swift agreed with Gay that a bad example at Court corrupted the whole of society. In his *Project for the Advancement of Religion and Reformation of Manners* he urged Queen Anne to appoint only virtuous courtiers and to bar the vicious from her Court. Such a policy would have the beneficial effect of improving morality throughout the realm.

Swift even thought that the law itself should not be confined to the negative role of deterring or punishing crime, but should be used to reward the law-abiding. In *Gulliver's Travels* he created societies in keeping with these ideals. Of the Lilliputians he wrote that 'in choosing persons for all employments they had more regard to good morals than to great abilities.' Anybody who could prove that they had strictly observed the laws for a specified period was entitled to certain privileges, including a financial reward and a title. 'And these people thought it a prodigious defect of policy amongst us', observed Gulliver, 'when I told them that our laws were enforced only by penalties, without any mention of reward.' The king of Brobdingnag also expresses his disapproval of the way people in England acquired promotion. 'You have clearly proved that ignorance, idleness and vice are the proper ingredients for qualifying a legislator', he informs Gulliver.

> It doth not appear, from all you have said, how any one perfection is required, towards the procurement of any one station among you; much less that men are ennobled on account of their virtue, that priests are advanced for their piety or learning, soldiers for their conduct or valour, judges for their integrity, senators for the love of their country, or counsellors for their wisdom.

The king can only make these points without hypocrisy if public officials are advanced in Brobdingnag on account of the qualities lacking in their equivalents in England. Not that the Brobdingnagian Court was a model of virtue. On the contrary, the maids of honour are lascivious, one of them using the diminutive Gulliver as a sex object. Nor was the country completely free from crime, for Gulliver himself witnessed the execution of a murderer. But the crime rate is very low in comparison to England, since there are very few precedents for criminal cases.

There is no crime at all among the Houyhnhnms, so that a system of rewards and punishments is irrelevant. Not only were there no 'pickpockets, highwaymen, housebreakers, attorneys, bawds ... ravishers, murderers, robbers ... or ... encouragers to vice, by seducement or examples', nor were there 'scoundrels raised from the dust upon the merit of their vices; or nobility thrown into it, on account of their virtues'.

Henry Fielding also contributed to this debate on law and order. But where other writers can be identified as advocating either that the state should crack down hard on crime or that the Court should provide a good example he, as ever, is ambivalent. In his *Proposal for Making an Effectual Provision for the Poor* he offered a draconian system to deter the lower orders from begging, robbing and stealing. Any of them found in an alehouse after ten at night could be brought before the justices as vagrants. They were not to be allowed to travel without a pass. Yet in his *History of Jonathan Wild the Great* he drew a parallel between criminals and cabinet ministers every bit as explicit as that drawn by Gay in the *Beggar's Opera*. Wild, like

Walpole, is constantly referred to as 'the Great Man'. He asserts that 'in civil life, doubtless, the same genius, the same endowments, have often composed the statesman and the prig, for so we call what the vulgar name a thief'. Fielding also notes how the thieves 'have the words honesty, honour and friendship as often in their mouths as any other men', which 'may appear strange to some, but those who have lived long in cities, *courts*, jails or such places will perhaps be able to solve the seeming absurdity'.

Yet, in the late 1740s he himself moved in Court circles. Thanks to the patronage of the duke of Bedford, Fielding became high steward of the New Forest, and justice of the peace for both Middlesex and Westminster. It was in his capacity as a justice that he became involved in the case of Bosavern Penlez, which provides an ideal case study for the Augustan debate on law and order.

The case of Bosavern Penlez[4]

On 30 June 1749 two sailors were robbed of thirty guineas and their watches while their attention was distracted by the diversions they were enjoying in 'The Crown', a brothel in The Strand, London. The following day, 1 July, they persuaded their shipmates in 'The Grafton', a man-of-war moored in the Thames, to retaliate on their behalf by gutting the tavern and burning its contents in the street. According to one eye-witness, the bonfire 'caused so violent a flame, that the beams of the houses adjoining were heated thereby'. Next night some 400 sailors went down The Strand 'threatening that they would pull down all bawdy houses'. They attacked 'The Bunch of Grapes', burning its contents in an even bigger fire. Then they went to 'The Star' in Devereux Court, which they proceeded to sack, throwing the goods of the owner, William Wood, into the street. Fortunately for Wood, a constable managed to call out troops, who dispersed the crowd before they could set fire to the goods. When it was rumoured that 4,000 sailors planned further attacks against disorderly houses on 3 July the proprietors of several evacuated them, while troops patrolled The Strand all day.

Several men were arrested during these disturbances. Four were rescued immediately by fellow rioters, who broke into places where they were confined, threatening the lives of their jailors. The rest

---

4. The account of the case is based mainly on *The Proceedings on the King's Commission of the Peace, Oyer and Terminer and Gaol Delivery for the City of London . . . held at Justice-Hall in the Old Bailey . . . September . . . 1749*, pp. 131–5.

were conveyed under armed guard to Newgate 'the mob frequently endeavouring to break in upon the soldiers and crowding towards the coach doors'.

One of those taken up was Bosavern Penlez, the 23-year-old son of an Exeter clergyman. Penlez had lived in London since 1747, working as a journeyman peruke maker. He was found asleep in the early hours of 3 July in possession of some linen, 'to wit 10 laced caps, 4 laced handkerchiefs, 3 pair of laced ruffles, 2 laced clouts, 5 plain handkerchiefs, 5 plain aprons and one laced apron'. When brought before a magistrate he could not account for his possession of these items. At first he said that they belonged to his wife, then to a woman who had robbed him and again that he had found them in the street. Jane Wood, the wife of the proprietor of 'The Star', later swore on oath that they belonged to her.

Penlez was consequently brought to trial in September 1749 at the Old Bailey. He was indicted along with two others 'for that they, together with divers other persons to the number of forty and upwards, being feloniously and riotously assembled, to the disturbing of the public peace, did begin to demolish the dwelling house of Peter Wood.' Wood, his wife and James Reeves, a waiter in the tavern who boarded there, all swore that they recognised Penlez as a ringleader in the riot. According to Reeves, 'he was the first man that went up the stairs, he was the greatest rascal amongst them all: I saw Mr. Wood lying on the stairs, and heard Pen Lez say to him, you dog are you not dead yet?' The testimony of these witnesses was, to say the least, suspect. They could not even agree on the size of the stick Penlez was alleged to have been carrying and to have used to demolish glasses, pictures and birdcages. John Nixon, who collected the scavenger's rate in Devereux Court, admitted that he 'would not hang a dog or a cat' upon the evidence of Wood or his wife. Wood was evasive and equivocal about who actually paid the rates for the premises, which he confessed constituted a disorderly house. Seven associates of Penlez, on the other hand, including his present and former employers, testified to his good character. Notwithstanding their pleas, he and another of the three accused were found guilty by the jury and sentenced to death by the judge. Although the Court recommended mercy, while his fellow convict was pardoned, Penlez was duly executed for his crime on 18 October 1749.

The Penlez case provoked a popular outcry. There were many reasons for the wave of sympathy which arose on his behalf. First, there was the fact that he was not a sailor, and everybody who saw the riots agreed that they were instigated by seamen. Secondly, he was found guilty on the testimony of persons of ill repute. Thirdly, he seemed to have been singled out in order to make an example of him, for of those arrested only Penlez was condemned to death, even though the Court recommended mercy. But perhaps above all was the fact that he was not charged with stealing linen, though that alone would have been enough to hang him in the eighteenth century. Indeed, his being found in possession of the linen was not mentioned at the trial, and when it was later adduced in justification of his execution his sympathisers denied the truth of the accusation.

At the actual trial Penlez was charged with being involved in a riot. The Riot Act of 1715 is best known for its provision requiring a crowd to disperse after a magistrate has ordered them to do so, failure to do so being a capital offence. But Penlez was not accused of violating the reading of the Riot Act, for instance by obstructing the magistrate so that the proclamation could not be heard. It is therefore irrelevant whether or not the order was proclaimed in July 1749, though there was some doubt about that. Instead, he was charged with breach of the clause making it a capital offence to demolish or begin to demolish any church or chapel or any building for religious worship, or any dwelling house, barn or other outhouse. The fact that it was a brothel which he was alleged to have helped demolish, and not a church or a chapel, seemed more deserving of commendation than condemnation to many.

At all events, petitions poured in for his reprieve, signed by hundreds from all walks of life. Some pointed out that in the thirty-four years since the passing of the Riot Act only two prosecutions had been brought under these clauses before Penlez was accused. Others expressed doubts that the attack on 'The Star' was a riot within the meaning of the Act. Most assumed that Penlez was not guilty or at least was deserving of a pardon. According to one account, 'several gentlemen of rank and credit, accompany'd by a reverend Divine, went in a decent solemn procession, all dress'd in black, to deprecate the execution of the sentence.' There was such fear that he would be rescued en route from Newgate to Tyburn by his sympathisers, especially among the sailors, that the authorities took elaborate precautions to prevent any attempt to get him out of their clutches. After his death he was buried by private subscription in St Clement Dane's, Westminster. Some of his subscribers were prepared to place an inscription on his tomb deploring the fact that 'of 400 persons concerned in the attempt he alone suffered though neither principal nor contriver.'

The chosen church is a clue that there were political motives behind the proposed inscription. St Clement Dane's was a high Anglican place of worship with tory and even Jacobite associations. The Young Pretender was alleged to have attended a service there during his last surreptitious visit to England following his flight from Scotland after the failure of the 'Forty-five. Had the inscription to Penlez been put up there it would have documented the anti-government sentiments of his sympathisers in thinly veiled irony. Thus it was to have stated that

> . . . activated by principles in themselves truly laudable (when rightly directed and properly restrained) he was hurried by a zeal for his countrymen and an honest detestation of public stews (the most certain bane of youth and the disgrace of government) to engage in an undertaking which the most partial cannot defend, and yet the least candid must excuse . . . Learn hence to respect the laws – even the most oppressive. And think thyself happy under that government that doth truly and indifferently administer justice, to the punishment of wickedness and vice, and to the maintenance of God's true religion and virtue.

Although the inscription was never made, the message it was intended to convey found expression in several publications, the most notable of which was a pamphlet by John Cleland, the author of *The Memoirs of a Woman of Pleasure*. Cleland published *The Case of the Unfortunate Bosavern Penlez* on 7 November 1749. Perhaps surprisingly for the creator of Fanny Hill, he opened his defence with a swingeing attack upon brothels, As Roger Lonsdale observes, 'his description of the brothels and their inmates is far removed from the world in which Fanny Hill had eventually thrived and had taken and given cheerful sensual pleasure.'[5] Cleland pictures Penlez as 'a harmless unthinking lad', unluckily a little the worse for drink, who got caught up in the sacking of Wood's tavern. 'It is to be presumed', Cleland maintained, 'that few will push the want of all candour and humanity so far as to maintain that this unfortunate person went into this riot (since riot is the word that the approvers of his tragical fate have got by the end, and found so high against him) with a riotous intention to break the public peace or fly in the face of the government. Alas! poor young man! Such a thought probably never once entered his head.'

5. Roger Lonsdale, 'New attributions to John Cleland', *The Review of English Studies* (London, 1979), xxx, 273.

Cleland himself denied any intention 'to arraign, or reflect, on a public judgment or on the wisdom of the executive power'. Yet the whole tenor of his pamphlet was a condemnation of the government. At one point he even cited 'a political aphorism, than which not one is strictly truer, than that nothing begets a greater contempt or irreverence to the laws than the partial administration of them; and above all, when the partiality is seen to run with too staring a bias in favour of the rich, in contradistinction to the poor'. That the ministers regarded his *Case of the Unfortunate Bosavern Penlez* as a reflection on their wisdom is indicated by the fact that the day after its publication a warrant was issued for his arrest as the author of *Fanny Hill.*

The warrant was issued from the office of the senior secretary of state, the duke of Newcastle. The junior secretary, the duke of Bedford, also showed an interest in the case. For Bedford was then the patron of Henry Fielding, and Fielding had already become involved in the Penlez case, since he was the magistrate before whom Bosavern appeared after being arrested in possession of the linen. Not surprisingly, therefore, he took a very different view of the matter from that of his fellow author Cleland.

Fielding supported the government's decision to proceed with the utmost rigour in *A True State of the Case of Bosavern Penlez.* He defended the Riot Act as a necessary protection of life, liberty and property, as 'the most necessary of all our laws for the preservation and protection of the people'. 'No statute law had ever less the mark of oppression', he insisted, 'nor is any more consistent with our constitution or more agreeable to the true spirit of our law.' Indeed, 'the public peace and the safety of the individual are much secured by this law.'

The case thus provoked a political confrontation between the government and the opposition largely because it involved the enforcement of the Riot Act. This was regarded by the opposition as a particularly repressive measure. It was repeatedly linked with other legislation passed after the succession of the House of Hanover, such as the Septennial Act of 1716 and the Waltham Black Act of 1723, as evidence of a concerted attack upon English liberties by the Court whigs who triumphed on the death of Queen Anne. Thus an opposition newspaper denounced it as 'a ministerial law, obtained in the times of party violence, when the rage of the whigs carried them beyond the excesses they had imparted to the tories'.

The whigs who triumphed at the Hanoverian accession have been seen as representing the interests of the financial-military complex which had profited from the wars against Louis XIV and now sought to protect their acquisitions with such repressive laws. Thus, where the first whigs of Charles II's reign had been a radical party whose slogan 'Liberty and Property' epitomised their populist ideology, by the early eighteenth century they had largely shed their former radicalism and its emphasis on 'liberty', being far more concerned to protect property.

Certainly, some of the arguments which Fielding employed to justify the execution of Penlez lend substance to this view. He pointed out that 'The Star' was opposite a banker's, so that if the rioters had set fire to its contents,

> what must have been the consequence of exposing a banker's shop to the greediness of the rabble? or what might we have reasonably apprehended from a mob encouraged by such a booty and made desperate by such atrocious guilt? . . . the cry against bawdy houses might have been easily converted into an outcry of a very different nature, and goldsmiths might have been considered to be as great a nuisance to the public as whores.

Peter Linebaugh, who subscribes to the view that the whigs upheld the rights of the propertied few by repressing the propertyless many, rightly rebukes Fielding for special pleading in this passage. Yet his discussion of the case employs no less tendentious language in order to sustain his own interpretation that Penlez was the victim of a repressive ruling class. Thus, the sailors who sacked the brothels are depicted as 'honest tars' wreaking a just vengeance on such 'parasites' as 'bum bailiffs, sharpers, panders and bawds'. Penlez, whose actions are excused on the grounds that he must have been drunk at the time, is said to have been 'hanged for stealing the ruffles of a cock bawd'.[6]

There are, however, serious problems in seeing the fate of Penlez in terms of class conflict. The greatest difficulty is to reconcile this interpretation with the facts that his reprieve was sought by persons from all walks of life and that he was buried by private subscription in one of the more fashionable churches in Westminster.

The case of Bosavern Penlez in fact divided society vertically rather than horizontally. It polarised the supporters of the administration and its opponents. This became clear in the Westminster by-election held in November 1749, shortly after his execution.

---

6. P. Linebaugh, 'The Tyburn Riot against the Surgeons', in D. Hay, P. Linebaugh and E. P. Thompson (eds), *Albion's Fatal Tree: Crime and Society in Eighteenth-Century England* (London, 1975), pp. 89–101.

The election came about because Lord Trentham, one of the sitting members for the City, had been appointed to an office in the administration, which obliged him under the terms of an Act of 1706 to quit his seat and offer himself to the constituency for re-election. Ironically, in view of the role of sailors in the recent riots, he had been promoted to the Admiralty. Sir George Vandeput stood against him. The election was very hard and closely fought. The unprecedently high number of 9,500 inhabitants polled, and although many of the votes cast were subsequently discounted at a scrutiny, over 8,000 were allowed. On 7 December, when the polls closed, Trentham was declared the winner by a mere 170.

During the contest Penlez emerged as an electoral issue.[7] The opposition pointed out that Trentham's brother-in-law, the duke of Bedford, could, as secretary of state, have obtained a pardon for the unfortunate Bosavern. Trentham issued a statement after the polls closed claiming that 'as to the affair of Penlez, who suffered by due course of law, no application either publick or private was ever made in his favour.' Amongst the handbills distributed during the election several alluded to the case.[8] One satirically solicited votes for Peter Wood, who 'has lately made it manifest to the whole world his particular love of justice'. An acrostic on Trentham purported to have been published by Penlez' ghost. At one stage 'a person carried about in a coffin dressed in a shroud, attended by a number of lights, etc, designed to represent Penlez . . . frequently sat up and harangued the populace for his unhappy Fate etc.' Fielding, who as Bedford's client was drafted in to respond to opposition propaganda, put on a tone of righteous indignation to respond to this charade, complaining 'when we see what Penlez's ghost has done at this juncture can any juncture be without scarecrows of such base materials?'

An analysis of the poll books at this by-election has revealed the social distribution of the votes cast.[9] There was indeed a rough-and-ready division between the more affluent parishes in the west of the city, where the gentry and aristocracy had their town houses, which tended to support Trentham, and the eastern parishes bordering London, inhabited mostly by tradesmen, who inclined to support

7. See Nicholas Rogers, 'Aristocratic clientage, trade and independency: popular politics in pre-radical Westminster', *Past and Present* (London, 1973), 61, 98–100.

8. *A collection of the advertisements and hand-bills serious satyrical and humourous published on both sides during the election for the City and Liberty of Westminster begun November 22d 1749* (Dublin, 1749).

9. Nicholas Rogers, *Whigs and Cities: Popular Politics in the Age of Walpole and Pitt* (London, 1989), pp. 174–96.

Vandeput. But this division was not exclusive. While aristocrats connected with the Court who had property in Westminster, like the duke of Bedford, were prominent in Trentham's campaign, others associated with the opposition, including the Prince of Wales, made interest for his opponent. Tradesmen who were clients of courtiers polled for Trentham and were crucial to his success.

Although the division was more partisan than social, it did not simply divide whigs from tories. The support of the Prince of Wales for Vandeput's cause is enough to discount a straight party fight. In fact Vandeput was put up by the self-styled Independent Electors of Westminster who, while they included tories and even Jacobites in their ranks, also represented disaffected whigs. The by-election is better seen as a contest between Court and Country.

Insofar as Penlez was more than an electoral gimmick, his case can also be seen as symbolising Court and Country ideologies. As we have seen, supporters of the government maintained that its role was the simple one of deterring subjects from breaking the law, while its opponents argued that it should set an example in maintaining order. They also criticised the regime established under the early Hanoverians for failing to do so. So far from setting a standard of civilised behaviour, ministers and courtiers were themselves guilty of the most flagrant corruption and the most shameless hypocrisy. The result was that crime and vice were increasing alarmingly in direct response to the corruption of the Court.

The Penlez affair provided a perfect touchstone for these divergent attitudes. As far as the government was concerned the riots were an unacceptable affront to the forces of law and order, and had to be suppressed if the fabric of society were not to be endangered. Penlez therefore had to suffer the death penalty as a sacrifice to the concept that the state must deter rioters, whatever the motive for their behaviour. The opposition maintained that the existence of brothels was living proof that the corrupt Court was not setting a good example, and that when private subjects took the law into their own hands, and did what the government should have done by suppressing them, Penlez was made the scapegoat.

PART THREE

The Age of the French Revolution:
1789–1820

CHAPTER EIGHT

The Breakdown of the Constitutional Consensus

The general agreement that the British constitution was the most perfect that human ingenuity could devise had always been subject to the qualification that, while theoretically this was so, in practice it did not operate ideally. Quite soon after the Revolution settlement there were complaints that the independence of the two houses of parliament, essential for the realisation of the ideal, was being jeopardised by the encroachments of Crown influence. Thus as early as 1696 *The Danger of Mercenary Parliaments* asserted that a majority of MPs had been reduced to Court cyphers.[1] There were complaints when clauses in the Act of Settlement of 1701, particularly one eliminating placemen from parliament, were repealed in Anne's reign. And the outcry was loud against the passing of the Septennial Act in 1716 as an evasion of the electorate.

Critics of these developments argued that they should be reversed in order to restore the pristine perfection of the constitution. They advocated the elimination of placemen and a greater frequency of elections. There were even occasional advocates of abolishing rotten boroughs in order to reduce the susceptibility of electors to corruption.[2] These were, however, isolated cases before the 1760s, when they were orchestrated into a sustained campaign by the Wilkites.[3] Even they spoke in terms of restoring rather than reforming

---

1. G. Holmes and W. A. Speck (eds), *The Divided Society: Party Conflict in England 1694–1716* (London, 1967), pp. 146–7. The pamphlet was reprinted in 1722, presumably for the general election in that year. A prefatory note claimed 'that 'twas wrote in King William's time by Lord Shaftesbury's direction, and printed and dispers'd privately at his expence'. *The Danger of Mercenary Parliaments* (London, 1722), p. xi.

2. Linda Colley, 'Eighteenth-century Radicalism before Wilkes', *Transactions of the Royal Historical Society* 5th series (London, 1981), xxxi, 1–19.

3. Brewer, *Part Ideology and Popular Politics at the Accession of George III* (London, 1976), pp. 163–200.

the constitution. It is true that they employed radical language in their pursuit of this goal. They drew attention to the fact that the constitution had been brought into being by the resistance to the Stuarts in the seventeenth century, culminating in the Glorious Revolution. If the Hanoverians and their mercenary parliaments refused to restore the liberties of Englishmen established in 1689, then they had the right to resist them in turn.[4]

By insisting that the Commons should be the representative of the people, and not of the Crown, the Wilkites were reviving claims for popular sovereignty which had been overwhelmed under Walpole by the notion that the king in parliament was sovereign.[5] The contrary notion of the sovereignty of the people had never completely disappeared during the middle of the century, though it tended to be marginalised as republican. In the 1760s it revived, especially when the king in parliament seemed to be abusing their sovereignty by expelling Wilkes from the Commons and declaring his opponent in the Middlesex by-election rightly returned, even though he had obtained a minority of votes cast by the forty shilling freeholders. The spectacle of a Commons' majority consisting of MPs from small and allegedly corrupt constituencies flying in the face of the majority of voters in a populous county raised afresh the dispute over the locus of sovereignty. 'Junius' reminded George III that his government was a trust from the people 'and while he plumes himself upon the security of his title to the crown, should remember that, as it was acquired by one revolution, it may be lost by another'.[6] Even Burke, reflecting on the causes of the discontents of the 1760s, could 'see no other way for the preservation of a decent attention to public interest in the representatives, but *the interposition of the body of the people itself*, whenever it shall appear, by some flagrant and notorious act, by some capital innovation, that these representatives are going to overleap the fences of the law, and to introduce an arbitrary power'.[7]

What also brought parliamentary sovereignty to the top of the agenda in that decade was the conflict with the American colonies over the right to tax. Parliament claimed that it was sovereign over the colonies and could impose taxation on the colonists without

4. Kathleen Wilson, *The Sense of the People* (London, 1995), p. 208.

5. W. A. Speck, 'The Glorious Revolution and the Hanoverian Succession, 1660–1734', in *House of Commons: seven hundred years of British tradition*, R. Smith and J. S. More (eds), (London, 1996), pp. 100–8.

6. *The Letters of Junius*, ed. John Cannon (London, 1978), p. 173.

7. *Edmund Burke on Government, Politics and Society*, ed. B. W. Hill (London, 1975), p. 190.

so much as a by-your-leave. Americans objected with the slogan 'no taxation without representation'. They dismissed the notion that they were virtually represented at Westminster and, in doing so, drew attention to the vast numbers of Englishmen who were taxed without being represented there either. This led Wilkites to raise the claim that taxpayers in England should also be enfranchised. Although in theory they were still advocating the restoration of the constitution of 1689, this measure would have reformed it. The Society for Constitutional Information and the Association Movement would have gone yet further. Supporters advocated the abolition of rotten boroughs and the redistribution of their seats to counties. Some even urged universal manhood suffrage. Even the parliamentary opposition under the marquis of Rockingham, though wary of Wilkes and other radicals, began to espouse measures to implement their desire to reduce the influence of the Crown. When they came into office in 1782 they passed some legislation implementing so-called economic reform, for instance abolishing sinecures which the Hanoverians had used to reward members of both houses of parliament. It was this development which led Keir to date the end of the classical age of the constitution precisely in the year that the second Rockingham administration was formed.

The following year, 1783, saw the publication of the last volume of Catherine Macaulay's *History of England*. Twenty years earlier the first volume had announced a whiggish thesis in the introduction. 'Patriots who have sacrificed their tender affections, their properties, their lives, to the interest of society, deserve a tribute of praise unmixed with any alloy', she declared. 'Men that with the hazard and even the loss of their lives, attacked the formidable pretensions of the Stewart family, and set up the banners of liberty against tyranny which had been established for a series of more than one hundred and fifty years.'[8] By the time she reached her conclusion in the Glorious Revolution, however, it was far from being a tribute to the whigs. On the contrary, she accused them of having been induced 'to give way to the settlement of the crown, without adding any new trophies to the altar of Liberty, or even of renovating those sound principles in the Constitution which, in the length of time, had fallen a sacrifice to the lusts and the opportunities of power'.[9] Thus they should have enlarged the franchise, restored

8. Catherine Macaulay, *The History of England from the accession of James I to that of the Brunswick Line* (8 volumes, London, 1763–1783), i, viii–ix. Despite the stated aim of covering the years 1603 to 1714, the History in the event was concluded in 1689.

9. Ibid, viii, pp. 329–30.

annual parliaments and eliminated placemen from the Commons. Such measures 'were so necessary to the rendering the British constitution . . . the best of all possible constitutions, that it opens a wider field for more corrupt abuses than ever were produced by all the monarchical, oligarchical and aristocratical tyrannies in the world'. This was 'because under the specious appearance of democratical privilege, the people are really and truly enslaved to a small part of the community' – the venal voters in tiny parliamentary boroughs. Disfranchising these and adding their seats to the counties, along with an extension of the franchise, would probably remedy the shortcomings of the Revolution settlement, but if not, 'the introducing the mode of election by ballot, a mode used in every wise government in all cases of election, would infallibly remedy the ruinous evil.'[10]

Mrs Macaulay was only too aware that there was still widespread support for the traditional constitution. As she admitted, the Glorious Revolution 'has formed such an epocha in the annals of our country, so universally celebrated by the voice of all factions, that a writer must be possessed of the enthusiasm of a martyr whose regard to the strict letter of truth, leads to neglect or contradict the opinion of his countryman in this important point'.[11] When the younger Pitt could command a parliamentary majority following the general election of 1784, he acknowledged the support of reformers at the polls by introducing a bill to abolish a number of boroughs and to redistribute their seats. He did so, however, not as prime minister but as a private member, and the bill was soundly defeated. While the constitutional consensus suffered considerable strain from the radical forces unleashed by the Wilkite and colonial agitation, therefore, it survived through much of the 1780s.

Towards the end of the decade, though, there are signs that the constitutional relationship of the state to the established church was under pressure for reform. Dissenters, many of whom had sympathised with the cause of the rebels in the War of American Independence, began to press for full admission into citizenship. Three times proposals to repeal the Corporation and Test Acts were introduced into the House of Commons, only to be defeated, albeit by a narrow margin on the second occasion.

The consensus broke down altogether under the challenge posed by the French Revolution. On 4 November 1789 Richard Price delivered a *Discourse on the Love of our Country* to the members of the

10. Ibid, p. 330.   11. Ibid, p. 329.

Revolution Society, which was commemorating the centenary of the Glorious Revolution. He welcomed recent events in France, and expressed the hope that they would have a better outcome for the French than 1688 had held out for the British. For in Price's view the Glorious Revolution had not gone far enough. While it had replaced hereditary with contractual kingship, it had still denied civil rights to dissenters and had not expanded the electorate:

> though the Revolution was a great work, it was by no means a perfect work; and [that] all was not then gained which was necessary to put the kingdom in the secure and complete possession of the blessings of liberty. – In particular, you should recollect, that the toleration then obtained was imperfect . . . there still exist penal laws on account of religious opinions . . . the Test laws are still in force . . . But the most important instance of the imperfect state in which the Revolution left our Constitution, is the Inequality of our Representation. I think, indeed, this defect in our constitution so gross and palpable, as to make it excellent chiefly in form and theory.

Burke reacted to this *Discourse* with the most celebrated defence of the Revolution settlement and the hallowed constitution, *Reflections on the Revolution in France*. He parried the plea for the dissenters and the unenfranchised by defending the constitution in church and state. Thus, he hinted that Price threatened the established church and claimed 'that our representation has been found perfectly adequate to all the purposes for which a representation of the people can be desired or devised'. He was particularly scathing about the notion that the men of 1688 had endorsed contractual kingship. Quite the reverse, they had gone out of their way to ensure that there was the slightest breach possible with the hereditary principle. They had done their utmost to preserve the country's historic institutions, whereas the French revolutionaries, whom Price admired, were bent on destroying theirs.

It could be argued that both Price and Burke misrepresented the events of the Glorious Revolution, one exaggerating and the other minimising the breach it made in constitutional continuity. But at bottom the dispute was not about the historical facts of 1688–89. Rather, it concerned the legitimate basis of constitutional authority. To Price and other radical thinkers it rested in the people. They appealed to an original contract and to natural rights as the sources of popular sovereignty. Burke did not deny that power originated in the people. As he put it in *An Appeal from the New to the Old Whigs* it was 'a position not denied nor worth denying or assenting to'. What he condemned were the conclusions which the radicals derived from that position, which he characterised as

> that in the people the same sovereignty constantly and unalienably resides; that the people may lawfully depose kings, not only for misconduct, but without any misconduct at all; that they may set up any new fashion of government for themselves, or continue without any government, at their pleasure; that the people are essentially their own rule, and their will the measure of their own conduct.

In his view the Revolution of 1688 was not justified because James II had violated a contract with the people at large, but one with the Lords and the Commons. He had committed

> that is to say, a breach of the *original contract*, implied and expressed in the Constitution of this country, as a scheme of government fundamentally and inviolably fixed in King, Lords, and Commons – that the fundamental subversion of this ancient Constitution, by one of its parts, having been attempted, and in effect accomplished, justified the Revolution; – that it was justified *only* upon the *necessity* of the case, as the *only* means left for the recovery of that *ancient* Constitution formed by the *original contract* of the British state . . .

In essence, where radicals advocated popular sovereignty, Burke upheld parliamentary sovereignty.

Burke's eulogy of the constitution prompted Thomas Paine to launch a swingeing denunciation of it in *Rights of Man*, part one of which appeared in 1791, to be followed by a second part in 1792. Part two referred to the Bill of Rights as 'a bill of wrongs'. 'The defect', Paine insisted, 'lies in the system. The foundation and the superstructure of the government is bad.' He asserted the sovereignty of the people against that of parliament. To Paine the representation of the people was much better catered for in revolutionary France than it was in conservative England. Thus, the number of French representatives was proportional to the number of taxable inhabitants. In Britain the tiny county of Rutland had two knights of the shire, as many as Yorkshire, while Old Sarum, with hardly any inhabitants, returned two MPs and Manchester, with over 60,000, sent none. 'Is there any principle in these things?' demanded Paine. His answer, of course, was 'No'. The electoral system was not based on any rational principle, but had developed haphazardly over centuries. This was precisely what commended it to Burke.

Paine also initiated an attack upon the hereditary basis of monarchy and aristocracy which was picked up and elaborated by William

Godwin in his *Enquiry Concerning Political Justice* published in 1793. To Godwin monarchy and aristocracy were inherently not only absurd but pernicious and evil. In the fifth book, 'of legislative and executive power', he argued against both and in favour of democracy. Thus he maintained that 'every king is by unavoidable necessity the enemy of the human race.'[12] This was because the artificiality of the office led monarchs to be surrounded by sycophants and flatterers who kept them from the truth. The result was, he insisted, that 'Royalty inevitably allies itself to vice', and he referred to 'that system of universal corruption without which monarchy could not exist'.[13] Godwin was no Leveller, but a meritocrat, who felt that monarchy, so far from rewarding genuine merit, promoted servile defenders of the hereditary principle. This was why he was even more scathing about the institution of aristocracy. 'Aristocracy, like monarchy, is founded in falsehood,' he asserted. 'Its empire, however, is founded in principles more gloomy and unsocial than those of monarchy.'[14] 'It is not satire', he protested, 'but a simple statement of fact, when we observe that it is not easy to find a set of men in society sunk more below the ordinary standard of man in his constituent characteristics than the body of the English, or any other, peerage.'[15] 'The features of aristocratical institution are principally two: privilege and an aggravated monopoly of wealth,' he went on to argue. 'They are both of them in direct opposition to all sound morality and all generous independence of character.'[16]

---

12. W. Godwin, *Enquiry concerning Political Justice and its Influence on Modern Morals and Happiness*, ed. I. Kramnick (London, 1976), p. 422. 'It is now twelve years since he became satisfied that monarchy was a species of government essentially corrupt,' Godwin wrote in the Preface. 'He owed this conviction to the political writings of Swift . . .' (Ibid, p. 69). It is not clear which of Swift's works led him to this conclusion. The only one he cites is *Gulliver's Travels*, though it contains the rather sympathetic figure of the king of Brobdingnag, who does not reinforce Godwin's conclusion. However, when advocating the efficacy of pure reason in the debates of a national assembly of enlightened rational men he claims that,

> such is the idea of the author of *Gulliver's Travels* (Part IV), a man who appears to have had a more profound insight into the true principles of political justice than any preceding or contemporary author. It was unfortunate that a work of such inestimable wisdom failed at the period of its publication from the mere playfulness of the form, in communicating adequate instruction to mankind. Posterity only will be able to estimate it as it deserves.
>
> (Ibid, p. 553)

To read the debates in the Houyhnhnm assembly as a prescription for the resolution of human disputes is a measure of how far Godwin's utopian rationality differed from Swift's gloomy cynicism.
13. Ibid, pp. 424, 437.   14. Ibid, p. 479.   15. Ibid, p. 468.
16. Ibid, pp. 471–2.

Godwin's theories prompted several replies, including one from the bishop of Llandaff, previously regarded as a radical sympathiser.

> The liberty of the press is a main support of the liberty of the nation; it is a blessing which it is our duty to transmit to posterity; but a bad use is sometimes made of it, and its use is never more pernicious than when it is employed to infuse into the minds of the lowest orders of the community disparaging ideas concerning the Constitution of their country ... There are probably in every government upon earth, circumstances which a man accustomed to the abstract investigation of truth, may clearly prove to be deviations from the rigid rule of strict political justice.[17]

Godwin's bulky two-volume tome, priced at three guineas, could scarcely have reached 'the lowest order of the community', unlike Paine's *Rights of Man* which, as a tract, sold for sixpence. This difference allegedly led prime minister Pitt to ignore Godwin while prosecuting Paine. Subversive literature was regarded as more dangerous when it could be read by the lower orders. Burke had played into the hands of popular radicals by insulting the masses as 'the swinish multitude'. It was to combat the effects of Paine and others who appealed to them that Hannah More wrote her *Village Politics addressed to all the Mechanics, Journeymen and Day Labourers in Great Britain, by Will Chip, a Country Carpenter*. This cheap tract, which has been dubbed 'Burke for beginners', sold for '2d or 25 for 3s' in 1793. In it More imagines 'a dialogue between Jack Anvil the Blacksmith [John Bull] and Tom Hood the mason [Tom Paine]'. Tom, discovered reading *Rights of Man* by Jack, demands 'a new constitution ... liberty and equality and the rights of man'. When Jack denounces him as 'a leveller and a republican', he replies that he is 'a friend to the people' and merely wants reform. The ensuing dialogue reveals that, in More's view, radical demands for liberty, democracy and equality were not reforming but revolutionary. When Tom claims that he is as fit to govern as any man, Jack refutes him thus:

> No, Tom, no. You are indeed as good as another man, seeing you have hands to work, and a soul to be saved. But are all men fit for all kinds of things? Solomon says 'How can he be wise whose talk is of oxen?' Every man in his way. I am a better judge of a horse shoe than Sir John; but he has a deal better notion of state affairs than I ...

---

17. Appendix added on 25 January 1793 to a sermon on 'the wisdom and goodness of God, in having made both rich and poor', *Gentleman's Magazine* (London, 1793), lxiii, 635.

When Tom replies that all men are equal, Jack accuses him of quarrelling with Providence and not with government. 'For the woman is below her husband, and the children are below their mother, and the servant is below his master.' Jack defines a democrat as 'one who lives to be governed by a thousand tyrants, and yet can't bear a king'. Yet, paradoxically, he also tries to persuade Tom that Britain is a virtual democracy already with the startling claim that 'few are so poor but they may get a vote for a parliament man'! What Jack really fears is not democracy but republicanism, and he asserts his faith in constitutional monarchy:

> we have a king so loving that he would not hurt the people if he could. We have the best laws in the world, if they were more strictly enforced; and the best religion in the world, if it was but better followed. While old England is safe, I'll glory in her, and pray for her, and when she is in danger, I'll fight for her and die for her.

By getting the village politician to refer to Anglicanism as 'the best religion in the world', More expressed her concern that political radicalism was allied with religious dissent and even atheism. The fact that radicals like Price and Joseph Priestley were nonconformists, while many expressions of sympathy for the American and French Revolutions came from dissenters seemed to confirm her view that the constitution in church and state was under siege. In her cheap repository tracts she defended both church and state from the dangers which threatened them. How far radical dissent did pose a danger to the constitution is difficult to gauge. Certainly Priestley, who at one time hoped to achieve full citizenship for fellow dissenters by restoring what he held to be the principles of the Glorious Revolution, came reluctantly to the conclusion that it could only be achieved by another revolution in England. 'I sincerely wish (if the genuine spirit of the original constitution cannot be revived, which would no doubt be still the best for that country)', he wrote in 1801, 'for some more radical change than I have hitherto thought necessary, tho' I wish it may be effected peaceably, and without the interference of any foreign power.'[18]

However, as the French Revolution developed into an attack upon Christianity itself, so political extremism became identified with atheism. This impression was apparently confirmed by Tom Paine's publication of *The Age of Reason*, which was a scathing critique of

---

18. J. Priestley, *Letters to the Inhabitants of Northumberland [Pennsylvania]* (London, 1801), p. 24.

scriptural revelation and organised churches.[19] 'Of all the systems of religion that ever were invented', Paine concluded, 'there is none more derogatory to the Almighty, more unedifying to man, more repugnant to reason and more contradictory in itself, than this thing called Christianity.'[20] In response to such onslaughts there was a closing of ranks among Christians of all denominations. No longer was the constitution in church and state threatened by radicals and republicans, so was Christianity. As the bishop of Llandaff put it in 1795, 'When religion shall have lost its hold on men's consciences, government will lose its authority over their persons, and a state of barbarous anarchy will ensue.'[21] 'Those who are hostile to the British constitution', asserted the bishop of London, 'are almost always hostile to the Christian revelation.'[22]

The evangelical revival rallied the ranks of the faithful to the defence of the constitution. It is particularly associated with the Methodists, whose conservatism has been seen as a major counter-revolutionary force ever since Elie Halevy identified it as a significant reason why there was no English revolution to accompany the French.[23] 'It was of incalculable benefit to the nation', claimed the bishop of London, 'that such a power of Methodism existed just at the time when otherwise the revolutionary torrent would have swept away multitudes in its course.'[24] Evangelicalism was not confined to Methodists, however, but affected most denominations in England. There was even a group of 'Evangelical Friends' among the Quakers. The Church of England was also influenced by the evangelical movement. Evangelicalism among Anglicans took many forms, including agitation for the abolition of slavery and the slave trade, missionary activity, and the crusade for moral regeneration known as the

19. Thomas Paine's *Age of Reason: Being an Investigation of True and Fabulous Theology* came out in two parts, the first in 1794 the second in 1796. Paine's argument was more that of a deist who believed in natural religion than of an atheist, but his denunciation of cherished Christian beliefs in the name of 'reason' discredited his reputation even with dissenters, as Cobbett was to learn to his cost when he brought Paine's bones back to England from America.

20. Paine, *The Age of Reason*, ed. G. Edwards (London, 1993), p. 178.

21. Quoted in Irene Collins, *Jane Austen and the Clergy* (London, 1994), p. 191.

22. Beilby Porteous, *A Charge delivered to the Clergy of the Diocese of London in the years 1798 and 1799*, cited in V. Kiernan, 'Evangelicalism and the French Revolution', *Past and Present* (London, 1952), 1, 45.

23. There has been considerable discussion of Halevy's thesis. For a recent summary of the state of play, which accepts a modified version of it, see David Hempton, *Religion and Political Culture in Britain and Ireland from the Glorious Revolution to the Decline of Empire* (London, 1996), pp. 31–8.

24. Porteous, cited in Kiernan, 'Evangelicalism and the French Revolution', p. 47.

reformation of manners. These brought together all the evangelicals in a broad ecumenical movement.

Sympathy was expressed even for Catholics, especially when émigré priests arrived in England from France with horror stories of the most violent anti-clericalism. Among those who sympathised with Catholics were Lord Byron, who spoke in the House of Lords in favour of a bill granting them relief.[25] This ecumenical trend helped to lay the foundations for Catholic Emancipation.

William Cobbett in his radical phase espoused the cause of Catholics, though by then he was no friend of the evangelicals.[26] Earlier, in the 1790s, when he was still a conservative, he had been one of Hannah More's admirers. When he became a radical in the 1800s, however, he came to despise her as 'the old Bishop in petticoats'. Cobbett's move from Burkean conservatism to Painite radicalism was the direct opposite of many major writers, who went in the reverse direction in these years. Thus his first essay in journalism was a denunciation of Joseph Priestley, who arrived in Philadelphia, where Cobbett then resided, in 1794 to a rapturous welcome from radical Americans. Rebutting Priestley's claim that he was a refugee from oppression at home, where his house and laboratory in Birmingham had been destroyed by a 'Church and King' mob, Cobbett pointed out that he had successfully sued his opponents, two of whom had been executed, while the city of Birmingham had been obliged to pay him compensation!

Cobbett admired Burke and the younger Pitt when he was in the United States, but shortly after his return to England he was disillusioned by what he regarded as 'Pitt's system', which sustained its power by corruption. This was especially exemplified in the impeachment of Pitt's ally Lord Dundas for peculation in the public funds. Cobbett was so disgusted at this that he turned his formidable journalistic talents into a condemnation of the system which kept corrupt aristocrats and boroughmongers in power and denied the people their natural rights. He kept up this campaign in the pages of his *Weekly Political Register* which was published continuously from 1802 to his death in 1835. In it he denounced the aristocracy as 'a prodigious band of spungers, living upon the labour of the

25. Speech of 21 April 1812. One of Byron's charges against George III in *The Vision of Judgement* was that he was

> The foe to Catholic participation
> In all the licence of a Christian nation.

26. J. Stevenson, 'William Cobbett: Patriot or Britain?', *Transactions of the Royal Historical Society* (London, 1996), vi, 134–5.

industrious part of the nation'. In November 1816 he brought out
a twopenny edition aimed at 'the journeymen and labourers of
England, Wales, Scotland, Ireland'. This 'had an immense circulation, reaching an estimated 200,000 within two months'.[27] 'The writings of William Cobbett suddenly became of great authority', claimed
a contemporary observer of their impact.[28]

> They were read on nearly every cottage hearth in the manufacturing
> districts of South Lancashire, in those of Leicester, Derby and Not-
> tingham; also in many of the Scottish manufacturing towns . . . he
> directed his readers to the true cause of their sufferings – misgovern-
> ment; and to its proper corrective – parliamentary reform.

The appeal by conservatives and radicals to those whom Burke
had characterised as the 'swinish multitude' testifies to the emergence of a new participant in the ideological debates of the eighteenth century. There is an obvious hardening of class distinctions
in the 1790s, the decade in which E. P. Thompson located the
start of the 'making of the English working class'. It is particularly
noticeable in the prints of the decade. When plebeian characters
had appeared previously in prints they were generally depicted
sympathetically, as, for example, the robust beef-eating artisans
in Hogarth's 'Beer Street'. But after 1790 they are represented as
sinister, almost subhuman, creatures, threatening the very fabric of
society, as in Gillray's print of the London Corresponding Society.

If the decade witnessed the origins of the class warfare of the
nineteenth century it also saw an intensification of the war between
the sexes. To be sure there had been plenty of complaints by women
before about their subordination to men. Mary Astell, who has
been dubbed 'the first major English feminist', expressed them in
A Serious Proposal to the Ladies in 1694 and *Reflections upon Marriage*
in 1700. 'If all men are born free', she asked in *Reflections upon
Marriage*, 'how is it that all women are born slaves?'[29] Lady Mary
Chudleigh had protested that

> Wife and servant are the same,
> But only differ in the name

and advised women to 'shun that wretched state'.[30]

---

27. Ibid, p. 123.
28. Samuel Bamford, *Passages in the Life of a Radical*, quoted in ibid, p. 123.
29. Bridget Hill, 'The first feminism', in R. Samuel (ed.), *Patriotism* (3 vols, London, 1989), ii, 130–1.
30. 'To the ladies', *The New Oxford Book of Eighteenth-Century Verse*, ed. R. Lonsdale (London, 1984), p. 36.

But such objections did not add up to a sustained critique of the discrimination against their sex which can be described as feminist. Feminism really came into its own with the publication of Mary Wollstonecraft's *Vindication of the Rights of Women*. She accused men of seeking to keep women in a perpetual state of childhood, as inferior objects of affection rather than as equal companions. Yet 'fondness is a poor substitute for friendship.' Education was the key to forming truly independent individuals. Men's education was geared to that end, whereas women were taught how to please men. 'She was created to be the toy of man, his rattle, and it must jingle in his ears whenever, dismissing reason, he chooses to be amused.' Wollstonecraft advocated that women should be educated like men, for independence. This was not so that they could live independently. On the contrary, her whole thesis was that an educated woman would make a more companionate wife: 'the woman who strengthens her body and exercises her mind will, by managing her family and practising various virtues, become the friend and not the humble dependent of her husband.'

Wollstonecraft's feminist manifesto was bolstered by what she saw as the prevailing political trend: 'The divine right of husbands, like the divine right of kings, may, it is to be hoped, in this enlightened age, be contested without danger.' And yet the radicalism of the emergent working class, and perhaps even more of women, in the period 1780 to 1830, has been exaggerated. During the years of war with France loyalism was not only cultivated from above by the government and such agencies as John Reeves's Association for the Protection of Liberty and Property against Republicans and Levellers; it was also genuinely popular. As Coleridge observed '. . . in England, when the alarm was at its highest, there was not a city, no not a town or village, in which a man suspected of holding democratical principles could move abroad without receiving some unpleasant proof of the hatred in which his supposed opinions were held by the great majority of the people; and the only instances of popular excess and indignation were in favour of the Government and the Established Church'.[31] This was demonstrated in the Paine-burning ceremonies of the 1790s. Frank O'Gorman calculates that there were some 25,000 occasions when effigies of Thomas Paine were ceremoniously 'executed' during that decade. These were not spontaneous occasions, to be sure, but had to be carefully

---

31. *The Friend* no. 10, 1809, quoted in S. T. Coleridge, *Biographia Literaria*, ed. G. Watson (Cambridge, 1975), pp. 119–20.

stage-managed. Nevertheless, their organisers were not the aristocracy and gentry but the tradesmen and manufacturers, while they
attracted considerable support from the lower orders. Although
their attraction could be attributed to free drink and food, the fact
that none were broken up by radical counter-demonstrations speaks
volumes for the exiguous support such attempts would have mus-
tered. Indeed, there are few signs of radicalism during the period
of the wars with revolutionary and Napoleonic France. Political
agitation has been detected behind the naval mutinies in 1797, the
food riots of 1800–1 and the Despard conspiracy of 1802. Yet the
mutinies and the riots were inspired by genuine economic griev-
ances which radicals tried to exploit, while the Despard conspiracy
was primarily an Irish plot. In Britain there is so little evidence of
subversive activity that historians of radicalism have been reduced
to arguing that it went underground during these years. By its very
nature such conspiring is almost impossible to prove or disprove,
but it seems equally likely that the upsurge of loyalism created a
situation in Britain, unlike in Ireland, where revolutionaries could
not count on the sympathy of a significant section of the population,
an essential ingredient for sustaining an underground movement.

Irish support for insurrection in 1798 led to the incorporation of
Ireland into the United Kingdom in 1800. The Act of Union considerably altered the British constitution by abolishing the Dublin
parliament and bringing to Westminster one hundred Irish MPs.
Prime minister Pitt thought that the logical corollary was to remove
the legal penalties on Catholics, and when the king refused to grant
Catholic Emancipation he resigned. For the rest of the reign of
George III the question could not be reopened. After his death in
1820, however, it was to be reopened by the Irish themselves, who
defied the ban on their returning Catholics to parliament by electing
Daniel O'Connell as member for county Clare. That event was to
break the log jam on reform which had built up during the years
of reaction to the radicalism associated with the French Revolution.

CHAPTER NINE

Novels and the War of Ideas

Novelists of the era before 1789, as we have seen, while they could be critical of aristocrats, rarely attacked aristocracy or the social order itself. On the contrary, after enduring many changes of fortune their heroes and heroines generally acquire or succeed to landed estates themselves. The objective of joining the gentry remained central even to bourgeois aspirations. Addison and Steele set the pattern for this in *The Spectator,* that significant prototype of the novel. When Sir Andrew Freeport resigned from the Spectator Club he informed its members that he was leaving business to set up as a landed proprietor: 'as the greatest part of my estate has been hitherto of an unsteady and volatile nature, either tost upon seas or fluctuating in funds; it is now fixed and settled in substantial acres and tenements.'

In the 1790s, however, novels appeared which did call in question the power wielded by owners of landed estates. Both Gothic and Jacobin novels challenged the authority of the aristocracy and the church. Two outstanding Gothic novelists, Ann Radcliffe and Matthew Lewis attacked them indirectly, while four 'Jacobin' novelists, Robert Bage, William Godwin, Thomas Holcroft and Elizabeth Inchbald tackled them head on.

The basic plot of Radcliffe's *The Mysteries of Udolpho* (1794) concerns the love of the French heroine, Emily St Aubert, for the hero Valancourt, and how their marriage is delayed for over a year by the death of her father making her dependent upon her aunt and uncle, who force her to accompany them to the castle of Udolpho. There her aunt dies and Emily is incarcerated by her uncle, the villainous Montoni. Eventually, she escapes from the Italian castle and makes her way back to France, where after more vicissitudes, largely due to Valancourt having to redeem himself in her eyes for his loose living in Paris during her absence, the hero and heroine are wed and presumably live happily ever after.

The theme is encapsulated in the key word in the title, 'mysteries'. These begin before the action moves to Udolpho, for strange happenings occur in Emily's family home of La Vallée in Gascony. In the very first chapter she comes across an anonymous sonnet written in pencil on the wainscot of a little fishing house belonging to her father. This incidentally is the first of several poems which Mrs Radcliffe introduces into the novel and which entitle her to be considered a poet as well as a novelist. Emily also hears her lute being played by an unseen visitor. Again, mysterious music features throughout the novel as an ingredient enhancing the foreboding atmosphere. Thus, after the death of her mother Emily and her father undertake a journey to Languedoc and stay near the chateau of the Marquis of Villeroy, where once more they hear haunting songs.

When Emily gets to Udolpho and finds herself a virtual prisoner there, disembodied singing adds to the air of suspense which characterises this central episode in the novel. The castle itself, a gloomy medieval pile, is a rabbit warren of dark corridors and chill rooms. These inspire terror and suspense which make the novel archetypally Gothic. To quote a typical passage:

> Her melancholy was assisted by the hollow sighings of the wind along the corridor and round the castle. The cheerful blaze of the wood had long been extinguished, and she sat with her eyes fixed on the dying embers, till a loud gust, that swept through the corridor, and shook the doors and casements, alarmed her, for its violence had moved a chair she had placed as a fastening, and the door, leading to the private stair-case, stood half open. Her curiosity and her fears were again awakened. She took the lamp to the top of the steps and stood hesitating whether to go down; but again the profound stillness and the gloom of the place awed her, and determining to enquire further, when day-light might assist the search, she closed the door, and placed against it a stronger guard.
>
> She now retired to her bed, leaving the lamp burning on the table; but its gloomy light, instead of dispelling her fear, assisted it; for by its uncertain rays, she almost fancied she saw shapes flit past her curtains and glide into the remote obscurity of her chamber. – The castle clock struck one before she closed her eyes to sleep.

It has been said that terror rather than horror is the stock in trade of the Gothic novelist. Mrs Radcliffe herself claimed that 'terror and horror are so far opposite, that the first expands the soul, and awakens the faculties to a high degree of life; the other contracts, freezes and nearly annihilates them.' While most of the mysteries of Udolpho inspire terror, there is one that can only be described as horrific. This is the episode in which Emily draws back a black veil covering 'an object that had overwhelmed her with horror; for on lifting it there appeared, instead of the picture she had expected . . . a human figure of ghastly paleness, stretched at its length, and dressed in the habilments of the grave. What added to the horror of the spectacle was that the face appeared partly decayed and disfigured by worms, which were visible on the features and hands.' Although Mrs Radcliffe is at pains to offer for this, as for all her mysteries, a rational explanation, it is not one that carries complete conviction. She reveals that the figure was in fact made of wax, and had been made by a member of the house of Udolpho as a penance for an affront to the church. While this explains the incident, it scarcely explains it away.

'Formal realism' might be a characteristic of other eighteenth-century novels, but clearly it is not a feature of the Gothic novel. The fantastic episodes, set in remote times and places, have even been seen as an escape from reality. Elements of escapism can indeed be detected in *Udolpho*. It is set in France and Italy in the late sixteenth century. Yet it is not a historic novel, for Mrs Radcliffe took very little trouble about the contemporary context. There are bandits and mercenary soldiers but these are only sketched in the vaguest way. Apart from such details, the action could be imagined as taking place in a remote Catholic country in the eighteenth century. Thus on one occasion we see Emily enjoying a cup of coffee! It could even have been the case that the novel was catering to a clientele debarred by the outbreak of war with revolutionary France from experiencing the continent at first hand.

Yet on another level *Udolpho* is not escapist at all, but deals with psychological and sociological realities. Psychologically, the castle of Udolpho has more in common with Kafka's *Castle* than with Walpole's castle of Otranto. Sociologically, it is a metaphor for English society in the 1790s.

The orphaned Emily finds herself in the clutches of her aunt and even more of her aunt's husband, the sinister marquis of Montoni. The couple exercise arbitrary power over her. Before leaving France they force her to distance herself from Valancourt and try to get her to marry Count Morano. When they get to Italy, Montoni becomes the dominant figure, confining both Emily and her aunt in his castle. After her aunt's death he puts enormous pressure on Emily to relinquish her claim to his wife's property in France, threatening to imprison her permanently if she declines to sign a deed alienating them to him. Emily even feels that he would not scruple to kill her in order to get his way. In this respect he appears as a tyrannical father figure, akin to Clarissa Harlowe's, though claiming even more absolute authority. Emily insists on her liberty to marry the man of her choice and to own her own property. Unlike Clarissa's her rebellion ends successfully.

In David Punter's view, 'condemnation of Montoni is limited by the fact that, for better or worse, he has been given a role in the bourgeois family.' 'We thus see in Radcliffe', he concludes, 'the familiar spectacle of a bourgeois stratum assimilating to itself those elements which it requires from the class which it has superseded, while simultaneously refusing to acknowledge the economic base which has in fact brought it to power.'[1] These Marxist assumptions raise the question of the novel's social significance. The principals are all members of the landed elite. Emily's father, we are told, 'was a descendant from the younger branch of an illustrious family'. Montoni was a marquis. On her return to France, Emily is sheltered in the chateau of the Count De Villefort. Villefort is the enlightened contrast to Montoni. Whereas the marquis tried to force Emily to marry Morano, Villefort, though he wishes his daughter Blanche to marry St Foix, makes it clear that she has a choice. He also warns Emily that her preferred partner, Valancourt, has been corrupted by the temptations to which he was exposed in Paris, where he became an inveterate gambler. The city is thus seen as a source of corruption, which scarcely squares with the advocacy of bourgeois values. So far from documenting the emergence of a dominant bourgeoisie, Radcliffe seems to be advocating an enlightened aristocracy.

Lewis' *Ambrosio, or the Monk* (1795) also upholds the values of the Enlightenment, this time not so much against a decadent aristocracy as a hopelessly corrupt church. The central plot concerns Ambrosio, whom Lewis makes the abbot of a Capuchin monastery in Madrid. He thus shows his ignorance of Catholicism, for the Capuchins were friars, not monks, and their houses were headed by guardians! Ambrosio is celebrated as the most pious and most effective preacher in Spain. But his downfall occurs when he is seduced by one of the 'monks', who turns out to be a woman in disguise, Matilda. His lust overcomes his guilt until he is glutted

1. David Punter, 'Social relations of Gothic fiction', in David Aers, Jonathan Cook and David Punter (eds), *Romanticism and Ideology: Studies in English Writing 1765–1830* (London, 1981), pp. 112–13.

with the enjoyment of her charms. Lewis in describing their sexual encounters shows himself the equal of Cleland as a pornographer, despite being only nineteen when he wrote the novel. Ambrosio then seeks fresh flesh, a quest in which he is aided by the diabolical Matilda. They plot for him to seduce Antonia, a visitor to Madrid with her mother. The implementation of the seduction involves necromancy on Matilda's part and leads to the murder of the mother by Ambrosio, who rapes and then murders Antonia. Ambrosio and Matilda are apprehended and brought before the Inquisition, which tries them for sorcery as well as murder. Both are found guilty. Matilda is ordered to be burned to death in an auto-da-fé, but escapes with the aid of the devil, with whom she claims she has made a compact for her soul. To escape a like fate Ambrosio makes a compact with the devil too. Lucifer gets him from the prison just as the door is being opened. But Ambrosio's escape from death is short-lived. The fiend throws him from a mountain ridge to die after lingering with broken bones for a week. Before flinging him down the devil informs him that the jailors were coming with a pardon, that Matilda was a spirit sent from hell to tempt him, and that Antonia's mother was also his own, so that matricide and incest were added to his enormous crimes.

Another story in this tortuous tale involves the priory of St Clare, a nunnery conveniently if not convincingly adjacent to Ambrosio's monastery. Agnes, one of the nuns, has previously been courted by Raymond de Cisternas in Germany. But their relationship was abruptly ended in one of the more bizarre passages in a literally fantastic novel. Raymond tried to rescue her from a German castle where she was incarcerated. To effect her release they arranged to elope on a night when an apparition, 'the Bleeding Nun', was to haunt the castle. Agnes was to disguise herself as the ghost and thus escape, helped by Raymond. Instead, he was deceived by the real ghost, whom he spirited away from the castle, leaving Agnes behind. She felt betrayed and returned to Spain to take the veil. Raymond goes there too to redeem his reputation with her and to release her from her vows. He contrives to enter the nunnery in disguise, and meet Agnes, where his efforts to convince her of his sincerity are so successful that as a result of one of their secret assignations she becomes pregnant. Their relationship is discovered by Ambrosio, who discloses it to the prioress. She determines to uphold the full rigour of the order, which prescribes solitary confinement on a diet of bread and water until the guilty nun dies. While serving this draconian sentence Agnes gives birth, but the baby dies of malnutrition.

Meanwhile, Agnes' brother, Lorenzo, obtains from Rome a dispensation for his sister, releasing her from her vows and therefore from the order. The fact that Lewis describes the document as a Bull again reveals his uncertain knowledge of Roman Catholicism. When Lorenzo presents it to the prioress, however, she avers that Agnes is already dead. Disbelieving this lie, Raymond and Lorenzo, aided by sympathetic nuns, contrive to rescue Agnes. They publically reveal the prioress' treatment of her during a procession promoted by the convent – another rather unlikely event in an enclosed order. Their revelations provoke the anger of the crowd, which proceeds to assassinate the prioress and to sack the nunnery.

After these sensational scenes the love interest of the novel is feeble. Agnes and Raymond are eventually married. At the same time Agnes' brother Lorenzo, who had hoped to marry Antonia, finds solace for his grief at her murder remarkably quickly by marrying Virginia, a novice nun whom Agnes persuades to leave the convent. Lewis concludes their story with the trite observation that 'the remaining years of Raymond and Agnes, of Lorenzo and Virginia, were happy as can be those allotted to mortals, born to be the prey of grief, and sport of disappointment.'

It has been truly said of *The Monk* that 'it is the wildest and most lurid of the Gothic romances'. Where Mrs Radcliffe contrives to give rational explanations for apparently supernatural phenomena, Lewis provides us with real ghosts and devils. Satan himself is a character in the novel. Also, where the sexual implication of a relationship between a dominant male character and a dependent female is barely hinted at in *The Mysteries of Udolpho*, it is made quite explicit in *The Monk*. While Radcliffe cannot fully escape the criticism that she inspires horror as well as terror, Lewis does not even try to avoid the charge. On the contrary, he positively revels in the gruesome and the grotesque. Thus, when Agnes' baby dies she refuses to bury it but hugs it to her bosom until 'it soon [becomes] a mass of putridity and to every eye [is] a loathsome and disgusting object.' Significantly, Lewis got into trouble over his tale not on account of its erotic or horrific passages but because of its alleged blasphemy. Antonia's mother presents her with an expurgated version of the Bible so that her thoughts will not be tainted by exposure to 'improper passages'. As Lewis put it, 'many of the narratives can only tend to excite ideas the worst calculated for a female breast; every thing is called plainly and roundly by its name; and the annals of a brothel would scarcely furnish a greater choice of indecent expression.' Lewis was taken to court, and undertook to remove offending passages, including the sexually explicit scenes, from future editions of the book.

Critics were shocked by the fact that Lewis' apparent condemnation of Catholicism spilled over into a critique of Christianity itself, Protestant as well as Catholic. Whether or not he intended this, it certainly is possible to see the novel as an attack on religion as well as superstition. The church is depicted as a repressive institution, stifling individuality. Ambrosio is as much a victim as an exploiter of its system of metaphysical sanctions for morality. He and the prioress are represented as hypocrites whose motives for their conduct are not genuine piety but pride and ambition. The church exploits the credulity and ignorance of its devotees. How credulous and ignorant the nuns of St Clare were is revealed in a passage wherein Raymond's servant, Theodore, gains entrance to the convent and 'amused himself with retailing to the credulous nuns for truths all the strange stories which his imagination could invent'. Thus 'he said that he was born in Terra Incognita, was educated at an Hottentot University and had passed two years among the Americans of Silesia.' Such remarks directed at the Catholic church by Protestants would have been unexceptionable earlier in the eighteenth century. But they hit a raw nerve in the 1790s. This was partly because respect for Roman Catholics, at least among the educated classes, had been growing in England since mid-century. They deplored the excesses of the Gordon riots of 1780 which had been inspired by a measure of Catholic relief passed by parliament. More immediately the attacks of the French revolutionaries upon ecclesiastical property and personnel had inspired sympathy for the church in France, even though it was Catholic. In this respect, Lewis' graphic description of the sacking of the convent and the assassination of the prioress perhaps came too close to home. The violent anti-clericalism of the French Revolution provoked a backlash in England in which Christians of all denominations, Anglican as well as nonconformist, felt that not only Catholicism but Christianity itself was in danger.

Where the Gothic novels criticised aristocrats and clergymen in remote times and places, 'Jacobin' novelists attacked the aristocracy and the church in contemporary England.[2] Gary Kelly observes that a central theme in all Bage's novels is an attack on aristocrats. His

---

2. The best account of the genre is by Gary Kelly, *The English Jacobin Novel 1780–1803* (Oxford, 1976). Kelly points out that 'the term "Jacobin" itself is misleading, since most of those in Britain who bore that label were in fact Girondins in their principles and beliefs'. (p. 7)

peers 'are rapacious, boorish, lustful, arrogant, and impecunious'.[3] Lord Auschamp in *Man as he is* fits this description. But he can at least restrain his authoritarianism. As he advises Sir George's mother, 'the young man is irritable, and the too free laws of this country will support him in disobedience. We must be cautious. I must confess too peremptory a tone lost us America.' By contrast, Lord Grondale in *Hermsprong* is a complete monster. In one scene he knocks down his daughter because she has refused to marry the man of his choice, and threatens her with forced solemnisation and consummation of the marriage. Furthermore, *Hermsprong*, unlike *Man as he is*, condemns not just the actions of one aristocrat but aristocracy itself. The earlier novel ends with the prospect of its hero and heroine one day being ennobled as an earl and a countess, 'a most agreeable metamorphosis, and likely to be relished in England, when titles shall be nick names only in the rest of Europe.' Aristocracy itself is condemned in the second novel in the views expressed by the hero, Charles Hermsprong. He is an American who recognises only merit and not rank in others, and has 'no respect' for a lord. When taxed with the levelling nature of the French he replies 'there may be many such shocking creatures among the men ... but the ladies ... are still addicted to rank and title.' Bage clearly shares these sentiments. Speaking through the fictitious 'author' he says of Lord Grondale's elevation to a peerage for selling his interest in Cornish boroughs to the Court that such ennoblements

> raise man far above man, and nearer to the divinity, since kings have once more become divine; and enable him to look down on the lesser inhabitants of this best of worlds, with a due consciousness of his great superiority.

One of the ways in which aristocrats use and abuse their position in Jacobin novels is to exploit the advantages which the law gives them. Grondale is no exception, and has recourse to the law to get rid of the troublesome Hermsprong. An obstacle in his path, however, is the latter's wealth. As Bage observes:

> To press down to the earth and under it a poor man is easy; it is the work of every day; but to make a man with money in his purse guilty of crimes he never committed requires a superior fund of knowledge of the more tortuous parts of the law.

3. Ibid, p. 30.

Hermsprong is charged with enticing a man to go to America, and with reading and distributing Paine's *Rights of Man* – he had lent his copy to a friend! He is also accused of having said that the 'French constitution though not perfect had good things in it and that ours was not so good', which his accusers think will carry because 'the bench of justices will not bear such things now.'. The 'leading charge' is that he took part in a riot of miners brought about by the rise in the cost of provisions. The other charges are easily dismissed as contemptible by Hermsprong himself, but the most serious is countered by a witness who testifies that he was instrumental in persuading the rioters to stop rioting. Some of the edge is taken off Bage's social satire, however, when it is revealed that Hermsprong is an assumed name – 'a very ugly name ... it sounds monstrous Germanish' – and that he is in reality Grondale's nephew, who has come to England to claim his father's rightful inheritance which the peer has usurped.

Godwin made no such concessions. A central feature of his *Things as they are* is the change in the behaviour of a principal character, Falkland. In the first volume he appears as a patriarchal figure befriending the victims of a patrician, Tyrell, who abuses his authority as much as any aristocrat in a Gothic or 'Jacobin' novel. In the second volume, however, Falkland becomes a tyrant himself, harassing Caleb Williams without mercy. Like Grondale, he abuses his privileged access to the law to destroy a victim. The explanation of this apparent character change is that Falkland, having been knocked down by Tyrell in front of an assembly of gentlemen, gets his revenge by murdering his assailant. Although at the time he manages to conceal his crime, and even has others condemned for it, Falkland's guilt is ascertained by Caleb. What makes Falkland kill Tyrell is the public affront to his honour at the assembly. He has been disgraced. As he himself expresses it, 'this it is to be a gentleman! A man of honour! I was the fool of fame. My virtue, my honesty, my everlasting peace of mind were cheap sacrifices to be made at the shrine of this divinity.' Falkland is thus corrupted by the genteel code of honour, which overcomes all other standards of morality. Once disgraced, he is ostracised from the company of gentlemen. Thus, the system itself is corrupt. Moreover, as Godwin observes, Falkland 'exhibited upon a contracted scale ... a copy of what monarchs are'.

Jacobin novels also attacked the church. In *Hermsprong* Bage depicted Dr Blick as an example of the reactionary Anglican clergyman who condemned radicals and dissenters alike. Thus, he gives a sermon on the anniversary of the Birmingham riots where 'a quantity of pious makers of buttons, inspired by our holy mother, had pulled down the dissenting meeting houses, together with the dwelling houses of the most distinguished of that unpopular sect.' The Reverend Dr Blick does not say this was exactly right; he only says that liberty had grown into licentiousness, and almost into rebellion.

> '[I]f ever the church can be in danger, it is so now' said the good Doctor. 'Now, when the atheistical lawgivers of a neighbouring country, have laid their sacrilegious hands upon the sacred property of the church; now, when the whole body of dissenters here have dared to imagine the same thing. These people, to manifest their gratitude for the indulgent, the too indulgent toleration shewn to them, have been filling the nation with inflammatory complaints against a constitution, the best the world ever saw, or will ever see; against a government, the wisest, mildest, freest from corruption, that the purest page of history has ever exhibited.'

While there are some worthy clergymen in Bage's novel, such as Mr Brown, there are none in Elizabeth Inchbald's *Nature and Art* (1796). The three representatives of the church, a bishop, a dean and a curate, are all shown as corrupt, hypocritical, worldly and utterly lacking in Christian charity. The neglect of their duties is directly responsible for the tragedy which overtakes Hannah, the daughter of a peasant family. The system, so far from punishing such ungodly churchmen, rewards them, for the dean becomes a bishop himself. The church itself, therefore, and not just individual undeserving clergymen, is depicted as an oppressive institution.

The clergy in Thomas Holcroft's *Hugh Trevor* (1794) are, if anything, even more repellent. The bishop is a particularly loathsome specimen, who uses the hero's writing skills to procure his own preferment, passing off Hugh's defence of the Thirty-Nine Articles as his own and thereby obtaining translation to another bishopric. This precipitates a breach between them, but before it Hugh is patronised by the bishop, who invites him to dinner. It is this experience which encapsulates Holcroft's view of the church. Hugh had often asked himself '[W]hy are butchers, tallow-chandlers, cookmaids and church dignitaries so inclined to be fat?' The question is answered in the case of churchmen at the bishop's dinner. Hugh could not finish the gargantuan first course, and flinched from the second, though he brought himself to start 'thinking that the engagement though hot would soon be over; but I little knew the doughty heroes, with whom I entered the lists. The chiefs of Homer, with their chines, and goblets, and canisters of bread, would have been unequal to the contest. I had time enough to contemplate the bishop; I thought I beheld him quaffing suffocation and stowing in apoplexy.' His grace was doomed to die of his excesses later in the novel. 'Neither did their eating end with the second course. The table was no sooner cleared of the cloth, and the racy wine with double rows of glasses again placed in array, than almonds, raisins, olives, oranges, Indian conserves and biscuits deviled, covered the board! To it again they fell . . .' The evening ends in drunken bawdy conversation. Despite the humour, the attack on greed and hypocrisy is deadly serious. As Hugh observes of the dinner, 'I must own that, in my mind, poor mother church at that moment made a pitiful appearance.'

Jane Austen's reaction to these criticisms of the major institutions in church and state was to defend them in *Northanger Abbey*. Although it was not published until 1818, it was originally written in the 1790s and belongs in many ways to that decade. It satirises the Gothic novels then in vogue, and especially Radcliffe's *Udolpho*. When Catherine Morland meets John Thorpe, he is revealed as a cad immediately in their discussion of Gothic novels, an obsession of Catherine's. She is currently reading Radcliffe's *Mysteries of Udolpho*, while he shows his ignorance of its author and admits that he has just read Lewis' *The Monk*, in his view the only 'tolerably decent' novel to have appeared since *Tom Jones*. Though Austen teases her heroine's suggestibility, she clearly approves of her reading Radcliffe and equally clearly disapproves of Thorpe's reading Lewis. *Udolpho* is acceptable in Austen's view presumably because it retains good taste despite its exploitation of terror, while *The Monk* is not because it goes over the top into horror and even pornography. Thorpe's sister is at first presented in a favourable light as possibly a suitable wife for Catherine's brother, John Morland. She shares Catherine's love of Gothic novels, and they debate what Emily would find behind the veil in the castle of Udolpho. Given Austen's aversion to *The Monk*, this is perhaps odd, since, as we have seen, the replica of a decomposing corpse is one of the few truly horrific passages in *Udolpho*. Perhaps it was more the pornographic elements in Lewis' novel than the horrific which made it unsuitable for Jane Austen's ladies.

General Tilney takes a great interest in Catherine and the prospect of her marrying his son, Henry, inviting her to spend some time at the family seat of Northanger Abbey. It is on this visit that Austen's teasing of her heroine is taken to its ultimate when

Catherine's lurid imagination, fired by the monastic associations of the house, leads her to suspect that General Tilney had either murdered his wife or kept her a prisoner in some remote room. The visit is abruptly ended when the general returns from a trip to London and orders Catherine to leave unceremoniously. Catherine fears that he might have heard of her suspicions, but it turns out that he has instead been with John Thorpe who has lowered the general's opinion of his guest.

Jane Austen not only makes fun of her heroine's obsession with Gothic novels but also challenges the notion that it was politically subversive. In conversation with Henry Tilney and his sister Eleanor, Catherine informs them that she had heard 'that something very shocking indeed will soon come out in London'. She means a new sensational Gothic novel, but Eleanor takes it to be a continuation of the last subject of the conversation, which was politics, and expresses the hope that 'if such a design is known beforehand, proper measures will undoubtedly be taken by government to prevent its coming to effect.' Henry resolves the misunderstanding, pointing out that Catherine only meant a new publication, whereas his sister 'immediately pictured to herself a mob of three thousand men assembling in St George's Fields; the Bank attacked, the Tower threatened, the streets of London flowing with blood, a detachment of the 12th Light Dragoons (the hopes of the nation) called up from Northampton to quell the insurgents . . .' Although such events had taken place quite recently, in the Wilkite disturbances of 1768 and the Gordon riots of 1780, it is clear from the context that Henry considers them to be highly unlikely, while Austen is apparently ridiculing the notion that the Gothic novel was encouraging them. The reason was that the ingredients of the Gothic novel might exist in Europe, and perhaps even in Scotland and Ireland, but not in England.

> Charming as were all Mrs Radcliffe's works, and charming even as were the works of all her imitators, it was not in them perhaps that human nature, at least in the midland counties of England, was to be looked for. Of the Alps and the Pyrenees, with their pine forests and their vices, they might give a faithful delineation; and Italy, Switzerland, and the South of France, might be as fruitful in horrors as they were there represented. Catherine dared not doubt beyond her own country, and even of that, if hard pressed, would have yielded the northern and western extremities. But in the central part of England there was surely some security for the existence even of a wife not beloved, in the laws of the land, and the manners of the

age. Murder was not tolerated, servants were not slaves, and neither poison nor sleeping potions to be procured, like rhubarb, from every druggist.

By implication the political circumstances were also different. There was no tyranny, no terror, no repression. There was therefore no need for radicalism, let alone revolution.

Jane Austen is often considered to have written in isolation from the great upheavals of her generation, the French and Industrial Revolutions. It is true that she is unconcerned with industrial changes, but then there is no reason why one should expect a novelist writing in rural Hampshire mainly about village life in the Home and southern counties to pass comment on industrialisation. It was only just beginning to have an impact on northern cities like Leeds, Manchester and Sheffield, and some historians have challenged the notion that it revolutionised the economies even of those areas until after Austen's death in 1817.

Although she did not directly address the Napoleonic Wars, however, she did engage, as Marilyn Butler has demonstrated, with the war of ideas unleashed by the French Revolution.[4] Thus *Sense and Sensibility* explores the challenge to the rationalism of the Enlightenment from early romantic notions that the heart should rule the head. It picks up themes enunciated in the dispute between Voltaire's rational philosophy and Rousseau's acknowledgment of the irrational. In the French Revolution the disciples of Rousseau had triumphed over those of Voltaire, with catastrophic results. Though Austen clearly did not envisage that the triumph of Marianne's sensibility over Elinor's sense would have similar consequences in England, she nevertheless regards it as socially subversive and sides with the conservative sister. Marianne's wildly romantic involvement with the utterly selfish Willoughby nearly leads to her death, for when he jilts her she neglects her health until she contracts a 'putrid fever'. As she herself admits, '[H]ad I died it would have been self destruction.' Letting the heart rule the head could be suicidal, not only for individuals but for society. On her recovery, Marianne vows that her recollection of her fondness for Willoughby 'shall be regulated, it shall be checked by religion, by reason, by constant employment'. Such restraints on irrational impulses were required to avoid a social breakdown too.

Similar restraints are also indicated in *Emma*. Emma's attempt to marry Harriet Smith to Mr Elton not only reveals her own naiveté

4. Marilyn Butler, *Jane Austen and the War of Ideas* (Oxford, 1987).

about social conventions but also displays the dangers of social engineering. As Marilyn Butler notes,

> Emma's presumption in thinking to direct Mr. Elton and Harriet into matrimony is an ingeniously comic revamping of the anti-jacobin plot in which some Julia or Marianne, ignoring the counsels of prudence, mistakes the nature of her man, transgresses, and does considerable damage to herself and to society.[5]

More disruptive both of individual happiness and social harmony is the invidious influence of Frank Churchill, a typical anti-jacobin male figure who insinuates himself from outside into a harmonious community and wreaks havoc. He likes to play games with people, and provokes Emma at Box Hill into insulting Miss Bates. The insult threatens not merely her relationship with a neighbour but the whole social fabric. As Mr Knightly observes when reproving Emma's appalling behaviour,

> Were she a woman of fortune, I would leave every harmless absurdity to take its chance; I would not quarrel with you for any liberties of manner. Were she your equal in station – but, Emma, consider how far this is from being the case. She is poor; she has sunk from the comfort she was born to; and if she live to old age must probably sink more. Her situation should secure your compassion. It was badly done, indeed! You, whom she had known from an infant, whom she had seen grow up from a period when her notice was all honour – to have you now, in thoughtless spirits, and the pride of the moment, laugh at her, humble her – and before her niece too – and before others, many of whom (certainly *some*) would be entirely guided by *your* treatment of her.

It is not just that Emma has been lacking in *noblesse oblige*. Civility and politeness were essential lubricants of an otherwise brittle social mechanism. Society would break down if the leaders of local communities did not honour their obligations.

As Butler observes, 'with the possible exception of *Sense and Sensibility*, *Mansfield Park* is the most visibly ideological of Jane Austen's novels.'[6] The Bertram family is a microcosm of a society torn between conservative and liberal values. Sir Thomas, his younger son, Edmund, and Fanny Price represent traditional order and restraint, while Tom, the elder son, and the two sisters, Julia and Maria, chafe at the restraint and wish to fulfil their individual potential. When Sir Thomas goes with Tom to Antigua in order to put his

5. Ibid, p. 252.   6. Ibid, p. 219.

estate there on a better footing the girls take advantage of his absence to realise their own selfish desires.

> Their father was no object of love to them, and his absence was unhappily most welcome. They were relieved by it from all restraint; and without aiming at one gratification that would probably have been forbidden by Sir Thomas, they felt themselves immediately at their own disposal, and to have every indulgence within their reach.

Their inclinations are reinforced by the arrival in the neighbourhood of Henry and Mary Crawford. The brother and sister represent the intrusion of an alien and sinister influence like that of Frank Churchill and Willoughby. They enter Northamptonshire 'with the true London maxim, that every thing is to be got with money'. They have already been tainted by their uncle and guardian, Admiral Crawford, 'a man of vicious conduct'. Even Mary admits that her brother has been 'quite spoiled' by 'the admiral's lessons'. She herself reveals its corrupting influence when she cracks a joke in very poor taste: '[M]y home at my uncle's brought me acquainted with a circle of admirals. Of *Rears* and *Vices*, I saw enough. Now do not be suspecting me of a pun, I entreat.'

The gulf between the Crawfords' values and those of Edmund and Fanny is clearly revealed in the visit to Mr Rushworth's house at Sotherton. As Alaistair Duckworth has demonstrated, the way that the owners of country houses treated the fabrics of their mansions in Austen's novels reveals their attitudes towards tradition and innovation.[7] Austen was no pure conservationist, but, like Burke, advocated improvements which built on the foundations of a structure and, in Pope's words, consulted 'the genius of the place'. Innovations, such as those the Crawfords urged Rushworth to make at Sotherton, severed the link between the building and its past, paying no heed to the environment.

The break with tradition is especially noticeable in the chapel. There they are told that it

> was formerly in constant use both morning and evening. Prayers were always read in it by the domestic chaplain, within the memory of many. But the late Mr Rushworth left it off.
>
> 'Every generation has its improvements' said Miss Crawford, with a smile, to Edmund ...
>
> 'It is a pity' cried Fanny, 'that the custom should have been discontinued ... A whole family assembling regularly for the purpose of prayer, is fine!'

7. A. Duckworth, *The Improvement of the Estate: A Study of Jane Austen's Novels* (London, 1971).

'Very fine indeed!' said Miss Crawford, laughing. 'It must do the heads of the family a great deal of good to force all the poor house-maids and footmen to leave business and pleasure, and say their prayers here twice a day, while they are inventing excuses themselves for staying away.'

'*That* is hardly Fanny's idea of a family assembling,' said Edmund.

Mary Crawford responds to the rebuke by reiterating her objections to compulsory devotions, adding a derogatory remark on the clergy, unaware that Edmund is about to be ordained.

The explicit Anglicanism of the central characters of the novel does add a new dimension to Austen's ideological message. For Edmund and Fanny are not only Anglicans but evangelicals, as Marilyn Butler points out.[8] Evangelicalism takes the place of anti-jacobinism in the earlier novels as a conservative ideology.

Another intruder, Mr Yates, younger son of a peer, is indirectly responsible for the biggest affront to conservative values, the per-formance of the play *Lovers' Vows* in Mansfield Park. He visits the house at the invitation of Tom, the elder son, who has returned from Antigua, where he left his father. Yates has just been to a house party where the play was to be performed but had been aborted following a bereavement in the family playing host. When he expresses disappointment, Tom, temporarily the head of the household at Mansfield Park, proposes staging the play there, despite the objections of his brother, Edmund. Their sisters and the Crawfords eagerly participate in the production. Fanny alone shares Edmund's complaint that it would be an affront to the absent owner of the house. Unlike the other females, she suppresses her selfish instincts on account of the moral impropriety of staging a play. 'For her own gratification she could have wished that something might be acted, for she had never even seen half a play, but everything of higher consequence was against it.' In the event she shows more integrity than Edmund, for he is persuaded, or rather persuades himself, to take the part of Anhalt, a clergyman, on the flimsy grounds that otherwise the others would have cast a stranger in this role. At the first rehearsal, however, the non-arrival of Mrs Grant obliges Fanny to read her part. The rehearsal is under way when the return of Sir Thomas to the house brings it, and the first volume of the novel, to an abrupt end.

The second volume opens with the question '[H]ow is the con-sternation of the party to be described?' Today it could be rephrased

8. Butler, *Jane Austen and the War of Ideas*, pp. 242–3.

to ask how it is to be understood. For amateur dramatics produced by a family in a private home, even if the head of the household is absent at the time, scarcely seem so earth-shattering as his unexpected return clearly makes them in *Mansfield Park*. 'For the greater number it was a moment of absolute horror.' Marilyn Butler, in a superb analysis of the situation, shows how acting, especially by women, was frowned on by evangelicals.[9] This would explain the dislike of the production by Edmund and Fanny, but scarcely by 'the greater number'. They seem like naughty children caught misbehaving by a severe father rather than as adults responsible for their own recreation. Yet, although Yates thought that Sir Thomas might permit the play to go ahead once he had been properly welcomed from his voyage home, even the worldly Crawfords accepted that, in the short run at least, there was no way that it could.

The main reason for Sir Thomas' disapprobation was that the order of the house had been disturbed. His own rooms had been physically altered to accommodate the theatre, and his first concern was to repair the damage and restore them to their former use. This restoration was not only of the material but also of the moral fabric of the house. He was particularly affronted that the play had been the libertine *Lovers' Vows*, and burned every copy that he came across. He thus reasserted his authority, which had been usurped in his absence by lords of misrule. The usurpation was brought directly home to him when he stepped onto the stage and, in Marilyn Butler's words, 'is confronted at the heart of his own terrain by a mouthing puppet who represents a grotesque inversion of himself'.[10] When he restores order, as Jane Austen observes, 'under his government, Mansfield was an altered place.'

The house is thus a microcosm of society. The family has rebelled against patriarchal authority. That authority is symbolised by silence. Throughout the novel, calm and peace represent order and restraint, while noise represents disorder bordering on anarchy. Fanny eventually contrasts the quietness of Mansfield Park with the commotion of her family's house in Portsmouth, and yearns for the former. Sir Thomas stresses his 'value for domestic tranquillity, for a home which shuts out noisy pleasures', while even Henry Crawford admits to Fanny that the play 'was more pleasant than prudent. We were getting too noisy.'

The tranquillity of Mansfield Park, however, depends on the cacophony of cries raised by the slavedriver's whip on a sugar

9. Ibid, pp. 231–2.   10. Ibid, p. 235.

plantation. For, as Edward Said has pointed out, the whole economy of Sir Thomas Bertram's estate in England depends on the prosperity of his property in Antigua.[11] It is precisely because his Antiguan plantation is undergoing economic difficulties that he has to absent himself from Mansfield Park, providing his rebellious offspring with the opportunity to defy him. In Said's words

> There is a paradox here in reading Jane Austen which I have been impressed by but can in no way resolve. All the evidence says that even the most routine aspects of holding slaves on a West Indian sugar plantation were cruel stuff. And everything we know about Austen and her values is at odds with the cruelty of slavery.[12]

This is even more paradoxical if the novel is held to be upholding an evangelical ideology. For although the evangelical movement took many guises, and can be misused if reified to explain moral trends in early nineteenth-century history, one element which did hold it together was the campaign to eliminate first the slave trade and then slavery itself from the British empire. Yet there is scarcely a hint of disapproval of the source of Sir Thomas' wealth. Fanny, indeed, at one stage asks him about the slave trade, but the subject is not pursued by her cousins, and her question is answered with 'a dead silence'. Sir Thomas rules over his English household like an absolute monarch and he inspires fear rather than love. Moreover, as Said observes, 'there is nothing in *Mansfield Park* that would contradict us . . . were we to assume that Sir Thomas does exactly the same things – on a larger scale – in his Antigua "plantations"'. And, in the event, his mismanagement of his family, especially of its education, is held to be the main cause of his children's flawed characters. But all this is of little consequence beside Fanny's avowed admiration for his values and role as head of the household. It would be a perverse reading of the novel that sees the moral corruption of the young Bertrams as stemming from the tainted source of the family's wealth. In this respect Said is right to say that the paradox of *Mansfield Park* cannot be readily resolved.

Another paradox about Jane Austen's ideological stance is that, while she was a conservative in her attitude towards society in general, on 'the woman question', as Warren Roberts observes, 'there can be little doubt as to her taking a feminist position'.[13] Feminism in her day did not mean the assertion of independence for women

11. Edward W. Said, *Culture and Imperialism* (London, 1993), pp. 95–116.
12. Ibid, p. 115.
13. W. Roberts, *Jane Austen and the French Revolution* (London, 1979), p. 177.

from the thrall of male hegemony. For one thing, in the circles in which Austen moved, the minor gentry of the southern counties of England, there were scarcely any opportunities to be independent. The only women in her novels who have this choice are Emma, who is financially secure, and Jane Fairfax, who is offered a position as governess. In the event both became wives instead. Marriage, indeed, was essential for most to avoid the fate of Miss Bates, whose spinsterhood condemns her to sliding down the social scale. All the novels are concerned with the strategies adopted by families to ensure that daughters found suitable husbands.

It is on the question of their suitability that Austen sided with Mary Wollstonecraft, whom otherwise she would have dismissed as a wild radical. For as we have seen Wollstonecraft advocated companionate marriages between equals. In her view, women should be treated in every way as men were in order to equip them to share their husband's interests. They should not merely be sexual playthings and otherwise pursue trivial and vapid pursuits, but should be educated to be intellectual companions to their spouses.

Austen heartily agreed. The disparity in the intellects of Mr and Mrs Bennett, and of Sir Thomas and Lady Bertram, make their marriages pitiful. Mr Bennett hides himself in his study amid his books to avoid his wife's 'mean understanding, little information and uncertain temper'. Lady Bertram is so stupid that in a whole evening she cannot learn the rules of a game of cards which Fanny picks up in three minutes. No wonder her husband has no emotional problem in leaving her for months on end to visit the West Indies! On the other hand, Austen's heroines – Fanny, Emma, Elinor Dashwood, for instance – can hold their own with the most sophisticated men. Perhaps the most liberated of all in this respect is Elizabeth Bennett. She is perfectly matched in wit and intelligence to Darcy, their inevitable marriage being only delayed by his pride and her prejudice. When eventually they are married Darcy confesses that he admired her not for her looks or her family but for the 'liveliness of [her] mind'. Elizabeth herself replies,

> You may as well call it impertinence at once. It was very little less. The fact is, that you were sick of civility, of deference, of officious attention. You were disgusted with the women who were always speaking and looking and thinking for your approbation alone. I roused, and interested you, because I was so unlike them.

Feminist critics, seeking to enrol Jane Austen as a sister in the subversion of male hegemony, accuse her of surrendering to it with this resolution of the plot of *Pride and Prejudice*.[14] Such criticism is essentially anachronistic since contemporary feminism sought not to subvert male hegemony by creating roles for women independent of marriage, but to make matrimony a union of moral and intellectual equals.

Maria Edgeworth made this point in her *Letters for Literary Ladies* (1795). 'I would have a woman early in life, know that she is capable of filling the heart of a man of sense and merit,' the sensible Caroline writes to her romantic friend Julia. 'That she is worthy to be his companion and friend.'[15] Caroline and Julia are in many respects early representatives of Austen's sense and sensibility, represented by Edgeworth as philosophy and enthusiasm. Caroline is a utilitarian who thinks that those who calculate felicity 'through the long perspective of distant years' are the wisest and happiest of human beings. She advises Julia, torn between marriage to Lord V and Caroline's brother, to decide which lifestyle would suit her better. As Lady V she would live in a style to which she was not accustomed, whereas Caroline points out that 'you would be certain of the mode of life you would lead with my brother.' Julia, however, lets her heart rule her head and chooses Lord V, with disastrous results. Five years into her marriage she leaves her husband and children and runs off to France. There she comes to her senses too late to save her marriage, and returns to England to die abjectly in Caroline's happy household.

Julia's fate would seem to be a sign of Jacobin enthusiasm run mad, and to place Edgeworth among the radical novelists of the revolutionary age. And yet in the conflict of ideas she did not come out consistently on the side of radicalism. On the contrary, her Irish novels won the approval of conservatives like Sir Walter Scott. And Marilyn Butler has suggested that the most famous of them, *Castle Rackrent*, could be read as 'a not unsympathetic account of the passing of old-fashioned landlordism'.[16]

How 'old-fashioned' the Rackrents were raises the problem of when the events in the novel were meant to have taken place. In the Preface, written in 1800, Edgeworth hoped her readers would 'observe that these are "tales of other times"',

> that the manners depicted in the following pages are not those of
> the present age; the race of the Rackrents has long since been extinct

14. Deborah Kaplan, *Jane Austen among the Women* (London, 1992), p. 200.

15. Maria Edgeworth, *Letters for Literary Ladies*, ed. Gina Luria (London, 1974), 'Letters of Julia and Caroline', p. 22.

16. Marilyn Butler, *Maria Edgeworth: A Literary Biography* (Oxford, 1972), p. 358.

in Ireland; and the drunken Sir Patrick, the litigious Sir Murtagh, the fighting Sir Kit and the slovenly Sir Condy, are characters which could no more be met with at present in Ireland, than Squire Western or Parson Tulliber in England. There is a time when individuals can bear to be rallied for their past follies and absurdities, after they have acquired new habits and a new consciousness. Nations as well as individuals gradually lose attachment to their identity and the present generation is amused, rather than offended, by the ridicule that is thrown upon its ancestors . . . When Ireland loses her identity by an union with Great Britain she will look back with a smile of good humoured complacency on the Sir Kits and Sir Condys of her former existence.

Butler cites this passage to claim that the novel's characters 'are not the same generation as the one on the point of uniting itself with England'.[17] Yet the storyteller, Thady Quirk, tells Sir Condy that he is 'now upwards of fourscore years of age'. Even though Edgeworth, as 'editor' of Quirk's *Memoirs of the Rackrent Family*, tells us that he 'several years ago . . . related to the editor the history of the Rackrent family', that could scarcely have been much more than a decade before the novel was published. Unless she was careless with her arithmetic, therefore, she can only have been making the chronological claims in the Preface ironically.

The degree of irony in the novel has been underestimated in other respects too. Above all, Quirk's claims that he was 'honest Thady' and boasts that 'as I have lived so will I die, true and loyal to the family' have been largely accepted at face value.[18] He is seen as an engaging, naive and, above all, innocent observer of his various masters, whose foibles, eccentricities and faults have to be deduced by the reader from Thady's rose-coloured description of them. Moreover, this process of deduction has to decode the brogue in which his observations are delivered. And this is not easy, for Edgeworth created in the character of Thady Quirk a plausible Irish steward whose very voice lilts off the page in the genuine rhythms and figures of speech of a native of Ireland of peasant stock. One can almost hear the voice of the Irishman Edgeworth used as a model for her creation. It was this literary feat which made the

---

17. Ibid, p. 356.
18. An exception is James Newcomer, *Maria Edgeworth the Novelist* (London, 1967), chapter ix, 'The disingenuous Thady Quirk'. Newcomer's interpretation has not been generally accepted. See Elizabeth McWhorter Harden, *Maria Edgeworth's Art of Prose Fiction* (London, 1971), chapter two. While there are problems with it, nevertheless it does add a dimension to Edgeworth's characterisation of Quirk which other accounts have missed.

novel the most popular between Sterne's *Tristram Shandy* and Scott's *Waverley*. Thady's deferential and sympathetic account of his masters' behaviour inspires in the reader the same respect for them that he seems to display. Hence, it can be concluded that the view of the landlord class conveyed in his memoirs is not unsympathetic. However, the relationship between an Irish peasant and his landlord was conducted in an extremely subtle discourse. It requires to be decoded as much as the vocabulary and speech patterns used by an American slave employed as a trusted domestic in the antebellum South. Behind Thady's deference there can be detected a shrewd and calculating mind which is fully aware of his masters' weaknesses and even minded to exploit them. He is by no means as disingenuous as he appears. Despite his disclaimers of his son Jason's exploitation of the Rackrents' total inefficiency as estate managers, he cannot be exonerated from having a share in it. As James Newcomer rightly observes,

> When Jason puts in for the possession of a valuable lease 'I spoke a good word for my son' Thady says 'and gave out in the county that nobody need bid against us.' Note the word *us* – inadvertent on Thady's part if we would keep him in character, but surely deliberate on the part of Miss Edgeworth.[19]

The import of the involvement of Thady in the auction for the estate would not have been lost on readers of Bage's *Hermsprong* four years before *Castle Rackrent*, for it was precisely to get a knock-down bargain in bidding for a house that Lord Grondale let it be known he was involved to deter others from bidding. It was in fact a way of cheating the Rackrents of the market price they might have realised for the estate if the auction had not been fixed by Thady Quirk. He might deplore the process by which his own family rose as the Rackrents fell, until his son owned the castle while Sir Gondy expired in the Lodge. But he was not averse from giving it a helping hand.

The rise of the Quirks at the expense of the Rackrents can be generalised as the inevitable outcome of two approaches to the management of a landed estate which might be termed the paternalistic and the patrician. The paternalist landlord regarded himself as the father of the local community, who protected his tenants from the adverse effects of market conditions by lowering rents when prices rose and even writing them off altogether. He also indulged in

---

19. Newcomer, p. 148.

hospitality and treated his neighbours to his largesse. The patrician regarded the estate as an asset to be exploited for profit, regardless of the price paid by his tenants. He was frequently an absentee, so in no position to exercise hospitality even if he had been that way inclined. These stereotypes were stock characters in eighteenth-century fiction. Thus, Addison's Sir Roger de Coverley exemplified the paternalist and Pope's Timon the patrician.[20] And both are displayed in *Castle Rackrent*. The very name would conjure up the typical patrician, a rack-renting landlord. Sir Murtagh and, to a lesser degree, Sir Kit live up to this expectation. But Sir Patrick and Sir Condy rather represent the paternalist. Sir Condy shows his similarity to the first Rackrent by putting up a monument to him 'of old Irish hospitality' and dying after quaffing a formidable bumper of whisky from Sir Patrick's horn. Marilyn Butler thinks this makes the novel broken-backed, since it defies the expectations raised by its title and depicts Sir Condy in a favourable light after the brutal behaviour of his predecessors.[21] But the title draws attention to the estate rather than to the family. And as far as the management of the estate is concerned, the tension between the two approaches continues and increases under Sir Condy, since his conspicuous consumption brings him to bankruptcy while his agent, Jason, exercises control over his lands, eventually buying him out. There is possibly a harbinger of less happy results of the Union than Edgeworth foresaw in the Preface in this outcome of her novel. For the paternalistic approach to the estate is symbolised by 'old Irish hospitality', while Sir Kit, who introduces the patrician approach, is accused of 'making English tenants of them'. The clash between Irish and English ideas of landownership were to make the history of Ireland in the nineteenth century tragic rather than happy.

Perhaps the clash of two cultures in *Castle Rackrent*, as well as its depiction of Irish characters, led Sir Walter Scott to admire it. He expressed his admiration in the first edition of *Waverley*, writing that he aspired 'in some distant degree to emulate the admirable Irish portraits of Miss Edgeworth'. In the Preface to the 1829 edition of the Waverley novels he observed that 'I felt that something

20. See W. A. Speck, *Society and Literature in England 1700–1760* (Dublin, 1983), pp. 46–52.
21. Butler, p. 357. It is possible to read Sir Condy's character as less favourable than it appears on the surface of Thady's account of his last master. Thus, Thady observes that Sir Condy was 'the most universally beloved man I had ever seen or heard of'. Yet, when his esteem is put to the test by his bizarre mock funeral, Sir Condy is disappointed by the poor turnout at his 'wake'.

might be attempted for my own country of the same kind with that which Miss Edgeworth so fortunately achieved for Ireland.' The Waverley novels both painted portraits of Scottish characters and depicted a conflict between two ways of life. Consequently, as many critics have pointed out, their heroes are confronted with two conflicting ideologies which oblige them to make a choice. In *Old Mortality* Henry Morton is confronted by the absolute pretensions of the Stuart court in the 1680s and the religious fanatics who are prepared to resist violently. Scott favoured neither absolutism nor rebellion, but in the end sympathises with Morton's decision to resist, even though he has to ally with rebels to maintain his rights. The nature of the choice Scott offered his heroes has been variously interpreted. Marian Cusac, for example, summarises it thus:

> The contrast of historical cultures as shown in the Waverley novels demonstrates symbolically Scott's belief in the intrinsic value of a rational, ordered society. The protagonist is used to show the necessity of choosing such a society rather than the older romantic (i.e. non-rational) heroic or barbaric society with which it is contrasted. For example, Frank Osbaldistone must reject the Highland outlaws represented by Rob Roy and must accept the responsibilities of filial duty and membership in the existing orderly social structure before he can be considered worthy of becoming a valuable member of society.[22]

In Bob Chase's view, however, Scott describes a Scotland containing two modes of production, a declining feudal system and an emerging capitalist economy. While the Marxist analysis can be questioned, his conclusion that Scott, though ultimately committed to one side in the cultural clash, sees virtues in both is valid.[23] It is certainly true of *Waverley*, where the Jacobites are treated sympathetically and their way of life nostalgically reconstructed, so that Waverley's dilemma in whether to choose the traditional Stuart or the modern Hanoverian culture can be understood, even though Scott himself sided with the latter. He was a conservative who, like Burke, accepted the inevitability of change. He therefore wished to preserve what was valuable in the old and to resist what was undesirable in the new. His imaginative sympathy for lost causes partly explains his

---

22. Marian H. Cusac, *Narrative structure in the novels of Sir Walter Scott* (London, 1969), pp. 100–1.

23. Bob Chase, 'Walter Scott: a new historical paradigm', in Bill Schwarz (ed.), *The Expansion of England: Race, Ethnicity and Cultural History* (London, 1996), pp. 92–129. This is a brilliant tour de force which applies McKeon's 'truth/virtue' model (discussed above p. 109) to Scott's novels.

appeal to Scottish readers. What they wanted, according to Nicholas Phillipson, was

> a passive ideology; one that would combine a stoical acceptance of the passing of an old Scottish way of life with a legitimate means of protesting against it without in any way harming the essential economic and political structure of the union. Scott provided such a formula.[24]

When in 1819 Scott turned from Scottish to English history with *Ivanhoe*, he again contrasted two rival cultures. Set in 1194 it represents the clash between Anglo-Saxon and Norman civilisation. This conflict fed two powerful myths, that of the Norman yoke and that of the feudal nature of English society. The notion that the Norman Conquest had imposed a tyrannical system onto Anglo-Saxon freedom informed a radical whig view of the middle ages which Scott appealed to in the characters of Ivanhoe himself and Robin Hood, who fight against the tyrants in joust and siege. Tories took the view that the Normans were legitimate rulers of England, whose concessions to their subjects in the form of representation in parliament were gifts granted by their grace rather than the restoration of lost rights. Scott recognises that view when he acknowledges the legitimacy of the claims of Richard I. As in his Scottish novels he seeks to reconcile the divergent views in a consensus drawing on the best of both traditions. This reconciliation is symbolised by the joint attack of Richard I and Robin Hood on Front-de-Boeuf's castle and, above all, in the marriage of Ivanhoe and Rowena.

24. N. Phillipson, 'Nationalism and Ideology', quoted in Francis R. Hart, 'Scott and the Novel in Scotland', in Alan Bell (ed.), *Scott Bicentenary Essays* (London, 1973), p. 62.

CHAPTER TEN

Poems on the State of Affairs

Traditionally, English poetry from the 1780s to the 1820s has been labelled 'Romantic'. But this label begs many questions. It was not a contemporary term, but was foisted upon the period by Victorians. It was also linked with literary trends on the continent, particularly in Germany. Yet, insofar as there was a change in the forms and subject matter of poetry towards the end of the eighteenth century, its origins can be detected earlier. Moreover, it can be argued that it derived more from English hymns than from European Romanticism.[1]

A central feature of so-called 'Romantic' poems is the relationship between the individual and the other – Eternity, Nature, Mankind, etc. This is conveyed by the opening line of the most famous Romantic poem in the language: 'I wandered lonely as a cloud'. Such concerns were, however, expressed in hymns before they found expression in poetry. Of course, the individual's relationship with God was a theme at least as old as the Psalms: 'The Lord is my Shepherd, I shall not want.' Moreover, psalmody informed much hymnody. Isaac Watts, one of the greatest of eighteenth-century hymn writers, began by versifying psalms.

Indisputably, the greatest hymn writer of the time was Charles Wesley, who wrote some six thousand hymns to inspire the Methodist movement. Charles and his brother John believed in the possibility of all men being saved through rebirth in Jesus Christ. Charles' hymns stressed this to counter Calvinist assertions by some Methodists that only the elect were saved:

---

1. For a reading of eighteenth-century hymns as poems see Donald Davie, *The Eighteenth-Century Hymn in England* (Cambridge, 1993).

> Come sinners to the gospel feast;
> Let every soul be Jesu's guest;
> Ye need not one be left behind,
> For God hath bidden all mankind.[2]

Many of the hymns deal with the intimate personal knowledge of Christ experienced by the believer.

> Come, O thou Traveller unknown
> Whom still I hold, but cannot see!
> My company before is gone,
> And I am left alone with thee;
> With thee all night I mean to stay,
> And wrestle till the break of day.[3]

Sometimes it was expressed in a very eighteenth-century manner.

> And can it be that I should gain
> An Interest in the Savior's blood?

But mostly the hymns express everyday experiences common to every age.

> When quiet in my room I sit
> Thy book be my companion still . . .
> I hold thee with a trembling hand
> But will not let thee go . . .

Spiritual experiences of an individual believer wrestling with Christ and seeking his own salvation were by no means confined to psalms and hymns, but found expression in many literary forms throughout the centuries. Thus in the seventeenth century they inspired Puritan confessional autobiographies, metaphysical poems and Bunyan's *Pilgrim's Progress* – to give but a few examples. But their expression in forms other than hymns was not a conspicuous feature of literature in the early eighteenth century. Isaac Watts' hymn 'When I survey the wond'rous cross' was as personal an expression of an individual's relationship with Christ as anything which Charles Wesley wrote. Yet Watts does not appear to have inspired a poetical response. Wesley himself, however, claimed that his hymns were also poems. Thus he wrote in the Preface to the Handbook of 1780:

> May I be permitted to add a few words with regard to the poetry?
> Then I will speak to those who are judges thereof with all freedom
> and unreserve. To these I may say, without offense: (a) In these

---

2. *John and Charles Wesley: Selected Prayers, Hymns, Journal Notes, Sermons, Letters and Treatises*, ed. F. Whaling (London, 1981), p. 179.
3. Ibid, pp. 192, 197, 215, 223.

hymns there is no doggerel, no botches, nothing put in to patch up the rhyme, no feeble expletives. (b) Here is nothing turgid or bombast on the one hand, nor low and creeping on the other. (c) Here are no *cant* expressions, no words without meaning. Those who impute this to us know not what they say. We talk common sense (whether they understand it or not) both in verse and prose, and use no word but in a fixed and determinate sense. (d) Here are (allow me to say) both the purity, the strength, and the elegance of the English language – and at the same time the utmost simplicity and plainess, suited to every capacity. Lastly, I desire men of taste to judge – these are the only competent judges – whether there is not in some of the following verses the true spirit of poetry, such as cannot be acquired by art and labor, but must be the gift of nature. By labor a man may become a tolerable imitator of Spenser, Shakespeare or Milton, and may heap together pretty compound epithets, as 'pale-eyed', 'meek-eyed' and the like. But unless he is born a poet he will never attain the genuine *spirit of poetry*.[4]

This almost anticipates passages in the Preface to *Lyrical Ballads*!

A major link between the religious and the Romantic expression of spiritual *angst* was William Cowper. He was also a Methodist, but a follower of the Calvinist George Whitefield rather than of the Arminian Wesleys.[5] He thus had more in common with the evangelicals than with Wesleyan Methodism, which is one reason why he became Jane Austen's favourite poet. His evangelicalism is implicit throughout his poems, becoming most explicit perhaps in those which deplore the slave trade.[6]

Cowper's belief in predestination drove him to madness with despair that he was not of the elect. Before his breakdown in 1773, brought on by the conviction that he was damned, Cowper wrote hymns. Thereafter, he turned to poetry. Some of the 'Olney' hymns he composed in collaboration with John Newton record his dark night of the soul. Thus, in 'The Shining Light' he confesses:

> My former hopes are fled,
> My terror now begins;
> I feel, alas, that I am dead
> In trespasses and sins.[7]

---

4. Ibid, p. 176.

5. He eulogised Whitefield in 'Truth'. *The Works of William Cowper*, ed. John D. Baird and Charles Ryscamp (3 vols, Oxford, 1980–95) [Hereafter Cowper, *Works*] i, 331–2.

6. Cowper, *Works*, i, 340; iii, 13–16, 26–7, 182–3. Elsewhere Cowper observes an evangelical concern for the reformation of manners and suppression of vice, lest an afflicting providence judge England. *Works*, i, 251–4; ii, 134–6.

7. Cowper, *Works*, i, 172.

In 'The Contrite Heart' he admitted that, though he went to church, he found 'no comfort there'.[8]

Yet, though he felt that he himself was literally beyond redemption, he still maintained the priority of religion in his poems. Thus, he imagines Alexander Selkirk soliloquising on the island of Juan Fernandez:

> Religion! what treasure untold
> Resides in that heav'nly word!
> More precious than silver and gold,
> Or all that this earth can afford.
> But the sound of the church going bell
> These vallies and rocks never heard,
> Ne'er sigh'd at the sound of a knell,
> Or smil'd when a sabbath appear'd.[9]

Cowper seems to have been aware that he was versifying a religious sentiment which had not recently found poetic expression. As he observed in 'Table Talk':

> Pity! Religion has so seldom found
> A skilful guide into poetic ground,
> The flow'rs would spring where'er she deign'd to stray,
> And ev'ry muse attend her in her way.
> Virtue indeed meets many a rhiming friend,
> And many a compliment politely penn'd,
> But unattir'd in that becoming vest
> Religion weaves for her, and half undress'd,
> Stands in the desert shiv'ring and forlorn,
> A wintry figure, like a wither'd thorn . . .[10]

He appreciated that religion and poetry were formerly allied:

> . . . in a Roman mouth, the graceful name
> Of prophet and of poet was the same,
> Hence British poets too the priesthood shar'd,
> And ev'ry hallow'd druid was a bard.[11]

Now he assumed, not the priestly but the bardic role. The idea of the bard, the priest-poet, was a central theme in the poetry of the period from Thomas Gray's *The Bard*, through 'the Immortal Bard' Burns, to Sir Walter Scott's *Lay of the last Minstrel*. 'Muse, hang this harp upon yon aged beech', Cowper exclaims in 'Expostulation', the harp 'still murm'ring from the solemn truths I teach'. He also

8. Ibid, p. 148.   9. Cowper, *Works*, ii, 403–4.   10. Cowper, *Works*, i, 260.
11. Ibid, p. 254.

imagines the wind stirring the harp's strings, an image of inspiration which was to become a feature of many Romantic poems.[12]

Cowper's most renowned contribution to Romantic poetry was his poem 'The Task', published in 1785. This differed from the collection he had published in 1782, all of which was written in rhyming couplets. By contrast, 'The Task' was in blank verse which anticipated in many ways Wordsworth's 'Prelude'. Yet the choice of that form was not his. As he explained, 'a lady fond of blank verse, demanded a poem of that kind from the author, and gave him the SOFA for a subject.' This was the trivial 'task' which 'brought forth at length, instead of the trifle he at first intended, a serious affair – a Volume'.[13] It became the classic set text in schools during the nineteenth century, and schoolboys learned by heart such lines as 'England with all thy faults I love thee still' and 'all flesh is grass, and all its glory fades'.[14] But the passages that resonate with romanticism are those autobiographical lines which inspired Wordsworth and other poets. Thus he opens the third book:

> So I, designing other themes, and call'd
> T'adorn the Sofa with eulogium due,
> To tell its slumbers and to paint its dreams
> Have rambled wide. In country, city, seat
> Of academic fame (howe'er deserved)
> Long held, and scarcely disengaged at last.
> But now with pleasant pace, a cleanlier road
> I mean to tread.[15]

This leads him to give 'some account of myself'.

> I was a stricken deer that left the herd
> Long since; with many an arrow deep infixt
> My panting side was charged when I withdrew
> To seek a tranquil death in distant shades.

And here the poem takes off to soar above the trivial and commonplace to 'sum up half mankind . . . And find the total of their hopes and fears dreams, empty dreams.' This is because they pursue fulfilment in secular rather than in religious goals.

Cowper was especially critical of those who sought salvation in political changes. Like the Wesleys he was deeply conservative in politics, a staunch defender of the existing constitution against radicals. Thus he deplored the American rebels who sought 'to rob their

---

12. Ibid, p. 316. The most famous expression of the phenomenon was Coleridge's poem 'The Eolian Harp'.
13. Cowper, *Works*, ii, 113.   14. Ibid, pp. 144, 169.   15. Ibid, p. 163.

royal master of his right'. At the same time, royal right was that of limited monarchy as established in the Revolution settlement, not the divine right of kings. 'There is no *true* Whig who wishes all the power in the hands of his own party,' he wrote in a letter. 'The division of it which the lawyers call tripartite is exactly what he desires, and he would have neither King, Lords nor Commons unequally trusted, or in the smallest degree predominant. Such a Whig am I . . .' Cowper warned George III not to attempt to step outside his constitutional limitations in 'The Task':

> we love
> The king who loves the law, respects his bounds,
> And reigns within them; him we serve
> Freely and with delight, who leaves us free.[16]

Yet above all, as Vincent Newey observes, Cowper 'elevates spiritual freedom, "liberty of heart, deriv'd from heav'n" . . . and . . . privileges heightened perception of the natural world as the gift, and sign, of a personal state of grace'.[17]

> Nature, enchanting Nature, in whose form
> And lineaments divine I trace a hand
> That errs not, and find raptures still renew'd,
> Is free to all men, universal prize.

He anticipates the Lake poets in deploring the way men have lost sight of nature in towns. Yet though earthly cities like London 'breathe darkness all day long', mankind is destined for a heavenly city, Salem.

> Bright as a sun the sacred city shines;
> All kingdoms and all princes of the earth
> Flock to that light; the glory of all lands
> Flows into her . . .[18]

Having glimpsed Sion, Cowper ends his poem with intimations of his own mortality:

> So glide my life away! and so at last
> My share of duties decently fulfilled,
> May some disease, not tardy to perform
> Its destin'd office, yet with gentle stroke,
> Dismiss me weary to a safe retreat
> Beneath the turf that I have often trod.[19]

16. Vincent Newey, 'Cowper and the condition of England', in V. Newey and Ann Thomson (eds), *Literature and Nationalism* (Liverpool, 1991), pp. 121, 126, 129, 135.
17. Ibid, p. 130.   18. Cowper, *Works*, iii, 257.   19. Ibid, p. 262.

In fact his last years were marked by depression, which infuses his last poem, 'The Cast-away'.[20] After recounting how a man swept overboard was abandoned by his shipmates and eventually drowned, Cowper concludes:

> No voice divine the storm allay'd,
>   No light propitious shone,
> When, snatch'd from all effectual aid,
>   We perish'd, each, alone;
> But I beneath a rougher sea,
> And whelm'd in deeper gulphs than he.

When Cowper died in 1800 William Hayley undertook to write his biography, and commissioned his protégé, William Blake, to make engravings for it which included portraits of Cowper and his mother. Apart from this coincidence, the lives of Cowper and Blake would appear to have no connexion. Cowper was educated at Westminster School, and studied law at the Middle and Inner Temples, being called to the bar in 1754. Blake was never formally educated before being apprenticed to an engraver. After his first attack of mental illness in 1763, Cowper left London and lived in the country until his death, whereas Blake remained a lifelong Londoner. Despite his rural retreat, Cowper was cosmopolitan, translating Voltaire and Madame Guyon from the French, Homer from the Greek and several Roman poets from the Latin. Blake was a metropolitan who affected to despise Greek and Roman models, and to prefer the Bible as a source of poetic inspiration.

Yet, as Peter Ackroyd has pointed out, 'the story of Cowper's life acted as both a lesson and a warning to Blake – a lesson on the need for courage and self-confidence, and a warning against self-doubt and melancholy.'[21] Their religious experiences also had something in common, both being possessed by inner demons which found expression in their poetry.

Blake's own religion will probably always defy categorisation. His parents were some kind of dissenters, though what kind is not known. It is perhaps a sign that they were not radical sectarians, at least when William was born, that they had their infant son baptised in St James's church, Piccadilly, in July 1757.[22] When he grew up Blake himself was exposed to several dissenting influences. As E. P. Thompson put it

20. Ibid, pp. 115–16.   21. Peter Ackroyd, *Blake* (London, 1995), p. 224.
22. Ibid, p. 19.

We will do best to think of a sectarian and antinomian gathering-ground in London, where heretical tracts were cherished, where sects suffered secessions and new hierarchs arose, where Behmenists disputed with Universalists and where seekers shopped around among preachers and little churches . . . And it was from this same gathering-ground that some of the first members of the Swedenborgian New Jerusalem Church were to be drawn.[23]

William and his wife were enrolled in a conference at this church in April 1789. For a while Blake seems to have espoused Swedenborgian doctrine, only to renounce it later. But the exact nature of those beliefs he accepted and rejected remains tantalisingly obscure. It seems possible that he was initially attracted to the church because it preached that at death the soul abandoned the physical body in the form of a new spiritual body. This could have appealed to the visionary in Blake, who himself claimed that when his brother died in 1787 he saw 'the released spirit ascend heavenward through the matter-of-fact ceiling "clapping its hands for joy"'.[24] The positive impact of Swedenborg's doctrine on his work, however, remains obscure. For instance, most commentators have taken Blake's poem 'The Divine Image' to be Swedenborgian.[25] E. P. Thompson, however, takes the diametrically opposite view that it is a confutation of the doctrines of the New Jerusalem Church.[26] Nevertheless, there is general agreement that 'The Marriage of Heaven and Hell', published in 1793, represents his rejection of Swedenborg and all his works.

The 'proverbs of hell' from this publication were widely disseminated in the 1960s. 'The tygers of wrath are wiser than the horses of instruction' even appeared on tee shirts. Blake appealed to that psychedelic decade because of his mysticism. The class of '68 read his bardic utterances stoned. It is a sign of his appeal to flower power that many editions of, and commentaries upon, his works appeared around that time. The standard edition of *The Complete Poetry and Prose* first appeared in 1965.[27] S. Foster Damon's *A Blake Dictionary* also came out in 1965, while David Erdman's *Concordance* was published in 1967. *Blake: An Illustrated Quarterly, The Blake Newsletter* and *Blake Studies* started life respectively in 1966, 1967 and

23. E. P. Thompson, *Witness against the Beast: William Blake and the Moral Law* (London, 1993), p. 107.
24. Ackroyd, *Blake*, p. 101.
25. Ibid, p. 104. Cf. Thompson, *Witness against the Beast*, pp. 150–1.
26. Ibid, p. 151. Thompson wrestles more convincingly with the problem.
27. Edited by David Erdman. Quotations here are from the newly revised edition of 1988.

1968. Previously, readers had sought – often in vain – for a meaning to his more mythic works, with their symbolic figures of Los, Orc Urizen and the Zoas. The Woodstock generation, which found its own bard in Bob Dylan and the cryptic messages of his songs, and turned to eastern gurus for inspiration, also found in Blake a near-contemporary voice. He even inspired the name of one of the more controversial rock groups of the decade, The Doors.[28]

In fact, much of Blake is readily accessible. Amongst the poems which English schoolchildren used to learn by heart is his 'The Tyger'.

> Tyger Tyger, burning bright,
> In the forests of the night;
> What immortal hand or eye,
> Could frame thy fearful symmetry?

People who would abandon reading, say, 'The Book of Urizen' after the first few lines, could sing lustily the following verses:

> And did those feet in ancient time,
> Walk upon England's mountains green?
> And was the holy lamb of God,
> On England's pleasant pastures seen?
>
> And did the Countenance Divine,
> Shine forth upon our clouded hills?
> And was Jerusalem builded here,
> Among these dark Satanic Mills?

There was even a film title taken from the last line of the next verse – 'Bring me my Chariot of fire'. Few people in England cannot have been roused by the closing lines:

> I will not cease from Mental Fight,
> Nor shall my Sword sleep in my hand:
> Till we have built Jerusalem,
> In England's green & pleasant Land.

Most people probably know this as a hymn called 'Jerusalem' rather than as verses in the Preface to Blake's 'Milton'. And that is the point – Blake not only composed Miltonic epics on biblical and mythical themes, he also wrote hymns, or at least meditations on spiritual themes. His most popular poems, titled 'Songs of Innocence and Experience', appeared in 1794 with the subtitle 'shewing

---

28. They took the name from one of Blake's 'proverbs of hell': 'if the doors of perception were cleansed every thing would appear to man as it is: infinite'.

the two contrary states of the human soul'. The Introduction to the 'Songs of Experience' exhorts the reader to

> Hear the voice of the Bard!
> Who Present, Past & Future sees
> Whose ears have heard
> The Holy Word.

The last song is 'The Voice of the Ancient Bard'. Blake was echoing Ossian in these pieces, and indeed the form in which they appeared was based on medieval illuminated manuscripts. The characteristically Blakean production of an engraved plate with hand-painted illustrations for the poems, which he used for the whole of 'Songs of Innocence and Experience' and extensively elsewhere, was at once an astonishing demonstration of eighteenth-century craftsmanship and a deliberately archaic Gothic device.

The illuminations are not just illustrations but an integral part of the poetry, so much so that the poems can only be read properly in an edition which reproduces the original plates. The interplay of text and print is an essential part of any reading. Often the engraving, especially when hand-painted, casts light on the meaning of the words. To give a simple example, the expression 'burning bright' associated with the 'tyger' has often been interpreted as referring to the tiger's eyes. But a glance at any print which Blake or his wife painted with watercolours shows at once that it refers to the stripes of its coat, which appear like flames.

Several of the Songs are sung by an individual identified in them as 'I'. Thus, the very first song of innocence has a narrator 'piping down the valleys wild', who refers to himself as 'I' no fewer than eight times in twenty lines. 'A Poison Tree' in *Songs of Experience* opens with four lines beginning with 'I'. The individual is not necessarily Blake himself. He is not, for instance, 'The Little Black Boy' who tells us that

> My mother bore me in the southern wild,
> And I am black, but O! my soul is white . . .

Nor is he the chimney sweep who laments that

> When my mother died I was very young,
> And my father sold me while yet my tongue
> Could scarcely cry weep weep weep weep . . .

Blake's ability to empathise with these children, forcing readers to put themselves in their shoes until the prejudice and exploitation they suffer become intolerable, shows how skilfully he could identify himself with others. This empathy makes it hazardous to use his verse for biographical information. He cannot, for example, have been 'The School Boy' who protested that 'to go to school in a summer morn . . . drives all joy away', since he himself received no formal schooling. One Song, however, 'London', is so Blakean that it can scarcely have been other than autobiographical.

> I wander thro' each charter'd street,
> Near where the charter'd Thames does flow,
> And mark in every face I meet
> Marks of weakness, marks of woe.
>
> In every cry of every Man,
> In every Infants cry of fear,
> In every voice: in every ban,
> The mind-forg'd manacles I hear.
>
> How the Chimney-sweepers cry
> Every blackning Church appals,
> And the hapless Soldiers sigh
> Runs in blood down Palace walls.
>
> But most thro' midnight streets I hear
> How the youthful Harlots curse
> Blasts the new-born Infants tear,
> And blights with plagues the Marriage hearse.

The first line originally read 'I wander thro' each dirty street'. E. P. Thompson has shown how the change from 'dirty' to 'charter'd' charged it with a political meaning, engaging the poem with the debate between Burke and Paine.[29] Burke used chartered rights as examples of the bulwarks of liberty against democracy and anarchy. Paine, by contrast, argued that charters took away liberty from people in general to grant it to a privileged few. Blake came out firmly on Paine's side, and 'thus chose "charter'd" out of the biggest political argument that was agitating Britain in 1791–2'. 'Mind-forg'd' first appeared as 'German-forg'd', which castigated the ruling house of Hanover, while the condemnation of the church and the palace also attacked the constitution in church and state. For Blake was a radical, a republican even – an ideological stance which informed his prophecies.

Blake saw himself as an Old Testament prophet. He published two 'prophecies', one on 'America' and another on 'Europe'. *America:*

---

29. Thompson, *Witness against the Beast*, pp. 175–9.

A Prophecy contained in draft four lines which he apparently can-
celled while it was being printed, for they survive in some first
editions.

> The stern Bard ceas'd, asham'd of his own song; enrag'd he swung
> His harp aloft sounding, then dash'd its shining frame against
> A ruin'd pillar in glittering fragments; silent he turn'd away,
> And wander'd down the vales of Kent in sick & dreary lamentings.

Again the 'stern Bard' is an Ossianic figure whose 'song' is presumably the visionary 'Preludium' of the *Prophecy*. The Preludium relates a visit by the daughter of Urthona to feed Orc, who has been
chained to a rock for fourteen years by her father. Orc explains
that while his body has been confined his spirit has roamed freely,
adopting various forms, sometimes an eagle, sometimes a lion,
sometimes a whale and sometimes a serpent. He then bursts his
bonds and immediately rapes the woman, who, so far from resist-
ing, 'joy'd'. She recognises her ravisher as 'the image of God who
dwells in darkness of Africa', as a serpent in Canada, an eagle in
Mexico, a lion in Peru and a whale in the South seas 'drinking my
soul away'.

> O what limb rending pains I feel, thy fire & my frost
> Mingle in howling pains, in furrows by thy lightnings rent.
> This is eternal death: and this thy torment long foretold.

The latest editor of the 'continental prophecies' concedes that
'many new readers . . . find in the poet's nomenclature an element
of mythmaking which at first is rather irritating and bewildering.'[30]
Indeed, the cosmic conflict between the forces of freedom and
repression, symbolised by the figures of Orc and Urizen, is couched
in language as ambiguous as an astrological prediction. Moreover,
Blake's 'prophecies' appeared along with many other gnomic pre-
dictions of the 1790s, some of which were expressed in arcane
language to avoid prosecution under a statute banning seditious
prognostications.[31]

---

30. D. W. Oorrbecker, editor, *Blake, the Continental Prophecies* (London, 1995),
p. 19. Of *Europe: A Prophecy* he even admits to doubt 'that its complexities could
possibly vanish altogether, however ingeniously a scholarly interpretation might be
crafted', p. 141.

31. John Mee, *Dangerous Enthusiasm: William Blake and the Culture of Radicalism
in the 1790s* (Oxford, 1992), p. 28. Prime minister Pitt even sponsored counter-
prophecies to encourage gratitude for the 'inestimable blessings' provided by church
and king, e.g. *A Prophecy of the French Revolution and the Downfall of Anti Christ.*

Their delphic language has enabled various readings to be made of Blake's prophecies. Traditionally, they were seen as on the side of Liberty, welcoming the American and French Revolutions and predicting similar triumphs for the radical over the reactionary cause in Britain. Recently, revisionist scholars have challenged this view, pointing out the ambiguities of the endings of the prophecies. It seems obvious that in *America: A Prophecy* Blake applauds the American cause and names such leaders of the conflict as Franklin, Paine and Washington with approval. He also disapproves of the measures taken by the British king and his agents to suppress the revolution. But at the end it is vague as to whether the forces unleashed by the freeing of Orc at the beginning will benefit Britain too. This could simply be an insurance against prosecution for seditious prophecy. But the ending of *Europe: A Prophecy* is even more ambiguous. Here Los is depicted as rising

> And with a cry that shook all nature to the utmost pole,
> Call'd all his sons to the strife of blood.

Does Los represent here the revolutionary poet-prophet of the traditional view? Or is he representative of the Counter-Revolution as some revisionists claim?[32] Both readings seem plausible, and this was perhaps deliberate on Blake's part. While he welcomed the opening stages of the French Revolution, along with many others he was disillusioned at the excesses of the Terror. By 1793 blood seemed to be the only way forward both for the revolutionaries and for their British opponents after France declared war on Britain in February of that year.

Robert Burns was also ambiguous about his attitude to the French Revolution and the radical forces which it unleashed. But this was to conceal his own radicalism at a time when he was employed in government service as an excise man.[33] Sometimes the concealment was insufficient. In 1792 he was accused of being disaffected from the government, and vowed when charges were dropped to 'set, henceforth, a seal on my lips, as to these unlucky politics.' Burns's 'unlucky politics' ran the gamut from Jacobitism to Jacobinism. In his Jacobite phase he wrote 'surely the gallant though unfortunate house of Stewart, the kings of our fathers for so many heroic ages, is a theme much more interesting than an obscure

---

32. Ibid, p. 152.
33. It has been claimed that he wrote anonymous radical articles in the Edinburgh press in the 1790s. Ian McIntyre, *Dirt and Deity: A Life of Robert Burns* (London, 1996). The attributions, however, have not been generally accepted and therefore are not used here.

beef-witted insolent race of foreigners whom a conjuncture of circumstances kickt up into power and consequence.'[34] This was a private note, but he could be equally outspoken in print. 'On seeing the royal palace at Stirling in ruins' contained the lines

> Here Stewarts once in glory reign'd,
> And laws for Scotland's weal ordain'd;
> But now unroof'd their palace stands,
> Their sceptre fallen to other hands . . .
> The injured Stewart line is gone,
> A race outlandish fills their throne;
> An idiot race, to honour lost –
> Who knows them best despise them most.

The poem provoked some hard questioning at a time when Burns was applying for his excise post. In all he wrote or adapted about thirty Jacobite songs.[35] Among them are some which are still sung, such as 'Charlie he's my darling'. The Jacobitism expressed by Burns was scarcely active so many years after the suppression of the last Jacobite rebellion in 1746. Yet the attachment to the House of Stuart went deeper than mere sentiment. It expressed a fierce Scottish nationalism in the only form that it could take under the Hanoverians. Burns deplored the Union of 1707 and was scathing about the Scottish commissioners who had negotiated it as 'a parcel of rogues in a nation'. He clearly considered that it had ended a long and proud history of Scottish independence, which he traced back to the days of Robert Bruce in 'Scots wha' hae wi' Wallace bled'.

He also seems to have equated Scottish independence before the Union with liberty. And this association links his nostalgic Jacobitism with his forward-looking Jacobinism. One of the many poems recited at Burns' night suppers every 25 January betrays his enthusiasm for the French Revolution.

> It's coming yet for a' that
> That Man to Man the warld o'er
> Shall brothers be for a' that.

Burns was accused in 1792 of joining in the singing of the French Revolutionary song 'Ca ira' – that will come. He excused his behaviour on the grounds that he was drunk at the time, which is plausible enough since he seems hardly ever to have been sober. Nevertheless, the sentiment is surely preserved still in 'it's coming yet'.

34. David Daiches, 'Robert Burns and Jacobite Song', in D. A. Low (ed.), *Critical Essays on Robert Burns* (London, 1975), p. 137.
35. Ibid, p. 145.

William Wordsworth, too, welcomed the onset of the French Revolution – 'bliss was it in that dawn to be alive' – and then became disillusioned. But his disillusionment came later than Blake's. He was in France in the years 1791–92 and shared the hopes of the Girondins, like his friend Michael Beaupuy, that a bourgeois republic could replace the monarchy.[36] He boldly declared himself 'a republican' in a reply he wrote to an attack on the revolution by the bishop of Llandaff. The bishop had previously been regarded as being sympathetic to radical causes, but in 1793 he published a new edition of a sermon on 'The Wisdom and Goodness of God in having made rich and poor', preached in 1785 and now printed with an Appendix which deprecated the French for having gone beyond constitutional monarchy to set up a republic.[37] He was convinced that a republic was the worst form of government since it subjected everybody to the tyranny of the majority. By contrast, 'the greatest freedom that can be enjoyed by man in a state of civil society, the greatest security that can be given him with respect to the protection of his character, property, personal liberty limb and life is afforded to every individual by our present constitution.' Wordsworth took exception to the whole Appendix, but particularly to this passage. 'You ask with triumphant confidence, to what other law are the people of England subject than the general will of the society to which they belong', he wrote in his reply to the bishop. 'If there is a single man in Great Britain who has no suffrage in the election of a representative the will of the society of which he is a member is not generally expressed; he is a Helot in that society.'

Hopes that a Girondin republic would be settled in France were dashed almost immediately after he wrote the 'letter to the bishop of Llandaff' by the more radical Jacobins, which is probably why he never published it. Nevertheless, Wordsworth still felt optimistic about the ultimate triumph of the Girondin cause throughout the Terror, and rejoiced on hearing the news that Robespierre was dead, taking heart that moderation would prevail. He opposed Britain's involvement in the revolutionary war, and deplored the measures taken by Pitt's government to suppress radicalism. It was only when the French turned from a defensive war to one of conquest and became 'oppressors in their turn' that he lost faith in the efficacy of

---

36. Ian Robertson Scott, ' "Things as they are": the literary response to the Revolution', in H. T. Dickinson (ed.), *Britain and the French Revolution 1789–1815* (London, 1989), p. 232.

37. The Appendix is published in *The Prose Works of William Wordsworth*, ed. Alexander B. Gossart (3 vols, London, 1876), i, 24–30.

the Revolution to transform the world for the better. Even then he did not become a supporter of the traditional order overnight, but turned for a while to the philosophic anarchy of William Godwin. Godwin postulated a society based on small communities more like the parish than the nation. In these the individual would be educated to see that anti-social behaviour was irrational. The few who refused to curb their irrational impulses would have their behaviour monitored and ultimately controlled by their neighbours. This utopian scheme depended upon an optimistic view of human nature which could be curbed by Reason. As he tested Godwin's assumptions about human nature, Wordsworth came more and more to doubt that it was possible to formulate laws about it. His play *The Borderers*, written about 1796, gave expression to these doubts. The action takes place on the borders of England and Scotland in the reign of Henry III. The complicated plot involves the hero, leader of a border gang, in the death of an old man, the father of the girl he hopes to gain, because he is persuaded by an Iago-like follower that she is going to be betrayed into the clutches of the dissolute Clifford. The play thus has a Shakespearean quality, and Wordsworth was alleged to have claimed that 'human nature is more effectively illuminated by William Shakespeare than by William Godwin.'[38] He himself gave a fuller explanation on the occasion of its publication in 1842.

> The study of human nature suggests this awful truth, that, as in the trials to which life subjects us, sin and crime are apt to start from their very opposite qualities, so are there no limits to the hardening of the heart, and the perversion of our understanding to which they may carry their slaves. During my long residence in France, while the revolution was rapidly advancing to its extreme of wickedness, I had frequent opportunities of being an eye-witness of this process, and it was while that knowledge was fresh upon my memory that the Tragedy of 'the Borderers' was composed.[39]

After rejecting Godwin's optimistic faith in human nature he apparently sought certainty in mathematics 'and their clear and solid evidence'. Samuel Taylor Coleridge rescued Wordsworth from these abstract speculations.

> Ah! then it was
> That Thou, most precious Friend! about this time
> First known to me, didst lend a living help
> To regulate my Soul . . .

38. John Turner, *Wordsworth: Play and Politics* (London, 1986), pp. 64–5.
39. *Wordsworth Poetical Works*, ed. E. de Selincourt (Oxford, 1949), i, 342.

Coleridge himself had gone through an even more radical phase than Wordsworth. In 1794 he had planned with Robert Southey to set up a 'pantisocracy' on the banks of the Susquehanna river. In it twelve men and twelve women would communally own land and wealth and share communal tasks. 'This plan', as Iain Robertson Scott observes, 'would have subverted all the traditional institutions and principles of the existing British constitution, but, by 1795, the scheme had fallen apart through lack of finance and sufficiently enthusiastic volunteers.'[40] In that year Coleridge began to give public lectures on politics which 'were very radical indeed'.[41] He even published a pamphlet with the title 'The Plot Discovered, or An Address to the People against Ministerial Treason'. Coleridge was a Unitarian, and even briefly became a Unitarian preacher – yet another connexion between Romanticism and dissent. Radical politics and religion were fused in 'Religious Musings', a long meditative poem written on Christmas Eve 1794 but not published until 1796. In it the excesses of the French Revolution are seen as 'regrettable but unavoidable conditions of the establishment of the "blest future state" which he approximated to the millenium itself.'

> Children of Wretchedness! The hour is nigh:
> And lo! the Great, the Rich, the Mighty Men,
> The Kings and the Chief Captains of the World,
> With all that fixed on high like stars of Heaven
> Shot baleful influence, shall be cast to earth,
> Vile and down-trodden, as the untimely fruit
> Shook from the fig tree by a sudden storm.[42]

The storm was the French Revolution. The poet deplored what he saw as the hypocrisy of Britain and its ungodly allies waging war on revolutionary France in the name of preserving Christianity.

In 1797 Coleridge met Wordsworth and struck up an immediate friendship which was to become the most celebrated partnership in English literary history. Together they wrote *Lyrical Ballads*, the publication of which in 1798 was epoch-making. Some date from it the beginning of the English Romantic movement. While to give something so anachronistic a precise moment of birth is unhistorical,

40. Ibid, p. 235.
41. Rosemary Ashton, *Samuel Taylor Coleridge: A Critical Biography* (London, 1996), p. 65. His first, delivered in Bristol, 'cleverly announced' in the advertisement that 'they who in these days of jealousy and party rage dare publicly explain the principle of Freedom must expect to have their intentions misrepresented and to be entitled like the Apostles of Jesus "stirrers up of the People and men accused of Sedition"'.
42. P. Kitson, 'Coleridge, the French Revolution and "The Ancient Mariner": Collective Guilt and Individual Salvation', *The Yearbook of English Studies* (London, 1989), xix, 200.

nevertheless historic claims have been made from the start for the slim volume of poems. Wordsworth himself claimed in the Preface to the edition of 1800 that 'it was published as an experiment'. This was 'to ascertain how far, by fitting to metrical arrangement a selection of the real language of men in a state of vivid sensation, that sort of pleasure and that quantity of pleasure may be imparted, which a Poet may rationally endeavour to impart'.[43] Wordsworth's boast did not go unchallenged either at the time or since. Coleridge himself, who later grew apart from his former collaborator, objected to the use of the word 'real', and would have preferred 'ordinary' language.[44] More seriously, Marilyn Butler has dismissed the notion that the ballads marked a significant moment in literary history, arguing that they could have appeared at any time in the previous decade.

While the language in which they were couched and the form in which they were expressed might not have been as novel as Wordsworth maintained, nevertheless, one claim he made for them does deserve to be taken seriously by historians.

> ... the human mind is capable of excitement without the application of gross and violent stimulants; and he must have a very faint perception of its beauty and dignity who does not know this, and who does not further know that one being is elevated above another in proportion as he possesses this capability. It has therefore appeared to me that to endeavour to produce or enlarge this capability is one of the best services in which, at any period, a Writer can be engaged; but this service, excellent at all times, is especially so at the present day. For a multitude of causes unknown to former times are now acting with a combined force to blunt the discriminating powers of the mind, and unfitting it for all voluntary exertion to reduce it to a state of almost savage torpor. The most effective of these causes are the great national events which are daily taking place, and the encreasing accumulation of men in cities, where the uniformity of their occupations produces a craving for extraordinary incident which the rapid communication of intelligence hourly gratifies. To this tendency of life and manners the literature and theatrical exhibitions of the country have conformed themselves. The invaluable works of our elder writers, I had almost said the works of Shakespeare and Milton, are driven into neglect by frantic novels, sickly and stupid German Tragedies, and deluges of idle and extravagant stories in verse.[45]

43. *Wordsworth and Coleridge: Lyrical Ballads*, ed. W. J. B. Owen (Oxford, 1969), p. 153.
44. S. Coleridge, *Biographia Literaria* (London, 1975), pp. 198–9.
45. *Lyrical Ballads*, pp. 159–60.

We have been here before too, of course. This is the disdain
which the self-appointed conveyors of Culture express for the mass
circulation of ephemeral literature. There are echoes of Pope's
attack on the 'dunces', the hack writers of Walpole's day. Only now
in addition to the newspapers they wrote are novels, German plays
and 'idle and extravagant stories in verse' – below the dignity of
poetry. But where the contagion was confined to London in the
'Dunciad', it has now spread throughout the land with 'the
encreasing accumulation of men in cities'. There is a bourgeois
infrastructure sustaining the demand for news, novels and verse.
The provinces are coming into their own. Moreover, English culture has become provincial as well. Where the leading writers of
the 'Augustan' period worked in London, the main authors of the
'Romantic' period, while they might have published in the capital,
wrote in the provinces. Wordsworth, Coleridge and Southey were
outstanding examples of this trend, choosing to live in the Lake
District.

The first poem by Wordsworth in *Lyrical Ballads* was set in the
Lakes: 'Lines left upon a seat in a yew-tree which stands near the
lake of Esthwaite'. Another, 'The Female Vagrant', begins 'By Der-
went's side my Father's cottage stood'. Wordsworth chose 'low and
rustic life' because he thought that

> in that situation the essential passions of the heart find a better soil
> in which they can attain their maturity, are less under restraint, and
> speak a plainer and more emphatic language; because in that situ-
> ation our elementary feelings exist in a state of greater simplicity and
> consequently may be more accurately contemplated and more for-
> cibly communicated; because the manners of rural life germinate from
> those elementary feelings; and from the necessary character of rural
> occupations are more easily comprehended; and are more durable;
> and lastly, because in that situation the passions of men are incorpor-
> ated with the beautiful and permanent forms of nature.[46]

Yet though he adopted the persona of many rustic characters,
including – perhaps surprisingly – several women, the most popular poem of his in the volume, judging by its appearance in
anthologies, is the autobiographical 'Lines written a few miles above
Tintern Abbey'. It records one of those 'spots of time' referred to
in 'The Prelude', those moments which etch a deep impression on
the memory as they acquire a permanent significance. They can
become the commonplace of romantic songs, like 'The way you

46. *Lyrical Ballads*, p. 156.

look tonight', or 'Things you said today'. But with Wordsworth it is
a spiritual experience, though not one of Christian orthodoxy. He
describes himself as 'a worshipper of Nature' who had 'learned

> To look on nature, not as in the hour
> Of thoughtless youth, but hearing oftentimes
> The still, sad music of humanity,
> Not harsh nor grating, though of ample power
> To chasten and subdue. And I have felt
> A presence that disturbs me with the joy
> Of elevated thought; a sense sublime
> Of something far more deeply interfused,
> Whose dwelling is the light of setting suns,
> And the round ocean, and the living air,
> And the blue sky, and in the mind of man,
> A motion and a spirit, that impels
> All thinking things, all objects of all thought,
> And rolls through all things.

These words might be the 'real' or 'ordinary' language of men, but
the ideas they convey are as visionary as anything in Blake's cryptic
myths.

Coleridge's main contribution to the Ballads, 'The Rime of the
Ancient Mariner', also contains a mythical element. The killing of
the albatross incurs a dreadful cosmic punishment. But this is a
traditional view of Providence, for the bird was 'a Christian soul',
and in shooting it with his crossbow the mariner 'had done an
hellish thing'. As he lamented,

> Instead of the Cross the Albatross
> Around my neck was hung.

When his shipmates mysteriously died, and he was left 'alone on
the wide wide sea', 'Christ would take no pity' on his soul. However, some kind saint took pity on him instead, and he was able to
pray, upon which the albatross dropped from his neck. Yet he still
had to do penance for the sin of slaying the albatross. Coleridge,
like Wordsworth, conceived of the universe as a moral entity; but
their metaphysical sanctions for morality were different. Where for
Wordsworth it was Nature, for Coleridge it was God. Religion was
a major theme in Coleridge's poems, from 'Religious Musings' to
his own Epitaph of 9 November 1833.

By then Coleridge was long past his radical phase. As he admitted
in 1817 'from the commencement of the Addington administration to the present day, whatever I have written in *The Morning Post*

or (after that paper was transferred to other proprietors) in *The Courier* has been in defence or furtherance of the measures of government.'[47] Wordsworth gravitated even more into establishment circles. In 1818 he made interest for a candidate supported by the Lowther family at the general election in Westmorland, writing two appeals to the voters in the county. In one he asserted that 'if the democratic activities of the great towns and of the manufacturing districts were not counteracted by the sedentary power of large estates, continued from generation to generation in particular families, it would be scarcely possible that the Laws and Constitution of the Country could sustain the shocks which they would be subject to.'[48] Wordsworth's transition from republican to Burkean admirer of the British constitution led Byron to castigate him as 'the converted Jacobin having long subsided into the clownish sycophant of the worst prejudices of the aristocracy'.[49]

The Romantic who travelled furthest from angry young man to staunch conservative was Robert Southey. In his younger days Southey had written a play praising Wat Tyler's stance against tyranny. He perhaps prudently did not publish it at the time, but was acutely embarrassed when it was published in 1817, even seeking to suppress its publication. By then he was poet laureate, and wrote a eulogy on George III when the king died in 1820: *A Vision of Judgement.*

In it Southey imagines himself looking out of his window towards Derwentwater 'at that sober hour when the light of day is receding' and light 'fades, like the hopes of youth'. His own youthful hopes of 'Pantisocracy' have faded so much that when he hears bells tolling the death knell of George III he exclaims 'Thou art released! . . . thy soul is delivered from bondage.' The mad, blind king has been released from 'mental and visual bondage' to 'yonder heaven'. Southey experiences a vision of George's reception at the pearly gates by the assassinated prime minister Spencer Perceval, who updates him on recent history, informing the king how England had triumphed over Napoleonic France. When asked if the spirit of faction has also been crushed in England, Perceval replies that it is still at work, plotting 'some accursed conception of filth and of darkness ripe for its monstrous birth'. Witnesses are then produced to testify whether or not the king deserves admission into heaven. Among the king's detractors are 'the souls of the wicked' in hell.

47. *Biographia Literaria*, ed. G. Watson, pp. 120–1.
48. R. Sales, *English Literature in History 1780–1830: Pastoral and Politics* (London, 1983), p. 52.
49. Byron, *Don Juan*, quoted in Robertson Scott, p. 245.

These include Wilkes and Junius, who now are too ashamed to testify against the monarch they had libelled on earth, and are cast back into hell by the Demon of Faction, who warns slanderers to 'bear in mind, that after death there is judgment.' With no witnesses against him, George enters a very English heaven, received by his predecessors on the throne of England and heroes mainly from his native land.[50]

In the Dedication to the new King George IV, Southey concluded 'that your Majesty may long continue to reign over a free and prosperous people, and that the blessings of the happiest form of government which has ever been raised by human wisdom under the favour of Divine Providence may, under your Majesty's protection, be transmitted to posterity'. By contrast, in the Preface he inveighed against 'those monstrous combinations of horror and mockery, lewdness and impiety, with which English poetry has, in our days, first been polluted', claiming that 'the publication of a lascivious book is one of the worst offences that can be committed against the well being of society.' He had in mind a group of poets whom he dubbed 'the Satanic school', and although he did not name them it was clear that he included amongst them Byron and Shelley. Byron could not resist the implied challenge. As R. Ellis Roberts put it, 'if he saw a man who, all unsuspecting, still had on his head the light paper fool's cap he had donned in a moment of heavy exhilaration, Byron had to go and ring the bells on it.'[51]

In *The Vision of Judgement*, a parody of Southey's *Vision*, Byron defended the poets whom Southey had appealed to parliament to censure, and drew attention to the poet laureate's own 'seditious publication', *Wat Tyler*, whose author had been criticised in the Commons as 'a rancorous renegade'. 'The way in which that poor mad creature the Laureate deals about his judgements in the next world', concluded Byron's Preface, 'is like his own judgement in this.' The poem imagines Southey being hoisted by a demon from Skiddaw, 'where as usual it still rained', to heaven on the occasion of George III's arrival there. Byron's *Vision* depicts the laureate in a ludicrous light. Satan, introducing him to the heavenly host, comments 'a sillier fellow you will scarce behold.' But Byron also had a serious point. Where in Southey's *Vision* George III gains admittance to heaven claiming, 'the desire of my heart hath been

50. Only Burke, Mansfield and 'the youth of Loch Leven' are not English, despite Southey calling them all 'worthies of Britain'.

51. R. Ellis Roberts, *A Vision of Judgement by Robert Southey and The Vision of Judgement by Lord Byron* (The Raven Press, 1932), p. x. a limited edition of 200 copies.

always the good of my people', Byron's accuses the king of having 'ever warr'd with freedom and the free'. Although he admits that George was 'no tyrant', yet he 'shielded tyrants'. Satan claims the king as his own, defying the archangel Michael to 'produce a reign more drench'd with gore, more cumbered with the slain.' To prove this he summons a host of witnesses from all around the world. Michael assures him that two will suffice, upon which Satan calls upon Wilkes and Junius. So far from remaining silent as in Southey's version, they willingly testify. Wilkes rather exculpates George, since 'his conduct was but natural in a prince' and puts the blame for his folly and wickedness on his ministers. Satan expresses impatience with this testimony, attributing it to the fact that Wilkes 'turned to half a courtier' before he died and has become a whole one since. Junius, who still refuses to reveal his identity even to the archangel Michael, stands by his former condemnation of the king, exclaiming 'I loved my country and I hated him.' Satan then asks Michael to summon George Washington, Horne Tooke and Benjamin Franklin to witness against the king. Before they can be summoned, however, Southey, whose vision had imagined the reconciliation of George III and Washington, arrives and creates confusion. Thus he relates his career, pleading 'his own bad cause'. When he recalls how 'he had written Wesley's life' he offers to write those of Satan and Michael. Then he begins to read his own *Vision* but the heavenly host find it so unbearable that St Peter knocks him down to earth with his keys. Meanwhile, in the confusion 'King George slipp'd into heaven.'

Like Junius, Byron loved his country but hated George III. Although he went abroad after his wife's separation from him ostracised him from society, he still felt nostalgic for his native land. His nostalgia found expression in 'Beppo', which he wrote in Venice. While 'with all its sinful doings . . . Italy's a pleasant place', this is largely due to the climate. Sunshine apart, Byron could still quote Cowper's line 'England with all thy faults I love thee still' when he reached Calais.

> I like the government (but that is not it);
> I like the freedom of the press and quill;
>   I like the Habeas Corpus (when we've got it);
> I like a parliamentary debate,
> Particularly when 'tis not too late;
>
> I like the taxes when they're not too many;
>   I like a seacoal fire when not too dear;

> I like a beef-steak too, as well as any;
>   Have no objection to a pot of beer ...
> And so God save the Regent, Church and King!
>   Which means that I like all and every thing.

Byron spelled out his own political position in *Don Juan*, which he dedicated to 'Bob Southey'. The dedication describes the poet laureate as being 'a Tory at last', and concludes 'that I still retain my "buff and blue"'. This identified Byron with the whig party of Charles James Fox and his nephew, Lord Holland, the poet's own mentor, who were out of power from the 1780s to the 1830s and therefore, like himself, 'born for opposition'.[52] Their watchword was 'Liberty', and in the mythology of the Romantic movement Byron was to die a martyr to freedom. But it was a patrician view of freedom in reality. Although he announced his 'downright detestation of every despotism in every nation', he also admitted that 'it is not that I adulate the people.'[53] He was in tune with the aims of the 'Friends of the People', that giveaway title for the whig reform society which implied that its members were not of the people themselves. He himself was a peer of the realm, and took part in debates in the House of Lords. In one he displayed his essentially whig rather than radical principles when he advocated the 'restoration of the true constitution of these realms'.[54] He wished to restore the Revolution settlement of 1689, not to introduce a Painite democracy. Thus, when Don Juan visits parliament 'at the closing session' he sees

> A King in constitutional possession
>   Of such a Throne as is the proudest station,
> Though Despots know it not – till the progression
>   Of Freedom shall complete their education.
> 'Tis not mere Splendour makes their show august
> To eye or heart – it is the People's trust.[55]

'The real difference between Byron and Shelley,' wrote Karl Marx

is this; those who understand them and love them rejoice that Byron died at thirty-six, because if he had lived he would have become a reactionary *bourgeois*; they grieve that Shelley died at twenty-nine,

---

52. *Don Juan* XV, 22. The following section on Byron's political attitude owes much to Malcolm Kelsall, *Byron's Politics* (London, 1987).

53. *Don Juan* IX, 24–5.   54. Kelsall, *Byron's Politics*, p. 37.

55. *Don Juan* XII, 83. Byron stresses that things changed between Juan's visit to London in the early 1790s and the time when the poem was composed.

because he was essentially a revolutionist and he would always have been one of the advanced guard of socialism.[56]

Certainly, Shelley was more radical than Byron. For where Byron was at heart a whig, Shelley was inspired by Godwin's philosophical anarchism.[57] An early poem, *Queen Mab*, written when he was only eighteen, is in many ways *Political Justice* versified. Mankind enslaved by kingly tyranny and priestcraft will be liberated by the exercise of reason to make love rather than war the basis of society. Yet it also contains Shelley's own critique of the existing system. His atheism, which had led to his expulsion from Oxford, is stressed. He also attacks the corrupting influence of commerce, and pointedly criticises Adam Smith's *The Wealth of Nations*. Godwin himself had used Smith's advocacy of *laissez faire* in the economic sphere to advocate it in the political. State interference was no more justified in man's social intercourse than it was in his economic transactions. Anarchy, meaning the lack of regulations, was preferable in both. This was a very intellectual approach. The young Shelley's was more emotional and utopian. As his widow put it in a note on *Queen Mab*, 'it was the cardinal article of his faith that, if men were but taught and induced to treat their fellows with love, charity and equal rights, this earth would realise paradise.'

In 1817 Shelley wrote 'Laon and Cythna', a poem later published as *The Revolt of Islam*. In the Preface he described it as 'an experiment on the temper of the public mind, as to how far a thirst for a happier condition of moral and political society survives, among the enlightened and refined, the tempests which have shaken the age in which we live.' That era he defined as 'an age of despair'. This was because the hopes raised by the onset of the French Revolution had been dashed by its excesses, which had justified the reaction of the conservatives. Shelley was still inspired by Godwin's philosophical anarchism, even though their personal relationship had been strained by the poet's elopement with Godwin's daughter Mary.[58] Thus, in the Preface he characterised Malthus's *Essay on*

56. Quoted in M. H. Scrivener, *Radical Shelley: The Philosophical Anarchism and Utopian Thought of Percy Bysshe Shelley* (London, 1982), p. 326, note 6.

57. In discussing Shelley's politics I have benefited principally from M. H. Scrivener, *Radical Shelley* as well as from P. M. S. Dawson, *The Unacknowledged Legislator: Shelley and Politics* (Oxford, 1980).

58. Significantly, where *Queen Mab* had been dedicated to his first wife, Harriet, *The Revolt of Islam* was dedicated to Mary: 'So now my summer task is ended, Mary, And I return to thee, mine own heart's home'. Shelley sent a copy of the poem to Godwin, whose response was so cool it provoked a spirited defence of his work from the poet.

Population as 'a commentary illustrative of the unanswerableness of *Political Justice.*'

Although the poem is set in the past, it addresses the present.[59] Shelley thought he detected the spirit of liberty stirring again in 1817, and wrote a tract in favour of parliamentary reform signed by 'the hermit of Marlow'. In *The Revolt of Islam* a hermit rescues Laon from imprisonment by a tyrant and urges him to fight for Liberty since the time is now ripe.

> In secret chambers parents read, and weep,
>   My writings to their babes, no longer blind;
> And young men gather when their tyrants sleep,
>   And vows of faith each to the other bind.

These lines apparently refer to the radicals whom Shelley had addressed in his own tract. Where that had urged reform, the poem prophesies the possibility of revolution if reform fails. It is, though, a curiously non-violent revolution, since Laon persuades the tyrant's soldiers to make common cause with the people. 'Thus the vast array of those fraternal bands were reconciled that day.' Laon recounts how

> Towards the City then the multitude,
> And I among them, went in joy – a nation
> Made free by love.

When they enter the City they are crowned with 'the token flowers of truth and freedom fair', placed on their heads by 'fairest hands' – shades of the flower-power of the 1960s!

There is, however, a counter-revolution in which the 'fraternal bands' are bloodily suppressed. This is done, though, by foreign troops brought in by the tyrant. It is thus more reminiscent of Tienanman Square in 1988 than of Peterloo in 1819, when the Manchester crowd was butchered by yeomanry from their own locality. Shelley's response to Peterloo was to urge the 'men of England' to behave much as the rebels led by Laon behaved in *The Revolt of Islam*. In *The Mask of Anarchy* he advises them to

> Stand ye calm and resolute,
> Like a forest close and mute,
> With folded arms and looks which are
> Weapons of unvanquished war . . .

---

59. Scrivener, *Radical Shelley*, p. 128.

> And if then the tyrants dare
> Let them ride among you there,
> Slash, and stab, and maim and hew,
> What they like, that let them do.
>
> With folded arms and steady eyes,
> And little fear, and less surprise,
> Look upon them as they slay
> Till their rage has died away.

This 'proposal for massive nonviolent resistance' is, in Scrivener's view, 'the key to understanding the uniqueness of Shelley's poem'.[60] It would, the poet assured them, shame the government into yielding concessions, while the army would take their side.

> And the bold true warriors
> Who have hugg'd Danger in wars
> Will turn to those who would be free,
> Ashamed of such base company.

It was all very well for Shelley to give this advice from Italy, where he had gone in 1818 for the sake of his health; but it was perhaps as well that he did not publish it at the time, for the government was in no mood to yield any concessions. On the contrary, it cracked down hard on the advocates of parliamentary reform who urged any kind of mass protest. 'Asleep in Italy', Shelley was surely out of touch.

Yet he felt that he himself and other contemporary writers were in tune with the spirit of the times. 'The great writers of our own age are, we have reason to suppose, the companions and forerunners of some unimagined change in our social condition or the opinions which cement it', as he expressed it in the Preface to *Prometheus Unbound*. 'The cloud of mind is discharging its collected lightning, and the equilibrium between institutions and opinions is now restoring or about to be restored.'

Among the authors Shelley had in mind was surely John Keats, whose death in 1821 moved him to write *Adonais*. In the Preface Shelley defended Keats' claim 'to be classed among the writers of the highest genius who have adorned our age'. Yet until recently Keats was not celebrated as a poet who anticipated social and ideological change. On the contrary, most commentators agreed with T. S. Eliot that he 'does not appear to have taken any absorbing interest in public affairs'. Of late, however, much critical energy has

---

60. Ibid, p. 208.

been expended on exploring the politics of Keats' poetry.[61] These investigations stress that contemporaries other than Shelley saw a political message in Keats' poems. Among these was John Gibson Lockhart who in a notorious review in *Blackwood's Magazine* certainly saw one in *Endymion*: 'Keats belongs to the Cockney School of Politics, as well as the Cockney School of Poetry.' This patrician and provincial disdain for the son of a London livery-stable manager was also a tory rebuke of a radical. For Lockhart quoted the opening twenty-two lines of *Endymion* book three to demonstrate that in them Keats had 'already learned to lisp sedition'. They meditated on how often power was undeserved and abused. This is a small nugget of political ideology in a poem of over 4,000 lines, and shows how determined Lockhart was to find fault with Keats. Recent writers also seem to rake through the canon seeking evidence for political reflections. They undoubtedly find it in *Isabella*, which even George Bernard Shaw claimed could have been written by Karl Marx. And Keats himself consciously modelled Apollo in 'Hyperion' on Napoleon. But when critics are driven to claim that in his 'To Autumn' the use of the word 'conspiring' to describe the season's collaboration with the sun to ripen crops carries a seditious resonance, then it becomes clear that the quest for political allusion in Keats' poetry has gone too far. While his letters document how far he was 'on the liberal side' in contemporary politics, his poems do not.

The paucity of political allusions in Keats' poems begs the question of whether there was such a thing as Romantic politics. There have been several attempts to detect an underlying ideology in English Romantic poetry.[62] On the whole, however, their theses have not been generally accepted. When even individual poets like Coleridge, Southey and Wordsworth went through several stages of political development, from ultra-radicalism to arch conservatism, then efforts to document a coherent and consistent political philosophy from their poems seem doomed to failure. But one theme does appear to run through the poems of the period from the 1780s to the 1820s. As we have seen, the politics of the era were increasingly polarised along class lines. The emergence of the English working class and the impact of the French Revolution combined

61. A forum in *Studies in Romanticism* (London, 1986), xxv, 169–229 was devoted to 'Keats and Politics'.
62. For instance, Crane Brinton, *The Political Ideas of the English Romanticists* (London, 1926); Carl Woodring, *Politics in English Romantic Poetry* (London, 1970); Jerome J. McGann, *The Romantic Ideology: A Cultural Investigation* (London, 1983).

to make this first period of modern class warfare particularly savage.
And despite their shifting political stance, the Romantic poets consistently spoke up for the working class. As *The Anti-Jacobin* observed,
a principle upheld by 'Jacobin' poets was 'the natural and eternal
warfare of the Poor and the Rich. In these orders and gradations
of society ... the Jacobin sees nothing but a graduated scale of
violence and cruelty. He considers every rich man as an oppressor
and every person in a lower situation as the victim of avarice and
the slave of aristocratical insolence and contempt.'[63] Blake's poems
shamed the upper and middle classes for their neglect of child
labourers like chimney sweeps, while Burns articulated the aspirations of cotters. Blake and Burns are often seen as spokesmen for
the lower orders because they were workers themselves. However,
as a skilled craftsman who sold his own engraved poems, Blake was
no labourer, while Burns was not the 'heaven-taught ploughman'
of legend but the owner of a family farm who was well taught by a
village schoolmaster. Only the English, whose educational system
was inferior to the Scottish, could consider him to be unlettered
because he did not go to university. As for the other Romantics,
they did not have to do a day's work in their lives. Yet Wordsworth
drew attention to the plight of leech-gatherers, reapers and shep-
herds. Byron made a speech in the House of Lords defending the
Luddites in which he said 'you call these men a mob, desperate,
dangerous, and ignorant ... Are we aware of our obligations to a
mob? It is the mob that labour in your fields and serve in your
houses – that man your navy, and recruit your army, that have
enabled you to defy all the world, and can also defy you when
neglect and calamity have driven them to despair!' Shelley spoke
out for the masses who supported parliamentary reform, urging
them to defy the ruling class, reminding them that 'ye are many,
they are few.' From this point of view, even Southey, whose politics
seem to have been the most inconsistent of all, remained consistent
throughout his life. One of his earliest poems, 'The Widow', recounted the desperate plight of a poor homeless wanderer making
her way through a pitiless snowstorm seeking shelter, to die of cold
and hunger before she found it. Thirty years later he defended the
working class against their exploitation under the manufacturing
system in *Sir Thomas More, or colloquies on society*. This earned a
magisterial rebuke from Macaulay in *The Edinburgh Review*. In some
respects this was the first major exchange in what has come to be

63. *Poetry of the Anti-Jacobin* (2nd edn., London, 1854), pp. 17–18.

called the standard of living controversy. Southey was the first 'pessimist' and Macaulay the first 'optimist'.

To some extent, the search for consistency in Romantic politics is bedevilled by labels. That Southey became a 'tory' seems a flat contradiction of his earlier radicalism. Yet in advocating social measures, such as Factory Acts, tories and radicals combined forces. Both protested against the exploitation of the working classes and sought to protect them from it. The ends were therefore the same. Only the means were different. Tories sought to extend the traditional protection of paternalism to the workers. Radicals strove to get them self-help in the form of the vote. Southey and others who moved from radicalism to toryism in these years were inconsistent in the means they chose to achieve political goals. But to a greater extent than is usually acknowledged they remained consistent about the ends.

Conclusion

'I want a hero': so begins Byron's *Don Juan*. His own choice of hero tells us more about him than about his fellow countrymen.[1] But, before deciding on the celebrated lover of epic proportions, he ran over lists of British and French heroes which offer significant clues to the heroic pantheon of eighteenth-century Britain:

> Vernon, the butcher Cumberland, Wolfe, Hawke,
>   Prince Ferdinand, Granby, Burgoyne, Keppel, Howe,
> Evil and good, have had their tithe of talk,
>   And fill'd their sign-posts then, like Wellesley now.

Admiral Vernon was a nine days' wonder in 1741, due to his popularity for his victory over the Spaniards at Porto Bello. His image was somewhat tarnished by his later defeat at Cartagena. 'Butcher Cumberland' is perhaps the most revealing name in Byron's list. At the outset of the Culloden campaign he was widely regarded as 'the martial boy' who would suppress the Highland host. Even after the battle he was greeted as 'the conquering hero', Handel writing an anthem with that title for the thanksgiving service in St Paul's. When stories of the atrocities committed by his troops after the battle reached England, however, his reputation suffered irreparable damage, and he became known ever after as 'the Butcher'. Wolfe's remains bright to this day, perhaps because he had the good fortune to die in the moment of victory at Quebec, a scene immortalised in Benjamin West's historic painting. Unlike Vernon and Cumberland, Wolfe was not a political figure. When military and naval leaders

---

1. Byron's real hero was Napoleon until his fall in 1814: Phyllis Grosskurth, *Byron* (London, 1997), p. 193. Although other Romantics, such as Coleridge, had welcomed Napoleon's rise, their disillusion with the emperor set in long before Byron's. R. A. Foakes, 'Coleridge, Napoleon and Nationalism', in V. Newey and Ann Thompson (eds), *Literature and Nationalism* (Liverpool, 1991), pp. 140–51. 'Once Coleridge's initial admiration had passed, he became convinced that Napoleon was not just a despotic ruler, but Evil Incarnate ... In his articles for *The Courier* he argued that Napoleon actively promoted evil like the Devil himself.' Iain Robertson Scott, '"Things as they are": the literary response to the Revolution', in H. T. Dickinson (ed.), *Britain and the French Revolution* (London, 1989), p. 242.

became involved in politics, like Wellington, the last of Byron's British heroes, they failed to sustain hero status.[2]

This is possibly why no names of men who rose to fame before 1740 appear in Byron's pantheon. There was no shortage of candidates for the role in previous years. Among those which spring to mind are William of Orange, 'our great deliverer', and the duke of Marlborough, the victor of Blenheim. When Sir Winston Churchill wrote the chapter in the life of his illustrious ancestor dealing with his return to England after the battle, he titled it 'the conquering hero'. Unfortunately, in the first age of party they were heroes to one side only, the whigs. Eulogies and encomiums were written almost entirely by whig authors. Tories hated 'Dutch William', and excoriated him in poems on affairs of state. Thus one actually compared him to Cromwell:

> As these two noble heroes t'other day
> Together hung, both as they ought and may . . .[3]

Another invited a painter to portray William in a dubious light.[4]

> First draw the Hero seated on the Throne,
> Spite of all Laws, himself observing none;
> Let English Rights all gasping round him lie,
> And native Freedom thrown neglected by . . .

Although Marlborough was a tory and even suspected as a Jacobite in William's reign, under Anne he became so dependent upon the whigs that he came to be identified as one himself. Thus, his reputation was sullied by the caustic remarks on his ambition, cupidity and miserliness by Mary de la Riviere Manley in the *New Atalantis* and by Swift in *The Examiner*. Manley claimed that 'he is excessive in nothing but his love of riches'. She also raised the question 'has he not been ungrateful to the Royal Bounty?', answering it, 'more than all mankind, because he was more beloved and trusted; but he has risen by it.'[5] Swift castigated his ungratefulness by comparing bills

---

2. The great exception to this rule was George Washington, whose retirement after being first President of the United States seemed to emulate the example of Cincinnatus, the Roman who saved his country and then went back to the plough. Washington thus became a hero to Romantic poets. Burns sang his praises in an Ode for Washington's birthday. Blake admired him in *America: A Prophesy*. Even Southey reconciled George III and Washington in his *Vision of Judgement*!

3. *Poems on Affairs of State* [*POAS*], v, 149–51; 'on the late metamorphosis'.

4. *POAS*, vi, 16.

5. Mary de la Riviere Manley, *Secret Memoirs and Manners of Several Persons of Quality of both Sexes from the New Atalantis, an Island in the Mediterranean written originally in Italian* (2 vols, 1709; reprinted with an introduction by Malcolm J. Boose, 1972), pp. 25–7. Manley had pilloried the duchess of Marlborough four years earlier in *Queen Zarah*.

of Roman Gratitude and British Ingratitude, showing that generals in ancient Rome were rewarded with a pittance while Marlborough had received a fortune, including Blenheim Palace, from an allegedly ungrateful nation. He also compared the duke's avarice and covetousness to that of Crassus.[6] The tories, with their 'blue water policy', preferred naval to military warfare, and sought heroes among admirals rather than generals. Some even tried to give Sir George Rooke equal status with the duke of Marlborough for his exploits in Spain, but the whigs would have none of it.

While martial exploits seem to have been the main criterion for inclusion in Byron's list, there was no lack of civilian heroes in the eighteenth century. In its opening decade the most famous of these was Dr Henry Sacheverell, the high church champion. Again, however, he was a partisan hero. To the whigs he was notorious, a careerist Oxford don who leaped aboard the bandwaggon of anti-dissenting hysteria. It was impossible to find a figure who would command universal consent as a hero in the first age of party. Even when they looked back into the past they had to go a long way before they could arrive at a consensus. Charles I 'king and martyr' was a hero to the tories, but not to the whigs. As for Cromwell, even whigs found it hard to have more than a grudging regard for him.[7] It was not until they reached the reign of Elizabeth that they could agree. The virgin queen was a heroine to the English. Queen Anne deliberately cultivated an Elizabethan image in order to capitalise on her ancestor's popularity. She even adopted her predecessor's motto 'Semper Eadem'. In their search for manly heroes, however, the Augustans went back as far as the ancient world.[8]

The choice of heroes is therefore an indication of the prevailing ideologies. The shift from the first age of party to the classical age of the constitution produced a parallel change in the heroic pantheon. Elizabeth remained a heroine throughout the two periods. In many ways Vernon was lionised because he emulated the feats of Elizabethan admirals like Drake and Raleigh by attacking the Spaniards. But other figures from the past were finding a niche in the hall of fame. When Lord Cobham went into opposition to Walpole over the Excise scheme in 1733 he asked William Kent to devise two temples in the gardens of his house at Stowe – one to modern

6. W. A. Speck, '*The Examiner* re-examined', *Prose Studies* (London, 1993), xvi, 36.

7. W. A. Speck, 'Cromwell and the Glorious Revolution', in R. C. Richardson (ed.), *Images of Oliver Cromwell* (Manchester, 1993), pp. 48–62.

8. James William Johnson, 'England 1660–1800: An Age without Heroes?', in R. Folkenflik (ed.), *The English Hero 1660–1800* (London, 1982), p. 31.

virtue, the other to British worthies. The first was a ruin, with a headless statue of the prime minister, who had deprived Cobham of a military commission for opposing the excise bill. The second contained the busts of King Alfred, the Black Prince, Elizabeth I, Raleigh, Drake, John Hampden, William III, Sir John Barnard, Sir Thomas Gresham, Shakespeare, Sir Francis Bacon, Inigo Jones, John Locke, John Milton, Sir Isaac Newton and Alexander Pope. Kent had previously designed a tableau of English figures for Queen Caroline at Richmond, which included Boyle, Locke, Newton, Samuel Clarke and William Wollaston, representing the mutual dependence of science and religion. After the creation of the temple of British worthies at Stowe, Caroline retaliated by having Merlin's cave constructed at Richmond, with Queen Elizabeth as well as Arthur's wizard. The fashion for such pantheons was followed by Bolingbroke's half-sister, Henrietta, at Barrells in Warwickshire, with the figures of Bolingbroke himself, Pope, Dryden, Milton, Shakespeare, Newton and Locke.[9]

Cobham's choice of 'worthies' was political. They represent a roll call of the heroes of the opposition to Walpole's Robinocracy. Two were contemporaries, Barnard and Pope. Barnard was regarded as a staunch independent member of parliament, whose own probity made him a formidable opponent of corruption. Pope, a personal friend of Cobham, was the prime minister's most eminent literary critic, with the possible exception of Bolingbroke. It is perhaps significant that Cobham did not include the latter among his worthies, leaving it to Henrietta St John Knight instead. King Alfred was counted by the opposition as a truly patriot king. Johnson was to compare his 'golden reign' to the Robinocracy in his first published poem, *London.* The inclusion of Milton indicates that the Cromwellian era was now being rehabilitated, while his appearance along with that of William III and John Locke demonstrates that this was by no means an exclusively tory pantheon. Cobham was a whig and his worthies represent 'patriots', heroes of Country ideology. In this respect it is noteworthy that two prominent whigs of the previous generation, Locke and Newton, appeared not only among the worthies at Stowe but also among the notables at Barrells and Richmond. There was a kind of consensus emerging about the recent past in the selection of heroes.

There was no such consensus about the present. Barnard, Bolingbroke and Pope are absent from Queen Caroline's pantheon at

9. David R. Coffin, *The English Garden: Meditation and Memorial* (London, 1994), p. 58.

Richmond. Vernon achieved a fleeting renown in 1741, but, apart from that brief fame, the Walpolian era was not regarded as a heroic age by contemporaries. On the contrary, it seemed to them that they were living through an era in which heroes were precious few and far between. The prevalent view that the nation's leaders in church and state, so far from being models to emulate, were fatally flawed by corruption created a need for heroes. Turning to the past for them was also suspect, since, where satirists exposed the inadequacy of contemporary politicians, historians were questioning the credentials of those in the previous century. David Hume, by rehabilitating the Stuarts in his *History of England*, called in question the motives of such whig heroes as Hampden and Pym. More seriously, James Macpherson of 'Ossian' fame published documents in his history of the Revolution of 1688 which revealed that the whigs who served William III had been intriguing with the exiled court at St Germain. Perhaps that was one reason why under the first two Georges people turned to fiction to provide them with role models. The 'heroes' and 'heroines' of novels gave them standards by which to govern their own lives, which their corrupt governors had failed and were failing to do. This could also help explain the popularity of biography in these years. There had, of course, been biographies of eminent men and women from time immemorial, those of the saints and martyrs being prominent among them. But the vogue for 'Lives', such as those of the poets which Johnson published, marked a new departure. Interest in the careers of contemporaries led to the appearance of the two most celebrated 'Lives' in the English language, Gibbon's autobiography and Boswell's life of Johnson.

As the consensus over the theoretical perfection of the constitution broke down, so that concerning past heroes and heroines of England also came into question. Blake was scathing in his denunciation of Locke and Newton, accusing them of making Reason a tyrant over Imagination. Even Elizabeth I was criticised. In *The White Doe of Rylstone or the Fate of the Nortons* Wordsworth wrote a sympathetic account of the Rising of the northern earls in 1569, and, although it refers to 'great Eliza's golden time', the queen is at least implicitly condemned for suppressing the rising so brutally.[10] Jane

---

10. The poem was based on a ballad in Thomas Percy's collection entitled 'The rising of the North'. It recounts how Richard Norton of Rylstone Hall in Yorkshire took eight of his sons up to County Durham to take part in the rising and how they were all sentenced to death at York after its suppression. The story largely involves the Protestant son, Francis, who stayed behind, to be butchered as he made his way

Austen in a juvenile history of England found nothing good to say about the 'wicked' virgin Queen, and instead made a heroine of the 'amiable' Mary Queen of Scots.[11] Mary's reputation rose as Elizabeth's fell. Burns extolled the virtues of Scotland's queen in several poems. Sir Walter Scott presented a very favourable picture of her in captivity at Loch Leven castle in *The Abbot* (1820). The following year he tried to do equal justice to Elizabeth in *Kenilworth*, but his heart was not in it. As he admitted in the Introduction,

> the candid Robertson himself confesses having felt the prejudices with which a Scottishman is tempted to regard the subject; and what so liberal a historian avows, a poor romance-writer does not disown. But he hopes the influence of a prejudice almost as natural to him as his native air will not be found to have greatly affected the sketch he has attempted of England's Elizabeth.

The trouble was that she was 'England's Elizabeth'. What was wanted was a hero who would rise above English and Scottish prejudices and become truly British. One was found in Admiral Nelson. Although his signal to the fleet before the battle of Trafalgar, 'England expects every man to do his duty', was scarcely tactful to the Scottish and Welsh sailors under him, he nevertheless became, in Byron's words, 'Britannia's god of war'. Robert Southey wrote the first and in many ways the best biography of Nelson. He strove to show 'what the country had lost in its great naval hero – the greatest of our own, and of all former times'.[12] Nelson's statue, towering on his column above the most central public space in the capital city, is a reminder to this day that the generation which endured the long wars against France unleashed by the French Revolution, though

---

back to Rylstone from York, carrying his father's banner. Yet, as Wordsworth admitted, 'the outward interest of the poem is in favour of the old man's religious feelings and the filial heroism of his band of sons'. *The Poems of William Wordsworth*, ed. Selincourt and Darbishire (Oxford, 1954), iii, 545. The Nortons were an old Catholic family who took part in the rising 'for the old and holy church'. This is another curious specimen of the sympathy shown by Romantic poets – and others – for Catholics when the question of Catholic Emancipation was at issue. It also marks a step in Wordworth's progress from radical to conservative, since he wrote it around 1807, though it was not published until 1815. In it he defends the motives of those who rose

> with free and open hate
> of novelties in church and state.

11. Jane Austen, *The History of England: A Facsimile* (London, 1993), pp. xxi–xxiii; Antoinette Burton, ' "Invention is what delights me": Jane Austen's remaking of "English" History', in Devoney Looser (ed.), *Jane Austen and Discourses of Feminism* (London, 1995), pp. 35–50.

12. R. Southey, *The Life of Nelson* (first published 1813; 1962 edn), p. 267.

divided on so many issues, could find in its hero, Nelson, a symbol of national unity.

A common theme which connects such heroes of the age as William III and Marlborough to Nelson and Wellington is that they earned their laurels fighting the French. They were linked with the conflict with France from the reign of Louis XIV to the regime of Napoleon in an 'Ode to my Country' of 1798

> To the great Batavian's name
> Ceaseless hymns of triumph raise!
> Scourge of tyrants, let his fame
> Live in songs of grateful praise.
> Thy turrets, Blenheim, glittering to the sun
> Tell of bright fields from warlike Gallia won;
> Tell how the mighty monarch mourn'd in vain
> His impious wish the world to claim.[13]

In this respect the era of the wars against France from 1689 to 1815, which has been seen as the second Hundred Years' War, is an epoch in English history. It stands apart from the decades before the Glorious Revolution, when Cromwell declared Spain to be England's natural and providential enemy, and Charles and James II became clients of Louis XIV; and it is distinguished from the Victorian age when Britain and France fought together against Russia in the Crimea.

Despite this endemic enmity there was an ambivalence towards French culture which found expression in the ideologies of the century. In the first age of party the whigs accused the tories of being Francophiles. They were alleged to prefer Bourbon-type absolutism to the mixed monarchy established in the Glorious Revolution. The treaty of Utrecht, negotiated by the tory govern-ment in 1713, was long held to be proof of the perfidy of the tories towards the Grand Alliance and their preference for the French. Under the Hanoverians Jacobitism was sustained from across the Channel, and in the 'Forty-five the rebels received succour from France.

Meanwhile, however, the English ruling class became suspected of Francophilia. The aristocracy were said to be Frenchified, aping French manners and emulating the fashions of Versailles. French cultural imperialism was accused of leading the English upper classes to betray the country's true interests. Anti-Gallican sentiment became

---

13. *Poetry of the Anti-Jacobin* (2nd edn., London, 1854), no. xxxviii.

a hallmark of middle-class distrust and detestation of French influence over the elite. Such fears were allayed by successes against the French in the Seven Years' War, when the aristocracy was perceived to be doing its patriotic duty in the fight against France. Although the alleged degeneracy of the aristocracy was again cited as a reason for the loss of the American colonies, it did not take the form of accusing the ruling class of being Frenchified. On the contrary, the entry of France on the rebels' side in the War of American Independence united the English in opposition to their by now traditional enemy, if not to the Americans.

The outbreak of the French Revolution renewed the ambivalence towards France. Attitudes towards the French revolutionaries polarised conservatives and radicals in the 1790s. Conservative followers of Burke denounced the revolution and dubbed their opponents 'Jacobins', stressing their alleged sympathy with the revolutionaries. Paine and his supporters greeted the initial phases of the French Revolution with enthusiasm, and, though they became disillusioned with subsequent developments, did not lose all hope of an acceptable conclusion to events in France until the rise of Napoleon.

As in other spheres of activity, literature both reflected and informed these perceptions. Poems on affairs of state repeatedly related the party conflict in England to the European struggle for power. 'I hate all monarchs with the thrones they sit on', concluded Rochester's 'Satyr on Charles II', 'from the hector of France to the cully of Britain.' As we have seen, the Tackers were depicted as giving succour to Louis XIV after the defeat of his troops at the battle of Blenheim.[14] Poems like 'Mat's Peace' accused the tories of betraying the allies in the negotiation of the treaty of Utrecht. John Arbuthnot rallied to their defence in *Law is a Bottomless Pit* in which he invented the character of John Bull to represent a Britain duped by its allies into needlessly opposing France.

John Bull was to become a symbol of the middle-class Englishman standing up for his liberties, not only against France but also against Frenchified aristocrats. Arbuthnot's Bull was a linen draper, but later others depicted him as various figures including a farmer as well as a tradesman. Hogarth gave expression to both anti-Jacobite and anti-French sentiments in such prints as 'The March to Finchley'

14. See above, pp. 39–40. The poem begins with the French king saying, 'I think I need never despair, though beaten at Blenheim full sore, for among the makers of laws I have one hundred and thirty four.'

and 'Calais Gate'. Tobias Smollett represented British rather than English dislike of French customs, especially in his hero, Peregrine Pickle, who disparages all things foreign to his taste in a fictional visit to France. Where Smollett also satirised the English aristocracy's penchant for French fashions, Fanny Burney made a peer of the realm the hero of her novel *Evelina*. But she still indulged the anti-French sentiments of her readers with episodes victimising her heroine's French relatives. Captain Mirvan is a character almost out of a Smollett novel, with 'a fixed and most prejudiced hatred of whatever is not English'. He perpetrates a grotesque trick on one Frenchified fop by dressing up a monkey à la mode to mimic him!

Literary responses to the French Revolution polarised writers into 'Jacobins' and 'anti-Jacobins'. As we have seen, novelists fought a war of ideas. 'Romantic' poets welcomed the initial events in France, to be criticised by writers defending the status quo, for instance in contributions to *The Anti-Jacobin*. The prospectus to the first number of 20 November 1797, probably written by George Canning, announced its intention to counter 'Jacobin' poets, whom it characterised as praising French victories while denigrating those of Britain or her allies.[15] 'The Jacobin' was alleged to maintain that

> Whatever is in France, is right;
> Terror and blood are my delight.[16]

The relationship between the rhetoric and the reality was complex. Tories in the first age of party were not a fifth column for the French king, though the fact that three tory MPs met Poussin, the French agent, in a London tavern in 1701 was used by whigs to smear all tories in parliament with the libel of supporting in the interests of France. Aristocrats under the early Hanoverians were not Frenchified to the extent of betraying English interests, though the duke of Newcastle felt obliged to dismiss his French cook at the height of the 'Forty-five! Romantic poets were not 'Jacobins' – if anything they were Girondins.

Ideologies, however, are not based on realities but on perceptions. Whigs perceived tories as Francophiles. Bourgeois Englishmen perceived aristocrats as Frenchified. Conservatives perceived enthusiasts for the French Revolution as Jacobins. These perceptions were informed and reinforced by literature, for eighteenth-century authors were well aware of the prejudices of their readers. Defoe's *Shortest Way with the Dissenters* backfired precisely because he could

---

15. *Poetry of the anti-Jacobin* (2nd edn., London, 1854), p. 14.   16. Ibid, p. 116.

get inside the mentality of a high-flying Anglican only too well. It was as though a black author today were to parody the sentiments of a racist with a diatribe on the shortest way with the immigrants. Racist ideology rarely deals with realities. It is of little avail to try to combat racism by statistical demonstrations of the numbers of immigrants and the ratio of them to native-born English people, or the relative contributions they make to the economy. Instead, as Enoch Powell showed when he gave his notorious 'rivers of blood' speech, racist stereotypes exist as ideological fantasies almost immune from rational argument. Henry Sacheverell was an Enoch Powell of his day, feeding the Anglican fantasy of the dissenters as an alien subversive element in society. Defoe only made explicit the implicit assumptions made by the high church clergy and their followers.

The changes rung on such stereotypes as the rabid dissenters and crypto-Catholics, the backwoods squires and upstart monied men of the first age of party to the conservative country gentlemen and 'Jacobin' tradesmen of the era of the French Revolution record shifts in the prevailing ideologies of the eighteenth century. Thus, literature documents not social realities but how they were perceived by contemporaries.

Select Bibliography

Introduction

For the historical background see the relevant volumes in Longman's Foundations of Modern Britain series:

ERIC J. EVANS, *The Forging of the Modern State: Early Industrial Britain 1783–1870* (1983).

GEOFFREY HOLMES, *The Making of a Great Power: Late Stuart and Early Georgian Britain 1660–1722* (1993).

GEOFFREY HOLMES and DANIEL SZECHI, *The Age of Oligarchy: pre-Industrial Britain 1722–1783* (1993).

For surveys of the literature see:

MARILYN BUTLER, *Romantics, Rebels and Reactionaries: English Literature and its Background 1760–1830* (Oxford, 1981).

J. A. DOWNIE, *To settle the succession of the State: Literature and Politics 1678–1750* (1994).

W. A. SPECK, *Society and Literature in England 1700–1760* (Dublin, 1981).

Chapter One – The First Age of Party

TIM HARRIS, GARY DEKREY, EDWARD ROSENHEIM, RICHARD GREAVES and JONATHAN SCOTT, 'Order and authority: creating party in Restoration England', *Albion* (1993), xxv, 581–647.

T. HARRIS, *Politics under the later Stuarts: Party Conflict in a Divided Society 1660–1715* (1993).

G. HOLMES, *British Politics in the Age of Anne* (2nd edn., 1987).

CLYVE JONES (ed.), *Britain in the first Age of Party: Essays presented to Geoffrey Holmes* (1987).

Chapter Two – Poems on Affairs of State

GEORGE DEFOREST LORD (ed.), *Poems on Affairs of State: Augustan Satirical Verse 1660–1714* (seven volumes, Yale, 1962–75).

GEORGE DEFOREST LORD (ed.), *Anthology of Poems on Affairs of State* (1975).

PHILIP HARTH, *Pen for a Party: Dryden's Tory Propaganda in its contexts* (1993).

Chapter Three – Party Ideology and Society

H. T. DICKINSON, *Liberty and Property: Political Ideology in Eighteenth-Century Britain* (1977).

P. G. M. DICKSON, *The Financial Revolution: A Study in the Development of Public Credit 1688–1756* (1967).

G. HOLMES (ed.), *Britain after the Glorious Revolution 1689–1714* (1969).

G. HOLMES, *Augustan England: Professions, State and Society 1680–1730* (1982).

J. KENYON, *Revolution Principles: the Politics of Party 1689–1720* (Cambridge, 1977).

J. A. SHARPE, *Early Modern England: A Social History 1560–1750* (1987).

Chapter Four – The Classical Age of the Constitution

LINDA COLLEY, *In Defiance of Oligarchy: The Tory Party 1714–1760* (Cambridge, 1982).

PAUL LANGFORD, *A Polite and Commercial People: England 1727–1783* (Oxford, 1989).

J. G. A. POCOCK, *The Machiavellian Moment: Florentine Political Thought and the Atlantic Revolution* (1975).

KATHLEEN WILSON, *The Sense of the People: Politics, Culture and Imperialism in England, 1715–1785* (Cambridge, 1995).

Chapter Five – Jacobitism and Patriotism

HOWARD ERSKINE-HILL, *Poetry of Opposition and Revolution: Dryden to Wordsworth* (Cambridge, 1996).

CHRISTINE GERRARD, *The Patriot Opposition to Walpole: Politics, Poetry and National Myth 1725–1742* (Oxford, 1994).

D. SZECHI, *The Jacobites* (1994).

HOWARD WEINBROT, *Britannia's Issue: The rise of British Literature from Dryden to Ossian* (Cambridge, 1993).

Chapter Six – The Emergence of the Novel

NANCY ARMSTRONG, *Desire and Domestic Fiction: A political history of the novel* (1987).

J. PAUL HUNTER, *Before Novels: The Cultural Contexts of Eighteenth-Century English Fiction* (1990).

MICHAEL MCKEON, *The Origins of the English Novel 1600–1740* (1987).

JAMES THOMPSON, *Models of Value: Eighteenth-Century Political Economy and the Novel* (1996).

IAN WATT, *The Rise of the Novel* (1957).

Chapter Seven – Literature and Law and Order

JAMES BEATTIE, *Crime and the Courts in England 1660–1800* (Oxford, 1986).

D. HAY, P. LINEBAUGH and E. P. THOMPSON (eds), *Albion's Fatal Tree* (1975).

JOHN H. LANGBEIN, 'Albion's Fatal Flaws', *Past and Present* (1983), **98**, 96–120.

P. LINEBAUGH, *The London Hanged: Crime and Civil Society in the Eighteenth Century* (1991).

Chapter Eight – The Breakdown of the Constitutional Consensus

H. T. DICKINSON (ed.), *Britain and the French Revolution* (1989).

ROBERT R. DOZIER, *For King, Constitution and Country: The English Loyalists and the French Revolution* (1983).

COLIN JONES (ed.), *Britain and Revolutionary France: Conflict, Subversion and Propaganda* (Exeter, 1983).

E. P. THOMPSON, *The Making of the English Working Class* (1968).

JAMES VERNON (ed.), *Re-reading the Constitution: New Narratives in the Political History of England's Long Nineteenth Century* (Cambridge, 1996).

Chapter Nine – Novels and the War of Ideas

MARILYN BUTLER, *Jane Austen and the War of Ideas* (Oxford, 1987).
GARY KELLY, *The English Jacobin Novel 1780–1803* (Oxford, 1976).

Chapter Ten – Poems on the State of Affairs

JEROME J. MCGANN, *The Romantic Ideology* (1983).
JOHN MEE, *Dangerous Enthusiasm: William Blake and the Culture of Radicalism in the 1790s* (Oxford, 1992).
CARL WOODRING, *Politics in English Romantic Poetry* (1970).

Index